DEMON
of the
LOST
CAUSE

SHADES OF BLUE AND GRAY SERIES

EDITED BY HERMAN HATTAWAY,
JON L. WAKELYN, AND CLAYTON E. JEWETT

The Shades of Blue and Gray Series offers Civil War studies for the modern reader—Civil War buff and scholar alike. Military history today addresses the relationship between society and warfare. Thus biographies and thematic studies that deal with civilians, soldiers, and political leaders are increasingly important to a larger public. This series includes books that will appeal to Civil War Roundtable groups, individuals, libraries, and academics with a special interest in this era of American history.

DEMON
of the
LOST
CAUSE

SHERMAN AND
CIVIL WAR HISTORY

WESLEY MOODY

UNIVERSITY OF MISSOURI PRESS
COLUMBIA AND LONDON

Copyright © 2011 by
The Curators of the University of Missouri
University of Missouri Press, Columbia, Missouri 65201
Printed and bound in the United States of America

5 4 3 2 1   15 14 13 12 11

Cataloging-in-Publication data available from the Library of Congress.
ISBN 978-0-8262-1945-9

 This paper meets the requirements of the
American National Standard for Permanence of Paper
for Printed Library Materials, Z39.48, 1984.

Jacket designer: Susan Ferber
Text designer: Stephanie Foley
Typesetter: FoleyDesign
Printer and binder: Thomson-Shore, Inc.
Typefaces: New Century Schoolbook and Minion

To Beth, my wife,
I owe all my success to her love, support, and good sense.

CONTENTS

ACKNOWLEDGMENTS

Thank you Wendy Venet, my professor, advisor, mentor, and friend. Your help has been invaluable. Thank you, John Ferling. Your example convinced me that I wanted to live the life of a scholar.

Lastly I want to thank my parents who have always had faith in me.

DEMON

of the

LOST
CAUSE

INTRODUCTION

I n 2004 the *Atlanta Journal Constitution* published on the front page of the opinion section an article about William Tecumseh Sherman. More than a quarter of the page was taken up by a photograph of a stern-looking Sherman, with his right hand resting Napoleon-like in his Brooks Brothers uniform, laid over an image of fire. The article is titled "Sherman Still Burns Atlanta," but it is subtitled "Despised Yankee General Wasn't as Evil as History Has Painted Him." The article quoted many historians who have written that a great deal of the history surrounding Sherman is simply myth.[1] To many of the newspaper's readers this story must have been proof that Atlanta with its numerous northern transplants was no longer a "real" southern city, at least its newspaper did not represent "real" southerners. To native-born southerners, Sherman is the symbol of the brutality of the North and no amount of scholarly work or Sunday newspaper fluff pieces is going to change that. On a recent visit to Eatonton, Georgia, I visited the Uncle Remus Museum and was regaled with stories of how Sherman had destroyed every home in the town. I then took a self-guided tour of Eatonton's beautiful antebellum homes.

Northerners have their own myths about Sherman. The northern myth is actually very similar to the southern myth. Sherman was brutal, but he was an innovator. He was a man who fought a hard war when others were too timid or too tied to tradition to do what had to be done. Sherman was the first truly total warrior. These views are amazingly close to one another and similarly flawed, for Sherman was as much a traditionalist as any general of the American Civil War. One thing cannot be argued though; William Tecumseh Sherman is by far the most controversial figure of the American Civil War. While debate may surround other men, none other elicits the emotion that Sherman does.

The modern image of Sherman has evolved over the years. In large part, it is the product of southern writers trying to justify the war and explain their loss, but it is also the product of Union generals' and politicians' attempting to glorify their own place in the history of the war, men with personal grudges against the general, and modern historians' using Sherman to make their own arguments about contemporary society. Sherman is also responsible for his own myth. From these different sources is born the complex William T. Sherman who through the years will become all things to all people. In this work I examine how Sherman's reputation has evolved over the years from accusations of being a Southern sympathizer and traitor at the end of the Civil War to the modern image of Sherman as the man who laid waste to the state of Georgia in 1864, who almost single-handedly invented the concept of "total war" and was the unprincipled destroyer of the old South. Any serious student of the war knows that much of what has been written is filled with myth. To present the accurate version of historical events is a critical step, but it is not the complete story. It is important to understand how and why the myth became accepted by the public and all too often the scholarly community. The creation of history has the ability to become larger and more interesting than the events themselves, even in the case of a man like William T. Sherman.

CHAPTER 1

The Prewar Years and the Early War

Although Sherman was unknown to the general public at the beginning of the war, the template for his future reputation began to emerge early on in the mind of the Southern public. Ulysses S. Grant, in his personal memoirs, described marching his regiment through a deserted Missouri town at the beginning of the war. People "had evidently been led to believe that the National troops carried death and devastation with them wherever they went," he recalled.[1] Before Union and Confederate troops met at the first battle of Bull Run, Confederate president Jefferson Davis in a speech to the Confederate Congress predicted how Abraham Lincoln and the Republicans would prosecute the war. According to Davis, "Mankind will shudder at the outrages committed on defenseless females."[2] Sherman was only an unknown colonel when Davis made this speech and was as far away from shaping national policy as was possible. A future generation of southerners and historians, however, will blame William T. Sherman for a brutality they implied did not exist in earlier wars or in other parts of the American Civil War.

Neither Jefferson Davis nor the people fleeing in the face of Grant and his single regiment had to look too far in the past to find examples of the kind of brutality they feared and that Sherman was credited with inventing in 1864. General Santa Anna ravaged a rebellious Texas, and both the British and the Americans would institute "hard war" in the American Revolution and the War of 1812. The most famous example, of course, was the burning of Washington, DC, during a British raid. Living off the land was the major strategy of Napoleon, who was studied intently by generals on both sides. The "On to Richmond" press and those sightseers who escorted the Union army to the battlefield at Bull Run may have believed that the war would be fought in one glorious battle, but the rest of the country knew that this would be the type of bloody war that had been going on between Kansas and Missouri for the previous five years.

There was nothing in Sherman's early life that would have led one to believe he was destined for greatness or controversy. With only a few exceptions, in his childhood and early life he was not that different from others of that era. On February 8, 1820, Charles Sherman, a prominent judge in Lancaster, Ohio, and his wife, Mary, had their sixth child, a boy they named Tecumseh. He was named after the Shawnee chief who had waged war against the United States prior to and during the War of 1812, and who had been killed during the Battle of Thames less than seven years prior to the birth of Tecumseh Sherman.[3] Giving a white child an Indian name was an oddity in the nineteenth century, as it was, but naming him after as dangerous and successful an enemy as the great Tecumseh was truly odd. This was obviously the first of many controversies in Sherman's life, and the fact that it occurred before he was born was very fitting.

When Tecumseh Sherman was nine years old, his father died while riding the judicial circuit. The obituaries printed by Ohio newspapers gave cholera as the cause of death, but typhoid fever was a more likely culprit. Mary Elizabeth Sherman was now a widow with eleven children. As was the tradition of the time, the children were taken in by family and friends. Tecumseh Sherman was taken in by Thomas Ewing, a prominent attorney and close friend of his father. His new home was in view of his old one, and he often visited his mother; it was not a traumatic move for the boy. He was taken in as part of the family, and he loved and was loved by the Ewings. Throughout his life he would view the Ewing sons as his brothers and would marry Thomas Ewing's daughter, Ellen.[4] Throughout his adult life, Sherman will be preoccupied with supporting his growing family, and this will affect all of his professional decisions. Perhaps the position his mother found herself in as a widow greatly affected his outlook on life.

In 1836, Sherman received an appointment to the US Military Academy. Ewing was then a senator from Ohio, so Sherman's appointment was all but guaranteed. According to his *Memoirs*, West Point was not Sherman's choice. He was informed by his adopted father that he would attend the academy.[5] In the age before grants and financial aid for students, West Point was the only free institution of higher learning in the country.

Sherman graduated sixth in his class in 1840. He would have graduated with higher standing had it not been for the large number of demerits he received. (According to Sherman's memoirs his demerits were due to uniform infractions, but according to his classmates he had a fondness for visiting Benny Havens, the local bar famous among cadets, and he also had a talent for procuring contraband food in the cadet quarters.) He graduated with George Thomas and Richard Ewell, both of whom would become generals in the Civil War.[6]

Graduating at the top of your class was no guarantee of success. The top student from the class of 1840 was the future governor of Louisiana and Confederate general, Paul Hebert. He, like most pre–Civil War graduates at the top of their class, had an undistinguished war record. Hebert may have had an almost perfect disciplinary record at West Point and excelled in his classes, but as a brigadier general in the Confederate Service he has been all but forgotten.[7]

After West Point, Sherman was assigned to the Third US Artillery. He was sent to the Florida territory to serve in the Second Seminole War that had been raging since 1836, but he saw little action in Florida. With the exception of isolated raids and ambushes, the Seminoles tried to avoid the soldiers, a tactic that made perfect sense since their goal was to remain in Florida. He did not see any action during the Mexican War, either. He was stationed in California, but he did not arrive until after the area was pacified. After this war he served as the commissary in New Orleans before resigning his commission from the army in 1852.[8]

Throughout his adult life Sherman was most concerned with supporting his family financially. As much as he loved army life, the low pay made it difficult for him to take care of his growing young family. Sherman moved to San Francisco to manage a bank owned by Lucas, Simonds and Company of St. Louis.[9]

Sherman first came to the attention of the press with local notoriety in the California newspapers in 1856. It was not his position as a bank president that brought him to the attention of the public. As a well-liked member of the business community and a West Point graduate, it was natural that Sherman would be made a major general in the state militia. San Francisco was still a wild boom town when he arrived. The city was poorly managed and corruption was rampant. In 1856, a policeman and a newspaper editor were murdered in two separate incidents. These deaths triggered a wave of vigilante violence.[10]

The local citizens formed a Committee of Vigilance, with the stated goal of restoring government to "its true functions, to correct abuses" and to give the law "force and effect." Sherman was offered command of the committee, but he refused that honor. The governor of California, J. Neely Johnson, ordered Sherman, as commander of the state militia district that encompassed San Francisco, to mobilize the militia. Very few men responded to Sherman's call since most of the militiamen were already members of the Committee of Vigilance.[11]

Most of the San Francisco newspapers supported the committee and attacked and lampooned Sherman in their pages. They ridiculed him for not being able to field a sufficient force to challenge the committee and also accused him of corruption, because some of the men lynched by the committee had large accounts invested with Sherman's bank.[12] The press's rough treatment of Sherman and his own inability to do anything about the situation led him to resign his position as head of the local militia. Sherman wrote to the newspapers about his reasons for resigning. He blamed his superiors for the failure to control the vigilantes, an act that only alienated the governor and the commander of the US Army Department of the Pacific, Brigadier General John E. Wool, a national hero from both the Mexican War and the War of 1812.[13] With this letter, Sherman began his long habit of writing the newspapers or making public statements when silence would have served him much better.

The committee eventually disbanded peacefully. Most of its members probably considered their work complete after having hung several men and run many more out of town. Although these events were covered in newspapers across the country, Sherman did not merit any mention outside the newspapers of northern California.[14]

For most of his life, Sherman lived under the shadow of his younger brother John, who was elected to the US House of Representatives in 1856 as one of the growing number of Republicans sent to Washington. John Sherman was extremely popular in his home state. He was young and handsome. He had a promising political career ahead of him and was the descendent of a signer of the Declaration of Independence.[15] William T. Sherman was just another West Point graduate trying to earn a living. Throughout their lives, John will be the most hated of the Sherman brothers among Southerners.

It was becoming increasingly difficult to support a family during the economic crisis of 1857. The San Francisco and St. Louis branches of his bank were both closed. Sherman lived for a short time off the kindness of his foster father, who was now his father-in-law, and then also practiced law in Leavenworth, Kansas, with his brother-in-law Thomas Ewing, Jr. The entire time he was looking for an opportunity to return to the army. In 1859 he accepted a position as commandant of the Louisiana Seminary of Learning and Military Academy.[16] This was not exactly the army, but it offered financial security and was closer to military life than banking.

While William T. Sherman was struggling to support his growing young family (his fifth child was born in September 1859), his brother was in the middle of possibly the largest controversy of the antebellum period. John Sherman was part of the congressional delegation sent to investigate the disputed elections and the growing violence between proslavery and antislavery forces in the Territory of Kansas.[17]

The congressional report accused the proslavery government of Kansas of committing massive voter fraud and acts of violence against midwestern settlers. Democratic newspapers responded by accusing Sherman and other members of the committee of falsifying the report. This issue dominated the headlines for nearly a month. The debate over what was happening in Kansas was so heated that it almost turned violent. Representative John Wright of Tennessee threatened Sherman with a pistol, making him the first in the Sherman family to face real danger in the conflict between North and South.[18]

As an active member of the new Republican Party and an outspoken opponent of slavery, Representative John Sherman was well known and controversial. He was disliked among Northern Democrats, and in the South he was hated and feared. When his older brother William was hired as superintendent of the newly formed Louisiana Seminary of Learning and Military Academy, his employers were concerned about his younger brother's political views. Louisiana's governor, Thomas Moore, suggested there was apprehension about him having an important government job since his brother was "the abolitionist candidate for speaker."[19] Moore was probably too much of a Southern gentleman to tell Sherman what he thought of his brother.

Sherman's assurances that his brother was not an abolitionist must not have been taken too seriously by his audience. Early that year, John Sherman had endorsed the highly controversial book *The Impending Crisis of the South and How to Meet It* by Hinton Helper. The North Carolina–born Helper argued that the South with its peculiar institution was a drag on the American economy. The book attacked the South and the Democratic Party and called upon non-slaveholders to unite against slaveholders.[20] Although the work would be considered racist by modern standards, especially those sections dealing with his fear of the "mongrelization" of American society, Helper was accurate in his portrayal of the Southern economy and of the damage slavery does to society.

Democrats, especially Southern Democrats, were extremely upset about the possibility of the young Ohio Republican becoming Speaker of the House. They wanted a moderate former Whig as opposed to the outspoken John Sherman who wholeheartedly believed in the Republican platform. The younger Sherman was accused of being the "standard bearer of [William H.] Seward" and the "Black Republicans," carrying the banner "upon which is inscribed: 'Slavery must be abolished and we must do it.'"[21] Although to modern readers this may seem positive accusations, to Southerners in 1859 there was nothing worse they could have said about John Sherman than that he was an abolitionist.

There was enough controversy stirred around Representative Sherman that his name was withdrawn from contention and William Pennington of New Jersey was elected Speaker. This did not satisfy Democrats either, since Pennington was only "the instrument of the Republicans, while Sherman is their master," but it was very unlikely that any Republican would have satisfied the Democrats.[22]

William T. Sherman's assurances to his new employers that his brother was a moderate may have been mere wishful thinking. His letters during this time are filled with appeals to his brother to be more moderate on the issue of slavery. He wrote asking him to make "reasonable concessions to the weaknesses and prejudices of the South."[23]

Sherman, himself, was a moderate on the slavery question. In his heart, he was a Whig, as was his foster father. He believed in rule by the elite, and as a young army officer stationed in the South he liked what he saw of Southern society. While Sherman did not own a slave, as did other officers stationed with him in Mobile and Charleston, this was more due to his financial situation than to any feeling of abhorrence toward slavery. While in Louisiana, he used slave labor at the academy and suggested that his wife should buy a few slaves to work as servants for the family. Unlike her husband, Ellen Sherman felt slavery was wrong. She refused.[24] Sherman was a man of his times. He felt slaves should be treated better, and perhaps he took pride in the fact that American slaves were treated better than slaves anywhere else, but he thought those who championed abolition were dangerous zealots.[25]

The election of Abraham Lincoln in the 1860 presidential election was the last in a chain of events that brought war. Regular army and naval officers resigned in droves to join the forces of their home states. State militias seized government installations, sometimes not even waiting for their state to secede. As a loyal former soldier, Sherman found himself forced by these events to leave the South. The state militia of Louisiana seized the US arsenal at Baton Rouge and sent two thousand muskets and a large supply of ammunition to Sherman at his academy. Sherman immediately wrote the governor and the president of the board of supervisors and resigned his position.[26]

He did not leave for the North immediately but, instead, spent a week in New Orleans finalizing his business with the academy and the state of Louisiana. He made a point in his 1875 memoirs to show that, when he left the Louisiana Military Academy, the institution was in no way damaged by his resignation. This stood in opposition to what he wrote his wife, Ellen, at the time, that he would "not for a day or even an hour occupy a position of apparent hostility to Uncle Sam."[27]

Like most people in 1861, Sherman was unsure what the next few years would bring. As the Southern states seized Federal property within their borders, most officers charged with its defense simply stood by and did nothing. While Sherman was still in the state, Major Joseph Haskins, the commander of the arsenal at Baton Rouge and a decorated veteran of the war with Mexico, with no resistance surrendered his post to the state of Louisiana. It is very likely that had Major Haskins and the many other officers in his position known the nature of the war to come or even what was expected of them by their government, they would have, as Sherman suggested was their duty, "defended their posts to the death." It is doubtful that Sherman would have acted differently had he known that the next four years would bring such death and destruction. Writing ten years after the war, Sherman seemed more concerned with the accusation that he "was guilty of a breach of hospitality" than with the possibility that he had committed treason by aiding the state of Louisiana after it had left the Union.[28]

The now unemployed Sherman returned to Lancaster, Ohio, where his wife and children were living, without a clear plan for the future. For a man for whom financial stability and the support of his family were top priority, this had to be a crushing blow. He did, however, have competing offers. His brother, then Senator Sherman, wanted him to come to Washington so he might use his political influence to find him a position in the new Republican administration. Sherman also had an offer from Henry Turner, who had secured him his position as bank president, to be the president of the Fifth Street Railroad in St. Louis. He quickly wrote Turner that he would accept the position, but since the position would not begin for a few weeks, Sherman traveled to Washington to see his brother.[29]

He was disappointed in what he saw in the capital. Sherman believed that the new government was not taking the threat posed by the South seriously. He was also not very impressed with the new president. When the brothers went to the Oval Office, Senator Sherman presented President Lincoln with a list of people who wanted appointments in Ohio and then introduced his brother, Colonel Sherman.[30] Lincoln was polite but dismissive of his warning about events in Louisiana. This angered Sherman, who told his brother that "the country was sleeping on a volcano and that might burst forth, at any minute, but that I was going to St. Louis to take care of my family." In Lincoln's defense, however, his first days as president were filled with meetings with office seekers and he must have believed Sherman was just another relative of a politician in search of an important position.[31]

Sherman moved his family to St. Louis and began his position as president of the small railroad. He declined the position as chief clerkship of the War Department and eventually assistant secretary of war. Sherman's refusal to accept a political position was seen by many as a sign that he would be another officer who would prove disloyal. Sherman would, of course, prove this belief false, but in the first days after secession as the letters of resignation flowed into the War Department, Lincoln's cabinet jumped to invalid conclusions. Sherman turned down the position for very practical reasons. Any government position outside of the regular army was only temporary. If Lincoln were removed from office in four years, Sherman would be once again unemployed.[32]

When Sherman was offered a command in the regular army, he quickly accepted. This was his true profession, and a regular commission offered the most job security. He moved his family to Lancaster, Ohio, where he correctly assumed they would be much safer than in Missouri. Commissioned a colonel, he reported to Washington, DC, to take command of his regiment, the Thirteenth Regular Infantry. Since the Thirteenth did not actually exist yet, Sherman was assigned to Lieutenant General Winfield Scott's staff to inspect the defenses around Washington, DC.[33] In July 1861, Sherman was given command of a brigade as part of the first ill-fated advance on Richmond. He received his first press coverage after the battle of First Manassas. Sherman could not complain about how the article portrayed him. The *Daily National Intelligencer* published his official report word for word.[34] Sherman would republish this report in his memoirs in 1875 and again in 1885. His view of those events was unchanged by later developments in the war. Sherman believed that the Union loss at the battle of First Manassas was the result of sending raw troops into battle. There are few modern historians who would disagree with his assessment.

Sherman assumed that after the disaster of First Manassas there would be dismissals of all the officers present at that battle. Instead Sherman was promoted to brigadier general and, along with George H. Thomas, was sent to Kentucky to serve under Brigadier General Robert Anderson, the former commander of Fort Sumter. In an interview with Lincoln, Sherman explained to the president that he was trying to avoid a position of overall command. According to Sherman, the president found this amusing, since he was surrounded by men jockeying for senior positions. Sherman was motivated to avoid a position of command for fear of failure. He predicted that the war's first commanding generals would not keep their jobs until the end.[35] Sherman was correct, but whether this was due to circumstances of war or the generals themselves can be debated.

Sherman's fear of failure can be linked to his motivation for rejoining the army in the first place. Sherman had been raised in a patriotic family. His ancestors included a signer of the Declaration of Independence who, fittingly, had attended the Hartford Convention during the War of 1812 to keep New England from seceding from the Union.[36] His overwhelming motivation, however, was to provide for his family. He had left the army because promotions had been slow to come. An officer had to wait for his senior to retire or die before he could be promoted and receive a pay raise. The seventy-five-year-old Lieutenant General Winfield Scott was the most famous example of why promotions were slow in coming in the old army. During the war, promotions would come quickly to those who survived the battles and the political axe. Sherman, time and again, would prove during the war that he feared losing his position much more than he feared death at the hands of the enemy. If

Sherman could avoid primary command, he could avoid the fate of so many officers who found themselves unemployed at the end of the war.[37]

Sherman was second in command to Major General Robert Anderson, commander of the Department of the Cumberland. Anderson is most often remembered as the commander of Fort Sumter. The department was made up mostly of the state of Kentucky. Anderson's command stretched from Paducah on the Ohio River to the Big Sandy River, Kentucky's border with Virginia. This was over three hundred miles of territory. Of the three major Union forces (Anderson in Kentucky, George McClellan in Virginia, and John C. Fremont, west of the Mississippi), Anderson had by far the smallest force, only about eighteen thousand troops in Kentucky.[38] It was an extremely important strategic position, however. The Ohio River formed Kentucky's northern border with Illinois, Indiana, and Ohio, and had the South taken Kentucky, the Confederate army would have been in a strong defensive position behind the river with the opportunity for offensive forays into three Union states.

In 1861, there were still questions about Kentucky's loyalty. In August the state's legislature had issued a proclamation of neutrality, a position that was not legally an option. Kentucky was a slave-owning state that would provide as many troops to the Confederate cause as to the Union, not to mention that it was also the birthplace of both Lincoln and Jefferson Davis.[39]

Anderson and his command were in a precarious situation. In a key strategic position, they were short of trained soldiers, weapons, supplies, and money. Both Sherman and George Thomas were forced to take out loans in order to supply their commands. On October 7, 1861, Anderson's request to be relieved from his command was accepted by General Winfield Scott. Anderson claimed the stress of his position was ruining his already fragile health. He requested that his senior subordinate, William T. Sherman, take his place.[40]

When Sherman was promoted to command of the Department of the Cumberland, James Gordon Bennett's *New York Herald* introduced Sherman to the public. The *Herald* called him a "well trained and long seasoned soldier" and "a scholar of rare endowments." However, he was still identified as "the brother of Senator Sherman."[41]

Sherman's prediction about the fate of those who took command early in the war came true. The three major commanders at the start of the war—McClellan, Freemont, and Anderson—were all relieved of their commands early in the war. The stress that had driven Anderson from Kentucky now belonged to Sherman. His visible signs of being overstressed led to rumors in Kentucky and in Washington that the general was perhaps mentally unstable. Secretary of War Simeon Cameron after a meeting with Sherman concluded the general was "touched in the head."[42]

Sherman was removed from command on November 13, 1861. The rumors that he was not mentally stable began appearing in midwestern newspapers after he had been sent on a twenty-day furlough. The first paper was the *Cincinnati Commercial*, which published an article titled "Sherman is Insane" on December 11, 1861, after Sherman had been replaced as the commander of the Department of the Cumberland by Don Carlos Buell. Sherman wrote that he first learned he was removed due to his mental health from articles in the New York papers. Before that he had assumed his removal from command had come from his own request to Lincoln that he not be put in command.[43]

This incident would have been the end for most general officers. A removal from command and accusations in the press of insanity are difficult to overcome. Sherman could have resigned from the army because his honor had been besmirched and spent the rest of the war writing anti-Lincoln editorials for the newspapers and maybe even run for Congress as a Democrat. Sherman, however, was heavily motivated to do otherwise. He needed a position in the army when the war ended so that he could support his family. There might have been more lucrative opportunities but nothing offered the stability of a place in the army when the war was over. He would need much more than a desire to remain in the army, however, if his career was going to survive those accusations. Luckily, Sherman had a brother who looked out for his interests in Washington. Senator Sherman's letters to his brother during this time period are filled with requests for justifications that he could pass on to the press and the government.[44] John Sherman was a tireless champion for his brother during the war years. Whether Senator Sherman expected a quid pro quo with his brother is not known. However, by the time General Sherman could be of political benefit to his brother, John's political place was already more than secure.

Sherman also had the willingness to take a position uncomplainingly under the command of junior officers. He was reassigned to St. Louis and assumed the command of the Benton Barracks, a training depot.[45] It is hard to believe that someone like McClellan, Pope, or Burnside would have taken such a position.

In the midst of the controversy surrounding his removal from the Department of the Cumberland and allegations of his mental instability, Sherman was quickly being overshadowed by another General Sherman. General Thomas West Sherman was referred to in the newspapers as T. W. Sherman. The Rhode Island native had graduated from West Point four years before William T. Sherman. Like W. T. Sherman, he served in the artillery upon graduation, but unlike the younger Sherman he actually saw combat in the Mexican War. T. W. Sherman remained in the army and began the war as a brigadier general of volunteers.[46]

In October and November 1861, Northern newspapers were filled with talk of T. W. Sherman's expedition to capture Port Royal, South Carolina. After the embarrassment of the first battle of Manassas, loyal newspapers celebrated a strike at the heart of the Confederacy.[47] The expedition achieved its goals. Port Royal was captured, along with several islands between Savannah and Charleston. T. W. Sherman was well on his way to proving W. T. Sherman's prediction about the fate of generals early in the war wrong. T. W. Sherman, however, then proved a victim of bad timing, bad luck, and geography. The leadership in Washington was more interested in Richmond at the time and did not follow up on the victory at Port Royal. The area between Savannah and Charleston, with its low swampy land, was not a suitable place to move forward.[48]

T. W. Sherman did not help his own cause when he issued a statement to the people of South Carolina saying that he and his command meant them no harm and would not "interfere with their social and local institutions."[49] The statement was controversial in the North especially among those with abolitionist leanings and was the subject of ridicule among Southern newspapers. The *Daily Morning News* of Savannah may have best summed up the feelings on both sides when it called Sherman's statement his "affectionate proclamation." It could not have helped his career when the *Charleston Courier* called him the only gentleman assigned to command by Lincoln. Port Royal became mostly a base for naval operations, and Sherman was transferred to the West where he never regained any of his earlier stature.[50]

T. W. Sherman became one of the many Civil War generals whose fame did not outlast the war. He retired from the army in 1870 and died nine years later in his Rhode Island home. Even his greatest military achievement is recorded as a purely naval operation by many Civil War historians.[51]

After William T. Sherman's resignation as commander of the Department of the Cumberland, little was heard from him until he joined Ulysses S. Grant's command after the battles of Fort Henry and Fort Donelson. Sherman would command one of Grant's divisions at the battle of Shiloh. Occurring in April 1862, this was the first great battle of the war. There were more battle casualties during the two days of fighting at Shiloh than during all earlier American wars combined. Sherman's orderly was killed, and he was shot in the hand. This bloodbath showed the American public, North and South, the true nature of this war. It was a decisive Northern victory, and the Union army secured both the Tennessee Valley and the upper Mississippi Valley, including Memphis.[52] Although in the postwar years, Sherman's critics would accuse him of being unprepared at Shiloh to the point of negligence, the press in the very aftermath of the battle proclaimed him the hero of the day.[53]

The *Daily Evening Bulletin* of San Francisco, after reporting Sherman's heroism at the battle of Shiloh, gave a brief biography of the general so its readers would not confuse him with Thomas West Sherman. The biographical sketch was favorable to him and reminded readers that Sherman had once called San Francisco home. It did leave out the fact that Sherman had commanded a military school in Louisiana, but this may have been due more to the limitations of space than to any other reason.[54]

Senator John Sherman used the opportunity of his brother's heroism at Shiloh to defend him from earlier attacks. The senator wrote a letter to the editor of the *Cincinnati Commercial,* which was widely republished, about its publication of the infamous "Sherman is Insane" article. He addressed the claims made by the paper nearly a year earlier. General Sherman neither defended himself at the time from this charge nor, according to his brother, allowed anyone else to do so either. John Sherman ended his letter with a call for the press and the politicians to be careful "in assailing military officers" as "they have no means of defense."[55]

John Sherman's advice to his brother over the issue of the press and his career could not have been better. He told General Sherman to let his service "answer those who have belied you" and to "be hopeful, cheerful, polite to everybody, even a newspaper reporter."[56] Sherman was correct in ignoring the much reprinted article. By the time Senator Sherman defended his brother in the pages of the *Cincinnati Commercial,* time had vindicated the general. His seeming paranoia over the number of troops he would need and the serious danger from invasion that was facing Kentucky had proved to be very accurate.

On July 21, 1862, General Sherman was placed in command of the recently captured city of Memphis, Tennessee. Many of his biographers portrayed Sherman's four months in command of this city as a turning point in his philosophy of war. Confederate guerrillas were active in the Memphis area. They often fired upon Union transports on the Mississippi River and disappeared before troops could be landed or cavalry brought up. These guerrilla tactics could be very effective. If the pilot was killed or disabled, the ship could run aground before control could be regained and her supplies seized or the ship destroyed. Sherman sent expeditions against the guerrillas, but these met with little success; the guerrillas simply blended into the local population.[57]

Sherman dealt with this problem in the most direct way available to him. He instituted a policy of reprisals. On September 24, 1862, he ordered the town of Randolph, Tennessee, to be burned in response for the attack upon the *Forest Queen*. Three days later, Sherman issued Special Order Number 254, which announced that, for every ship fired upon, ten families sympathetic to the Confederate cause would be expelled from Memphis. This was no empty threat. On October 18, 1862, Sherman forced forty families to leave Memphis. He then destroyed all the buildings that could have been used by the guerrillas for fifteen miles south of Memphis on the Arkansas side of the river.[58]

Not only have biographers unfriendly to Sherman often portrayed this as a sign of things to come, the first hints of the total war he would unleash upon Southern civilians, but they also credit him as being the originator of this policy.[59] Nothing could be further from the truth. When Sherman gave Special Order Number 254, it was a long accepted strategy for dealing with guerrillas. The order Sherman gave was very similar to the orders given by Admiral David Farragut as he led his squadron up the Mississippi River from New Orleans. When an officer and several sailors from the *Hartford* were shot at by mounted men on their way to shore in Baton Rouge, Farragut ordered the city to be shelled. When the mayor came out under a flag of truce to ask that the firing cease because it was the work of guerrillas and not the city, Farragut told him that any attack from the shore on his men or ships would be answered by the complete destruction of the closest city, town, or plantation. This was accepted naval policy. It was also accepted army policy. Both John C. Fremont and his successor John Schofield had adopted a policy of retribution in Missouri, and Major General Samuel Curtis while he was in Arkansas adopted an identical policy to Sherman's.

Sherman did not defend himself against these charges of brutality, more than likely because he did not feel it was necessary. Reprisals and hostage taking were an accepted part of war long before the Civil War. To defend those actions would make as much sense to him as defending an order to send out pickets or hold court-martial hearings. Southern papers, however, saw this as an outrage and an example that the commander at Memphis was issuing orders to "punish the women and children" for the acts of lawful combatants.[60] The legality of the combatants was a very debatable point.

Had Sherman felt it necessary to justify his actions at Memphis or any other action during the war he most likely would have referred his accusers to Emmerich De Vattel's *The Law of Nations*. This was considered the standard work on the laws of war. The Swiss-born Vattel was a diplomat in Saxony. His *Law of Nations*, first published in 1758, was especially popular with Americans. Vattel's philosophy justified the American Revolution and called for the neutrality of the sea, a cause that was precious to Americans in the early nineteenth century. Sherman's actions throughout the war not only were justified by Vattel's widely accepted philosophies but were actually quite tame compared to the laws put forward by Vattel. According to *The Law of Nations*, all the citizens of a country are at war when their nation is at war. Of course, he makes the distinction between combatants and noncombatants, but the rights of an army at war always supersede those of the enemy population.[61] Sherman kept a copy of Vattel with him throughout the war.

Northern newspapers would sometimes portray Sherman in a humorous light. Perhaps these stories emerged because the general had a good-humored nature at times. There are many examples of Sherman's sense of humor, but since they are always from secondhand sources (an unnamed junior officer, a reporter, or other civilians), there is no way to tell if they were true or simply urban legends. One example of this type of story was widely publicized while Sherman was the commander at Memphis. According to one story, a man from Arkansas came to Memphis to retrieve his runaway slave, and he wanted help from the army. Sherman, as the story went, told the man from Arkansas to see the US marshal, who under the Fugitive Slave Law of 1850 is obliged "to hunt him up for you." The man excitedly went to the provost marshal's office, per-haps confusing the military office for its civilian counterpart. The man was told that the US marshal was not in town. When he inquired as to his whereabouts, he was told the marshal had been run out of town when Tennessee left the Union.[62] This story was published throughout the North. These types of stories, which portray Sherman as being mischievous in his dealings with Southern civilians, would become common.

The story does portray one of the major issues facing Sherman and all other officers in occupation duty, which was the vast number of runaway slaves. To Northern politicians, the issue of escaped slaves was a complicated one. For military officers it was more so. According to the official stance of the Lincoln administration, the war was a rebellion and thus the laws of the United States were still in effect. This meant that fugitive slaves had to be returned to their owners. However, if an officer was too zealous in this duty he fell into quick disfavor with many politicians and a growing segment of the population. This had been the fate of Thomas West Sherman. As the war dragged on, returning slaves could hurt the morale of the soldiers, since they knew they would have to attack fortifications that had been made by the very same slaves or they would have to face soldiers freed from other duty by these slaves.[63]

On the other hand, if an officer ignored the law and paid more attention to the actual situation, both political and military, he could find himself in violation of US law. It was not likely that any prosecutions would take place, but it was not a comfortable position to be in if the political climate changed or an ambitious junior officer wanted his position. Generals who went to the other extreme—as Major General John C. Fremont did when he issued his own emancipation proclamation at the beginning of the war—could very quickly find themselves in disfavor with an administration that was trying desperately to hold on to the border states.[64]

While in command of Memphis, Sherman deftly avoided the political nightmare that came with the question of runaway slaves. All runaway slaves who came into Union lines around Memphis were put to work preparing the defenses of the city. In exchange, they were fed, housed, and paid. No abolitionist could find ground to complain about Sherman's orders dealing with this issue. The wages the slaves earned were held in escrow for them until their status was determined by the US government. If they were still property, their owners would be given the money they had earned while working for the US Army, so no anti-abolitionist could find fault with Sherman's policy.[65] Until the president issued the Emancipation Proclamation, which clearly stated the policy of the US government and removed officers on occupation duty from the uncertainty regarding the issue of runaway slaves, Sherman handled the issue as best as was possible.

Sherman avoided the controversy that the other General Sherman in South Carolina had fallen into, as well. T. W. Sherman had been widely criticized for being too soft on the Confederacy. This would never be a serious complaint about William T. Sherman in Memphis. Not only did he use slaves for his own military purposes and expel citizens from the city in response to guerrilla attacks, he also made his feelings about the Southern leadership well-known to the citizens of Memphis.[66] The arguments he made against slavery and Southern culture were as much John Sherman's as they were General Sherman's.

It was during his stay at Memphis that the general acquired his reputation for bias against the press. Sherman censored the newspapers and even closed down the *Memphis Union Appeal*, a paper the Northern press referred to as "an out-and-out loyal paper," for publishing information that might be helpful to the enemy. He also ordered a correspondent for the *Chicago Post*, a Mr. Corcoran, to leave the city.[67] Sherman took over the office of the *Appeal*, and the Union army began printing its own newspaper. It is very unlikely that any editorials complaining of Sherman's ill treatment of the press appeared in its pages.

Although there had been some complaints about Sherman's heavy-handedness in Memphis at the time, he was generally seen as equal to any other Union commander that occupied Memphis during the war. His destruction of personal property along the river and his expulsion of Confederate sympathizers in response to attacks on riverboats may have earned him some unkind words, but New Orleans residents who suffered under Benjamin "the Beast" Butler would probably have gladly preferred living under the rule of Sherman. He mostly tried to stay out of the lives of ordinary citizens, going so far as bringing back the city government that existed before occupation, a decision that would bring him minor admonishment in the Northern press for being too soft on the Confederates.[68]

Sherman was greatly relieved when he received orders from General Grant commanding him to move against Vicksburg with four divisions. As was usual, the newspapers printed the movement of Sherman's forces. They provided conjectures as to the army's probable objectives as soon as the forces began to move.[69]

Sherman was still enough of an unknown commodity that the *New York Herald* felt it was necessary to reacquaint their readers with him as he moved toward Vicksburg. The short summery of Sherman's military career included nothing negative about his previous military commands. The paper did not mention the reason he was removed in Kentucky. The last sentence reminded readers that he was the brother of Senator Sherman. *Frank Leslie's Illustrated Newspaper* published a similar introduction of Sherman to the general public during the campaign for Vicksburg, describing his heroism at Shiloh and dismissing his failures around Vicksburg as fruitless attacks. His less than successful tenure in Kentucky was conveniently left out.[70]

In the same weeks that some newspapers introduced General Sherman to the public, many newspapers reported his death. General T. W. Sherman had been wounded at Port Hudson, Louisiana, and when reports reached newspaper offices there was some confusion as to which Sherman had been killed. As it turned out neither of the generals was one of the over half a million men to die in the war. T. W. Sherman lost a leg but survived the war; the press had been much too quick to report his death.[71]

Sherman was a prolific letter writer during the war and throughout his lifetime. Often letters written to friends or family would reach the press, and as Sherman's fame grew these letters were printed by newspapers starved for news from the front. Many of Sherman's letters that reached the press during the war years are ones written to his brother John. If John Sherman felt his brother's words would help the general's reputation, they would be printed in the newspapers. One such letter, written outside of Vicksburg, described Sherman's view of war in 1863. It is the type of letter that a future generation of writers would use to portray Sherman as a savage. Sherman wrote that he deplored "the devastation and misery that attend our progress, but that all history teaches us that war, pestilence and famine are the usual order of things by which the Almighty allays the storms of human passion after the long calm of peace." It would be very easy to portray this type of quote as the beginnings of a philosophy of war that would culminate in the destruction of Georgia and South Carolina and the brutal campaigns against the Native Americans during the postwar years. It is much more likely that Sherman was trying to convince himself that the depravations faced by those in the path of the army were necessary for a later peace. By no means did he suggest that the suffering should be increased. Instead he believed that, for civilians in an area occupied by a nineteenth-century army, this suffering was unavoidable, and at least there was a positive aspect to that.[72]

The capture of Vicksburg was one of the most important victories of the war. It was also perhaps Grant's finest hour. He marched his troops south of the city on the opposite shore of the river. His gunboats and transports passed under the guns of Vicksburg, suffering only minor damage, and he ferried his army unopposed across the river thirty-five miles south of Vicksburg. Instead of coming directly at Vicksburg as the Confederates expected, Grant moved east toward Jackson. After capturing the Mississippi state capital and driving away an army under the command of Joseph Johnston, he turned back west toward Vicksburg. Grant took a great risk in this operation, because he abandoned his line of supply and communication. Washington could do nothing but wait until he reemerged at Vicksburg. Johnston, whose strategy was to sever Grant's supply lines, could not counter Grant's bold move.

John Pemberton, the Confederate commander at Vicksburg, was determined to hold the city, however. Strong fortifications forced the Union army to lay siege to Vicksburg. After six weeks of artillery bombardments and on the point of starvation, the Confederate garrison surrendered on July 4, 1863. The Fourth of July holiday would not be celebrated in the city of Vicksburg until the bicentennial in 1976.

Sherman received praise from the Northern press after the fall of Vicksburg and Jackson. He was hailed as Grant's most trusted lieutenant who deserved a great deal of the credit for the victories in Mississippi.[73] Sherman was promoted to brigadier general in the regular army, all but ensuring him a prominent position after the war. He even received a letter from his old instructor at West Point Dennis Hart Mahan, considered by many one of the great minds among American military thinkers, praising him for his role in the capture of Vicksburg.[74]

Tragedy struck the Sherman family, however, just as they were enjoying the success of the general. On October 3, 1863, nine-year-old William Tecumseh Sherman, Jr., died of typhoid fever. Sherman's wife, Ellen, and the four oldest children had been visiting the army at camp along the Big Black River in Mississippi. Sherman was devastated by the loss, but his responsibilities did not leave him time to grieve. General William Rosecrans's Army of the Cumberland had been defeated at Chickamauga and was now under siege in Chattanooga, Tennessee. Sherman was unable even to attend his son's funeral in Ohio.[75] The newspapers respectfully reported the story of the boy's death. In the midst of thousands of deaths in battle and from disease, reporters treated the death of Willy, as he was called by family and friends, as a senseless tragedy.[76]

General Sherman did find time to write a short letter to the commander of the Thirteenth Regular Battalion of the Army of the Tennessee. Before Willy's death, the boy had been adopted as a sort of mascot for that unit. He had been made an honorary sergeant of the Thirteenth and had drilled with them in the uniform the soldiers had made him. Sherman asked the commander, Captain C. C. Smith, to thank his men "for their kind behavior to my poor child."

Sherman promised that in future years, if any soldier from the Thirteenth during the Vicksburg campaign came to the door of his family, they would "share with them our last blanket, our last crust."[77] Sherman would keep this promise in the postwar years. Any veteran from the Western armies would be treated with kindness and charity by the general and his family.

After the disaster at Chickamauga, President Lincoln created the Military Division of the Mississippi and ordered Grant to take command. Grant rushed to Chattanooga, where the Army of the Cumberland was under siege. On Grant's recommendation, Sherman was given command of the Army of the Tennessee and ordered to move the army as quickly as possible to Chattanooga. Newspapers reacted positively to Sherman's promotion, one reporter viewing him as the natural choice and deserving of the honor.[78]

Sherman's West Point roommate, George Thomas, replaced Rosecrans as head of the Army of the Cumberland. He was given the order by Grant to hold Chattanooga "at all hazards." To this Thomas made his famous reply, "We will hold the town until we starve."[79]

Grant's position at Chattanooga was a precarious one. With the city situated in a valley surrounded by mountain ridges controlled by an enemy of nearly sixty thousand men, Grant's lines of communication and supply were almost completely cut off. Although Grant is best remembered for his victories along the Mississippi River and his defeat of Robert E. Lee in the East, the Battle of Chattanooga showed his greatness as a general. Inheriting an untenable position, Grant drove the enemy from its superior position and laid the groundwork for Sherman's invasion of Georgia.[80] Grant's victory was won on the most difficult terrain of the war. Any visitor to Chattanooga who follows the path taken by the men of the Army of the Cumberland will not be overly impressed with the gently rolling hills that George Pickett's men crossed at the Battle of Gettysburg.

After the war there was a great deal written about who deserved credit for victory at Chattanooga. Generals claimed they did not get enough credit and that their fellow officers got too much. In November 1863, this was not the case. Chattanooga was a complete success, and there were enough congratulations to go around. Newspapers credited Grant with the victory. His plan and his audacity carried the day. His subordinates carried out his plans and performed even better than the optimist Grant could have hoped for.[81]

Joseph Hooker, the disgraced former commander from the East, carried Lookout Mountain in the "Battle above the Clouds," putting his army in a position to move behind the Confederate army and cut off its retreat. Sherman's Army of the Tennessee attacked Tunnel Hill on the north end of the Confederate line. While both ends of the Confederate army were engaged, George Thomas's

Army of the Cumberland drove through the center and forced the rebels from Missionary Ridge. Although Thomas's supporters would always claim that he was never given the credit he deserved because he was a Southerner, the press at the time heaped praise on all three men and their leader.[82]

Sherman was praised for the speed at which his army reached the battlefield. In the decades that followed the Civil War there would be accusations that he was slow in reaching the battlefield and that he did not complete the tasks given to him by Grant. These would be arguments made by men writing their memoirs in the later years of their lives. In 1863, every man succeeded brilliantly on the battlefield, and Sherman's movement of an army from North Mississippi to the battlefield at Chattanooga was, in the assessment of the *Wisconsin State Register*, no less than "one of the most remarkable feats in the history of army marches."[83] This was a bit of an overstatement, of course, but it was an achievement that many Civil War generals would have been incapable of making.

Following the battle of Chattanooga, Sherman was on the verge of becoming one of the great generals of the war. He had gone from an unknown and unemployed former soldier to someone the newspapers were beginning to give credit to as bringing victory to the Union. He had overcome obstacles that would have ended the careers of most men. His West Point education and politically connected family had helped somewhat, but his willingness to loyally follow an officer junior in seniority was what would turn Sherman into a figure known, if misunderstood, by even the most casual students of history.

CHAPTER 2

The Atlanta Campaign and the March to the Sea

At the beginning of the Civil War, William T. Sherman had shunned high command. He understood that there would be a learning curve to be faced by both soldiers and politicians. He rightly predicted that commanding generals in the first few years of the war would be very unlikely to survive in their positions until the end. Sherman's goal was to have the job security of the army when the war ended. He knew that if he were relieved of another command, he would once again be unemployed when the army shrank to its prewar size following the Civil War.

He had great success following Grant. Sherman's loyal support helped Grant win, and as Grant rose with each of the great victories, Sherman would occupy his last position. By the end of 1863, Sherman would have to take independent command if he were to rise any further. It is in this last year and a half of war that Sherman gained his reputation and would be judged by future generations.

After the battle of Chattanooga, it was obvious to most that the armies of the Military Division of the Mississippi would move south along the railroad with Atlanta as the main target. Northern and Southern papers agreed that this was the next logical step for General Grant.[1] They did not, however, predict that Grant would be given command of all Union armies and that General Sherman would be the one to lead the Armies of the Tennessee, the Cumberland, and the Ohio south into Georgia.

When Sherman replaced Grant in command, the news generated no great surprise. Ever since his victory at Vicksburg, the Northern public regarded Grant as the savior of the Union cause who could do no wrong. This included his choice of Sherman as the commander of the Military Department of the Mississippi. By the time of his appointment, Sherman was the most prominent general in the West, second only to Grant himself. His raid into the interior of Mississippi had dominated the newspapers for weeks.[2]

In February 1864, with twenty-one thousand men, Sherman left Vicksburg for Meridian on the border with Alabama. The mission was to destroy the railroads around the city. Meridian was a railroad junction that connected Memphis, Mobile, and Montgomery. If this junction was cut there would be disastrous consequences for the Confederacy. What made Meridian a tempting target also made it a dangerous one. There were about seventeen thousand Confederate soldiers scattered throughout the area under the command of Lieutenant General Leonidas Polk. This was a sizable force on its own, but because Meridian was a railroad hub and the Confederates had the advantage of interior lines, reinforcements could be brought against Sherman from Atlanta and Mobile.[3]

To keep the Confederates from massing their forces against Sherman, Grant ordered all the forces under his command to make demonstrations against their closest opponent. The navy would maneuver outside Mobile Bay. Thomas was to move his Army of the Cumberland south as if he was beginning an advance toward Atlanta. General W. Sooy Smith's force of seven thousand cavalry would ride south from Memphis, sweeping the cavalry force of Nathan Bedford Forrest out of his way and join forces with Sherman in Meridian. After completing his objectives at Meridian, Sherman had the discretion to choose his next move. An invasion of Alabama was a real possibility. Sherman, in a letter to Halleck, wrote that Selma was the most likely target for his army after Meridian. The destruction of the Selma Cannon Foundry would have been a serious blow to the Confederacy. Pascagoula was also discussed by Sherman and Grant as a possible destination.[4]

Sherman was limited in what he could do by two things. Grant wanted him to be cautious in his operations. The loss of Sherman's force might threaten Union control of the Mississippi. Sherman, also, only had a limited amount of time. Nathaniel Banks's ill-fated Red River campaign was scheduled to begin the next month. It would include portions of Sherman's command. The Red River campaign was a priority for Lincoln, Halleck, and Grant and was strongly supported by Sherman. He could not operate in east Mississippi or west Alabama very long.[5]

The initial stage of the plan worked perfectly. Sherman reached Meridian on February 15, 1864, without fighting a battle. Polk fell back across the Tombigbee River into Alabama, assuming an advance to Mobile was the next step. Sherman's small army destroyed or captured 150 miles of railroad, sixty-seven bridges, twenty locomotives, twenty-eight cars, and several thousand bales of cotton. More than eight thousand escaped slaves followed Sherman back to Vicksburg.[6]

Smith's cavalry was defeated by a force under the command of Nathan Bedford Forrest at the battle of Okolona and retreated back to Memphis. When it was clear to Sherman that Smith would not reach Meridian in time for the combined force to move east, he returned to Vicksburg. Without cavalry support, he decided that a move against Polk's army lurking across the river in Alabama or any move east was too dangerous.[7]

The Meridian campaign has been called a rehearsal for Sherman's "March to the Sea." There is a great deal of truth in this. Sherman showed that a city and railroad hub can be made unusable by the enemy without occupying it. He also learned that by feint and deception he could achieve his goals without risking a battle. The most important lesson from the campaign was that an enemy with the interior lines can be defeated by an enemy with superior resources and a good plan. The fear of operating against the Confederacy with its interior lines had paralyzed the Union army at the start of the war.[8] Sherman showed that, if the enemy was kept engaged on all fronts, the fact that he could move reinforcements more rapidly did not matter, an argument Lincoln had been making since the beginning of the war. This was a lesson that would be put to great use in the spring campaigns of 1864.

The great similarity between the two operations was the reaction of the public and the press. The Northern press speculated endlessly about the status of Sherman's army and its final destination. Southern newspapers simultaneously decried the destruction accompanying Sherman's forces, downplayed its effect, and criticized their generals for not doing more to stop the hated invaders.[9] The press, both North and South, had created a template in which they only had to change a few names and dates from the coverage of the Mississippi campaign to report the Georgia campaign. Even the term "Sherman's Vandals," which would become a cliché among those writing about Georgia, originated in newspaper accounts of the Mississippi campaign.[10]

The movements of the Union navy near Mobile and Thomas in west Tennessee had so thoroughly convinced the South that Sherman's attack on Meridian was the beginning of a campaign against Mobile that they considered his return to Vicksburg a Union defeat. The *Daily Richmond Examiner* analyzed the reasons for this perceived Confederate victory. According to the editors at the *Examiner*, Sherman had introduced an ancient practice into modern warfare. By abandoning his military "base" and moving into the enemy's interior Sherman was using the "moveable column" favored by the ancient Romans and Greeks. Apparently this analyst had forgotten both Grant's operations around Vicksburg and Scott's successful capture of Mexico City when he had abandoned his supply lines and marched into the interior of Mexico.

According to the *Examiner*, "This system of operations is at war with all modern tactics, which places an extravagant estimation upon field artillery." The article went on to predict that if the Union army continued to use this tactic it would fail just as Sherman's expedition failed, because the interior of the South was filled with the "frightful face of bleak prairies and more alarming frowns of somber pine forests."[11] General Nathan Bedford Forrest would probably have argued that they gave credit to the wrong forest for Sherman's withdrawal. Not even the moveable columns of the ancient Greeks marched into enemy territory without the aid of a cavalry screen.

Pro-Republican Northern newspapers saw the operation as the success it was. Instead of discussing the reasons for Sherman's withdrawal they wrote about the destruction brought by the Union army. The Union army met its stated goals, destroyed a great deal of railroad, and thus disrupted commerce and the distribution of supplies.[12] Had Sherman been more open about his plans for after the capture of Meridian, and had the press and public known that his aim was Polk's army and Selma, the press might well have reported the campaign differently when he failed to meet those objectives. That victory was partially determined by how the press covered an operation was a lesson that General Sherman was not slow to forget.

On April 11, 1864, from his headquarters in Vicksburg, General Sherman wrote his brother about the military situation in the West. He included in the letter a set of instructions he had sent to one of his adjutants with the understanding that John Sherman would discreetly pass it to the press. The letter, obviously written for public consumption, dealt with the treatment of disloyal citizens in occupied territory. Unless the adjutant's question had been "What is your general impression of the righteousness of this war," it is difficult to believe that the letter answered it. Sherman's letter stated that he expected complaints against him in the press due to his railroad policies in Tennessee and Kentucky. He had ordered that no civilians be allowed to travel further south than Nashville. In the letter he put forward his views of the treatment of civilians. He argued that the army had "any and all rights which they chose to enforce in war." This was a letter meant for public consumption. It was a radical letter, written to get an angry response from the Southern papers. He understood that if the Confederate press was calling him "the prince of Barbarians," he was safe from the Republican press.[13]

After the promotions of Grant and Sherman, the two generals met in Cincinnati to discuss the spring campaign of 1864. In all likelihood they considered more technical details since the overall strategy had been decided by Grant long before this meeting. All Union armies in the field would begin offensive actions in early May 1864. This would prevent the Confederate army from massing its forces against one Union army, as they had done throughout the war. Sherman would command the combined Armies of the Tennessee, Cumberland, and Ohio against General Joseph Johnston's Army of Tennessee. The strategy was simple: if Sherman pressed toward Atlanta, a major Southern manufacturing center, and Grant pushed toward Richmond, the Confederate armies would destroy themselves trying to stop them.[14]

Civil War historians have a tendency to concentrate on the Eastern Theater of the war. Anything that did not happen between Washington and Richmond is delegated to the second tier. In their defense, however, that was how many people viewed the war at the time. Although it can very easily be argued that the war was won in the West, it did not catch the public's attention as much as the epic battles between the Armies of the Potomac and Northern Virginia. Lincoln and some loyal newspapers lamented this. Sherman became the major beneficiary of the response. In an attempt to overcome this fixation on the Virginia campaign, pages and pages were written about Sherman's successes leading to the capture of Atlanta and how extremely important this was.[15]

The Northern press followed all details of the advance toward Atlanta very closely. It is difficult to say whether the coverage was negative or positive as it was generally just the facts of the campaign with little or no editorial comment.[16] Even the much debated battle of Kennesaw Mountain was treated in the press as just another push south by the Union army.[17] The reports of Sherman's southern movements said it all.

Only the Southern press was forced to offer opinion and predictions of the future. They attempted to portray Johnston as a master of Fabian strategy. Named after the Roman general Quintus Fabius Maximus Verrucosus, Fabian strategy has in military terms come to mean a strategy of retreating to avoid a major defeat and drawing the enemy into a trap. This strategy best explained many of Johnston's decisions, but after the war Johnston vigorously claimed that he was not pursuing a Fabian policy. This was ironic considering his argument. He claimed his early removal led to Confederate defeat just as Fabius's dismissal led to a disaster for the Roman army against Hannibal and the Carthaginians. The *Atlanta Register* printed a quote supposedly from General Winfield Scott: "Beware of Lee when he advances—of Johnston when he retreats."[18] The fact that the quote was directed toward an unknown general sometime within a two-year period makes it less than believable. More doubt is cast on this story when the *Richmond Examiner* would eventually discover that it was to Sherman that Scott made this prophetic warning.[19]

On the day Confederate forces abandoned Atlanta to Sherman and the Union army, the *Daily Richmond Examiner* wrote that the campaigns of Sherman and

Grant were weakening and quickly approaching disaster. The article stated that Lincoln was frustrated with these two generals and would soon replace them. Northern papers were much kinder toward Sherman; some pro-Lincoln papers even erroneously reported that it was presidential candidate George McClellan who had Sherman removed from command in Kentucky.[20]

Although Southern newspapers tried to put the best spin possible on the loss of Atlanta, the Confederate citizens knew the city's importance. Not only was Atlanta the railroad hub that connected east to west, it also had one of the few rolling mills left in the South.[21] Although newspapermen and politicians of the day wrote at length about the importance of Atlanta, and so have scores of historians since the end of the war, the famous Southern diarist Mary Boykin Chesnut put it best: "Atlanta gone. Well—the agony is over. No hope. We will try to have no fear."[22]

The fall of Atlanta perhaps came just in time for Sherman as he was about to step into what might have become another controversy. In 1864 Congress passed a law allowing the individual states to recruit freedmen and count them as part of the number of troops their state was required to provide. Sherman did not think this good policy on the part of the Federal government. He felt it was an insult to the soldiers of his army "to place them on par with the level of recruits" that would be brought into the army.[23] Of course, by this Sherman meant the freed or runaway slaves, although Sherman's view of freedmen's regiments raised in the North was little better.

Like many of the controversies that Sherman faced throughout his life, he should have kept his opinion to himself or saved it for his memoirs. Instead he wrote a letter to a Massachusetts's recruiting agent suggesting that he set up his office in one of a number of cities deep within Confederate lines. Newspapers reprinted Sherman's letter where it received mixed reviews. Many newspapers such as the *Ohio Statesman* supported Sherman and saw the humor in his statements. However, the abolitionist newspapers, particularly *The Liberator*, accused him of being narrow-minded.[24] A discussion in the nation's newspapers of Sherman's views of African American soldiers was postponed by the news that Union forces had captured the city of Atlanta.

The loss of Atlanta with its railroads and foundries would be a defeat from which the Confederacy could not recover.[25] The *New York Tribune* called Atlanta the "Gibraltar of the Rebellion, . . . the territorial key to the Confederacy" and said that its capture "ranks in military importance beyond even Richmond." After the fall of Atlanta, Sherman's star was at its highest. The vast majority of historians credit Sherman's capture of Atlanta with Lincoln's reelection in 1864. Without Sherman's success, Lincoln may not have even received the Republican nomination.[26]

Southern newspapers naturally tried to downplay Sherman's success, at least those who were not using the fall of Atlanta to attack the Davis administration. Atlanta was presented as a target of little importance. The *Fayetteville Observer* in an attempt to strengthen the morale of its readers wrote that the fall of Atlanta did not compare with the twin disasters of Gettysburg and Vicksburg and that the South had recovered from those tragedies. While it is possible to argue that the fall of Vicksburg and the defeat at Gettysburg were worse than what had happened at Atlanta, it is a lot more difficult to say that the South ever recovered from July 1863. It was a common theme in Southern papers that the only benefit of the fall of Atlanta was the reelection of Lincoln. According to the *Fayetteville Observer*, this was actually a positive event because McClellan would have been so much more capable of handling the war.[27]

On November 16, 1864, Sherman left Atlanta with approximately sixty thousand men. He sent the rest of his men back to Tennessee to join the command of George Thomas with the hope that Thomas would move south into Alabama against Hood's battered army. Sherman sent two entire corps of veteran troops north to Thomas.[28] Every army has it stragglers and shirkers, often draftees or bountymen who would do all they could to avoid combat. These men probably assumed that as Sherman marched south out of Atlanta he was headed toward the next major battle and that safety lay north toward Chattanooga. One can only presume that as the excess equipment, non-combat troops, and wounded were loaded onto trains, these stragglers would have done everything possible to leave as well. As Sherman put it in a report to Grant, he sent back the "sick and wounded and worthless."[29] It is ironic that those who went to the rear to avoid combat found themselves in the middle of the worst fighting of the war, the battles of Franklin and Nashville.

Sherman reached Savannah on December 14, 1864. In those twenty-nine days, Sherman's army had fought no major engagements. They had covered nearly ten miles a day. With the exception of Savannah, the Union army had conquered no new ground in Georgia. Atlanta, which had been so difficult to take, had been abandoned to the enemy. It was those twenty-nine days that made Sherman a legend; some argued that it was the bold master stroke that helped bring the war to an end and others that it was the brutal offensive that ushered in twentieth-century total warfare.[30] It is perhaps because of this huge gulf that Sherman's March to the Sea is the most misunderstood aspect of the American Civil War.

Although it has been much debated by historians, Sherman's decision to march south out of Atlanta was an easy one for him to make. When he was in command in Memphis, he chaffed at having to remain stationary, and Atlanta would prove much worse than Memphis. With a major Confederate army threatening his lines of supply and communication, he would have to fight to keep the single line of railroad connecting Atlanta to Chattanooga open. People who met Sherman in person described him as a man who could not sit still, always pacing and fidgeting.[31] If he could not stay still in a room, it was much more difficult to sit still with an entire army.

The decision of where to go with his army was a more difficult one. Sherman would not fall back toward Tennessee. That would be the type of retreat that his superiors, especially Grant, and the public would not stand for. Jefferson Davis had only recently given a speech to John Bell Hood's army promising that Sherman would be driven out of Georgia. It was a challenge that Sherman could not ignore. Sherman also knew that moving back to Tennessee would not serve any purpose.[32] A westward move into Alabama would have very limited value. With the important railroad junction of Atlanta made useless, Mobile Bay in the hands of the Union navy, and the Mississippi River in Union hands, Alabama was essentially out of the war. An eastward move toward South Carolina would pay bigger dividends. Augusta, Georgia, had so far been untouched during the war and was the Confederate armies' largest source of gunpowder.[33] The eastward route was also the most direct way to General Robert E. Lee's rear. This idea was abandoned for the same reason that Sherman's March to the Sea is so applauded. Sherman would have to cut his supply line to move on Augusta. If he found himself in a siege of Augusta, as he had at Atlanta, he could easily have been cut off and placed in an untenable position. Sherman suggested to Grant that he would move against Augusta if the navy could take Savannah and supply his army using the Savannah River.[34] This proved improbable without diverting large numbers of troops then on the frontline pushing the Army of Northern Virginia.

Sherman ordered his army south. His orders were discretionary as to the final destination. Places as far west as Pensacola and Mobile were mentioned as possible destinations. Halleck was hoping Sherman would take Montgomery and Selma.[35] There is a famous quote attributed to both Lincoln and Grant (depending on the source) that Sherman was like a "ground-mole when he disappears under a lawn. You can here and there trace his track, but you are not quite certain where he will come out till you see his head."[36]

Sherman's preference was Savannah. If he could reach the East Coast, he would be supplied by the navy, and with uncontested mastery of the seas the rear of his army would be completely safe. If the commander of the Army of Tennessee, John Bell Hood, followed, which Sherman hoped, he could turn and fight with his back to the sea and no supply line to protect. If Hood did not follow, Sherman could move north and trap Lee and his Army of Northern Virginia between Grant and himself.[37] The Gulf Coast offered Sherman some good targets. Mobile was still in Confederate hands, although Admiral David Farragut's masterful battle of Mobile Bay had shut the city off from the outside. Montgomery and Tallahassee were both Confederate state capitals. Only the capture of Savannah, however, would put Sherman where he wanted to be, in position to move north against the Army of Northern Virginia. The lesson from the Meridian campaign was obvious. Had Sherman been more open about his desire to capture Selma and destroy Polk's army that campaign may have been seen as a failure instead of the success it was. Sherman will not state Savannah as his final goal. If military expediency had caused him to change direction and emerge on the Gulf of Mexico, he did not want the Confederacy to be able to claim victory, however minor.

To trap Lee between Sherman's armies and Grant's was the overall object of the movement toward Savannah. He told his officers, before leaving Atlanta, that they were destined for North Carolina, a probable location of Lee had he been able to evade Grant. Confederate Lieutenant General Wade Hampton wrote, after the war, that Sherman's purpose to meet up with Grant "was evident to everyone who had given a thought to the subject."[38]

Before Sherman began to move his army south through the state of Georgia toward saltwater, he gave two orders that would become the beginning of Sherman's black legend. Sherman ordered the city of Atlanta evacuated. Civilian residents would either be taken north to Chattanooga or be allowed to go south. If they went north, the Union army would transport them for at least the first leg of the trip. If they decided to go south, they would be the responsibility of the Confederate army. When an army captures territory, it has the moral obligation to ensure law and order. When an army moved forward, a force would have to be left to garrison a captured city. This drained the strength of an army on the move, "so that success was actually crippling our armies in the field by detachments to guard and protect the interests of a hostile population." The technical term for this is "strategic consumption," and it was a concept that every military leader more than understood.[39]

In a letter to General Halleck, Sherman wrote the oft-quoted line "that war is war, and not popularity seeking."[40] The quote is often seen by writers as a confession made by Sherman that he was guilty of whatever atrocity he was charged with. In fact, Sherman was referring to the forced evacuation of Atlanta, in which Union troops would help the residents get to their destination. His actual thought is a far cry from that of the destructive war dog this quote is meant to portray. Sherman would also forward a letter written from Major William Clare of the Confederate army complimenting the Union army for its "positive kindness" toward the over four hundred families and their belongings sent south.[41]

During the March to the Sea, very little information of the army's whereabouts reached the newspapers, either North or South. At any time, there was little doubt that Sherman's goal was the Atlantic Coast but how far his army was from the coast and its status could only be guessed. The lack of information has often been blamed on Sherman's "war" with the press and his banishment of them from the campaign. This is untrue; several reporters from major newspapers accompanied the army and submitted their stories when the army reached Savannah. The real reason the press and the public, North and South, were kept in the dark about Sherman's campaign was his systematic and effective destruction of the telegraph lines. Some Southern papers even concluded that the silence from Georgia was due to censorship by the Confederate government.[42]

The Southern press initially portrayed the March to the Sea as a retreat. Sherman was rushing to the coast where he could be rescued by the US Navy. This portrayal was probably based more on wishful thinking than anything else. According to some papers, Hood and his army had moved north of Atlanta and cut off the Union army from its supply line to Chattanooga, forcing this panic-driven retreat to saltwater. Hood's cavalry had moved into position to threaten Sherman's supply line, which had convinced Sherman that remaining on the defensive in North Georgia was a poor idea. Thanks to the navy, saltwater did mean safety for a Union army. To refer to the March to the Sea, however, as a desperate move was an extreme exaggeration. Southern papers also hoped against reality that Sherman was "marching on his Moscow."[43]

After the fall of Atlanta and Hood's movement into Alabama, and eventually Tennessee, the question of who commanded Georgia's resistance was as confusing to Confederate citizens as it is to modern historians. Gustavus W. Smith commanded the Georgia militia. Smith was a former general in the Confederate army as well as the secretary of war. He resigned when others were promoted ahead of him. Smith was appointed commander of the militia by Governor Joseph Brown. His command was made up of men who had been able to avoid the Confederate draft and was probably around thirty-five hundred. Smith took his command to Macon, believing this was Sherman's next logical target after Atlanta. To his lifelong embarrassment, Smith's Georgia militia was easily swept aside by a single brigade. Smith has become a footnote in Civil War history as the man who commanded the Army of Northern Virginia for twenty-four hours between Joseph Johnston and Robert E. Lee.[44]

Lieutenant General William J. Hardee, whom Hood blamed for the loss of Atlanta, took command of the defense of Macon. He did not, however, have command over the Georgia militia. General Braxton Bragg brought ten thousand troops into Augusta, Georgia, from North Carolina to defend that city. General P. G. T. Beauregard came east from Mississippi to Macon. Although he had overall command of all departments west of the Appalachians, he had no forces under his direct command. This situation was a case of too many chiefs and not enough Indians, and to make it even worse, Lieutenant General Richard Taylor, commander of the Department of Alabama, came to observe and report his findings to Lee in Virginia.[45]

The only real resistance facing Sherman's army was provided by the forty-five hundred men under the command of Major General Joseph Wheeler, one of the youngest generals in the war. Sherman's own cavalry—under the command of one of Wheeler's West Point classmates, Major General Judson Kilpatrick—was more than successful at keeping the Confederate cavalry away from the Union's three columns as they marched through Georgia. Wheeler's small force was unable to defend any of the state's cities or citizens from the Union army. Wheeler's only real success came in alienating the general population. There were enough complaints in Southern newspapers about the thefts and destruction carried out by Wheeler's men that the *Daily South Carolinian* felt obliged to publish a defense of Wheeler. According to the article, any loss at the hands of Wheeler's cavalry was the "legitimate results of the presence anywhere of an army" or was the result of "exceptional villains" who were "cowardly stragglers."[46]

Sherman reached Savannah, his target, without a great deal of difficulty caused by Confederate forces. Wheeler's cavalry harassed his flanks, and occasionally Georgia militiamen who were either too young or too old would block the path of one of Sherman's columns but would be quickly swept away by the Union veterans. At the closest thing to a battle, the engagement at Griswoldville, less than fifteen hundred Illinois veterans pushed aside forty-four hundred Georgia militiamen. They took few casualties, and the overall march was barely slowed. What impressed Sherman's contemporaries was the logistics of moving such a large force from Atlanta to Savannah. The invasion of South Georgia was truly a case of the very best of the Union army versus the dregs of Confederate resistance.[47]

When Sherman reached Savannah and reestablished contact with the outside world, two major pieces of news were waiting for him. Hood had been soundly defeated in Tennessee. This must have been a great relief considering that, if Nashville was taken and Hood was in a position to invade Kentucky, Sherman's march south would have looked foolish. Sherman also learned from the newspapers that his nine-month-old son, Charles, had died.[48]

Sherman also on his arrival in Savannah received a letter from Eliza Anderson, wife of his old friend and former commanding officer Major General Robert Anderson. She wanted Sherman to locate her two brothers who were serving in the Confederate army near Savannah. Duncan Clinch, Jr., had been seriously wounded in the defense of Fort McAlister, and the second brother, an aide of General Hardee, had been captured on a ship in the Savannah River. Sherman sent Kilpatrick to see the injured man and deliver Mrs. Anderson's kind words and jam. Sherman visited the younger brother himself. He gave the young officer "a terrible scolding" on the "rash crime" of secession against the "government his own father had been instrumental in establishing" and for joining forces "with those who aimed the shot at the noble gentleman and loving husband to his own sister."[49]

Sherman's March to the Sea was a total success if his goal was to reach Savannah and put his army into position to move north in order to trap the Army of Northern Virginia between himself and Grant. His army very quickly reached its destination with minimal losses. When it reached Savannah, it was in a position to be ferried anywhere along the Atlantic Coast to deliver a hammer blow to Lee's army, or it was ready to begin marching north, capturing those enemy capitals not yet in Union hands and putting pressure on the Army of Northern Virginia as it neared its rear.[50]

The March to the Sea was not a success, however, if, as many historians and a later generation of southerners contend, it was intended to break Southern resistance, "make Georgia howl," to use Sherman's phrase, or initiate a new era of total warfare. Sherman's intentions can best be judged by his actions. Sherman moved his army as quickly through Georgia as possible. While he did destroy the manufacturing capabilities of Atlanta and destroyed all the railroads in his path, he completely bypassed the industrial cities of Macon, Columbus, and Augusta. If Sherman's mission had been to destroy the ability of the enemy to wage war (the definition of "total war"), he left untouched three of the enemy's biggest assets. Macon and Columbus still had river access to the Gulf of Mexico, and Augusta with its powder works was still connected to Lee's army by railroad.

It has also been argued that Sherman pierced the outer shell of the Confederacy and showed it was hollow inside. This argument emphasizes that Sherman broke the morale of the Confederacy by showing it could not defend its interior and proved to the rest of the world that Union victory was inevitable.[51] To accept the argument that Sherman broke the morale of Georgians, you have to believe that Confederate morale was strong before his March to the Sea. This was anything but true. Georgia politicians were already debating making a separate peace. The lack of resistance that Sherman's army found in Georgia is the best evidence that the state was suffering a serious morale problem. As for showing the world that Union victory was inevitable, it can easily be argued that everyone but a handful of Confederate politicians knew this already. If, however, Hood in Tennessee and Lee in Virginia had won a victory, things may have been different.

Sherman knew what most historians believe today. The war would be over when the Army of Northern Virginia was defeated, and this was his goal. The March to the Sea was a change of base. Its entire purpose was to move his army into a position that would allow it to participate in the Eastern Theater of the war, where he rightfully believed final victory would come. If victory came while he was in transition and his army had not played a key role, his postwar place may not have been as secure. Thomas destroyed Hood, Grant destroyed Lee, and Sherman was touring the Georgia countryside. His claim to being one of the great generals of the war—and thus to a senior position in the postwar army—was the capture of Atlanta, and he had abandoned it. The March to the Sea had to stand alone as a military achievement.

The war ended before Sherman could reach Virginia and Lee, but he was in the position he wanted to be in, commanding a major army and receiving credit for destroying the South's ability to fight the war. This, and the loyalty of Grant, would guarantee him a position in the postwar army.

CHAPTER 3

The Commanding General versus the North

General William T. Sherman's status as one of the great generals and the cruelest fiends of the Civil War had not been established by the close of hostilities. Sherman was the most controversial of Civil War generals at the close of the war and the decades that followed, but this had little to do with Sherman's now infamous March to the Sea or his treatment of Southern civilians. The first battle concerning Sherman's reputation was fought among veterans (mostly Union) over how much credit he deserved for defeating the South and among politicians who were afraid that Sherman might march straight into high political office.

For most Civil War veterans, the decade that followed the war contained too many immediate challenges to worry about how future generations would view their contributions. Professional Confederate soldiers such as Robert E. Lee and Joseph E. Johnston had resigned their commissions and abandoned the only career they had ever known. They had to worry about earning a living in a region ruined by war.[1]

Employment was a major issue for Northern soldiers as well. As Sherman had predicted, the Union army was greatly reduced, and the postwar army was filled with junior officers who had been generals during the war.[2] Those who remained in the army, especially those of high rank such as Ulysses S. Grant and Sherman, still had a great deal of work to do. Native American unrest was growing rapidly; the South had to be occupied and US laws enforced, especially those dealing with over three million newly freed slaves; French troops occupied Mexico; and professional soldiers had to worry about promotion and retention in a greatly shrinking army.[3]

Regardless of the time constraints of veterans, there was a large market for histories of the late war. During the last half of the 1860s, this demand was met by professional writers and journalists from both North and South. Most of these histories were based on newspaper accounts published during the war and were thus thoroughly inaccurate.[4]

The first history of the war dealing exclusively with Sherman was also one of the first memoirs of the war to be published. Ironically, even though Sherman's dislike of the press is well documented, his aide-de-camp during the last year of the war was a former journalist who returned to that profession after leaving the army. A Maine native, George Ward Nichols was thirty-four years old and an experienced adjutant when he joined Sherman's staff after the Atlanta campaign. In 1865, he published *The Story of the Great March*. It was based closely on the diary he kept during the campaign. In the first year it sold nearly seventy thousand copies and has been in almost constant publication ever since.[5]

Nichols's history of the campaign is a much romanticized view. He idolized Sherman, describing him as a strategic genius and a master of the minutia of running an army. He compared Sherman's cutting his supply line and marching to the coast with Cortez's burning his ships and marching into the interior of Mexico.[6] It seems strange that Nichols did not compare the campaign to Scott's cutting loose his supply lines and marching into the interior of Mexico. Perhaps a historical figure closer to the knights of old better suited Nichol's romantic mind-set.

Nichols wrote that the purpose of the campaign was to reach Goldsboro, North Carolina. He described in detail a meeting between Sherman and his general officers when Sherman explained to them his intentions. Sherman told them that if they could reach the railroad junction at Goldsboro that Lee and the Army of Northern Virginia would be trapped in Richmond.[7] With the exception of the destruction of the railroads, Nichols did not present devastation as one of the goals of the March to the Sea.

The Story of the Great March is one of the most quoted works on Sherman, perhaps even more than the general's own memoirs, and this is for two reasons. Nichols's language is very quotable. His purpose in writing this book was to sell copies and make money. His writing style was aimed at a general audience, and individual sentences can stand alone powerfully. "Behind us we leave a track of smoke and flame." This is the type of quote that a historian who wanted to present Sherman the monster would be unable to resist. It is a misleading quote when taken out of context. Nichols is describing an isolated incident where Marietta was partially destroyed by stragglers as the army left the Atlanta area. Nichols stressed that this was not ordered.[8]

Nichols is also heavily quoted because he deals with the bummers more than any other narrative. The term *bummer* has different meanings. To Nichols, a "bummer" was "a raider on his own account." This was also Sherman's definition.

He differentiated between the pillagers and robbers called bummers and the foragers who had been authorized by their brigade commanders. Sherman, however, seems to confuse the term and will use it in an affectionate way when discussing his entire army.[9] Later writers, especially Southern diarists or anyone meaning to disparage Sherman, will refer to the entire army as bummers, for after all, there is little difference to the injured party if their cattle are taken to sustain an enemy army or for personal use. They will complain regardless of the legality of the seizure.

In 1866, a year after publishing *The Story of the Great March*, Nichols wrote a novel about the Civil War in Georgia. The hero was a Georgian who had joined the Union and participated in the battle for Savannah. *The Sanctuary* was as popular if not more popular than his nonfiction. These two works were, however, the highlight of Nichols's career. In 1867 he began a short career with *Harper's Magazine*. He wrote a series of articles on Wild Bill Hickok that launched the legend of that famous Western gunfighter but was so inaccurate that newspapers from Kansas raised an uproar. Nichols was fired and never worked in journalism again.[10]

In writing *The Story of the Great March*, Nichols probably had no higher purpose than the selling of books. He was a professional writer who had witnessed one of the great events of the war. The best way for him to advance his career and personal reputation was to write a best seller. He proved in his writings about Hickok, where the gunfighter killed hundreds of men, that he was more interested in selling copy than in historical accuracy.[11]

Nichols had a clear anti-Southern bias in his work. This is not surprising considering his wartime experience. He did not witness any of the great battles of the war where he might have earned a grudging respect for the Southern soldier.[12] He was writing for a mainly Northern audience that was still burying its dead.

Throughout the book Nichols encountered enraged Southern women or witnessed unnamed Union officers encountering incensed Southern belles. Whether these were true accounts or a literary device that allowed Nichols to make his point can never be known. These women were never told that what they suffered was comparable to what Unionists suffered in east Tennessee. They were not told that actual suffering was exaggerated by the Southern press, or that an army troops taking what they needed as they marched through enemy territory was an accepted practice as old as war itself. These women were told by Nichols, and the officers he quoted, that they had brought it on themselves.[13] There was no apology or justification.

In 1865 Nichols's book was exactly what Sherman's reputation needed. The greatest criticism that Sherman faced at the end of the war was that he was a

Southern sympathizer. His leniency in reaching the terms of surrender with General Joseph Johnston's army to end the war and his very unprogressive views toward African Americans brought accusations of leniency toward the defeated South. Sherman was accused of allowing President Jefferson Davis to escape with the Confederate treasury and possibly even making it possible for the South to become independent.[14]

The terms signed by Sherman and Joseph Johnston on April 18, 1865, went well beyond those signed by Ulysses S. Grant and Robert E. Lee, whose surrender at Appomattox Courthouse was a simple military affair. The Confederate soldiers turned over their arms and swore an oath of allegiance to the United States and were allowed to go home on parole. On the other hand, Sherman authored an agreement that accepted the surrender of all Confederate forces still in the field from the Army of Tennessee in his direct front to the Confederate naval raiders operating in the northern Pacific. Surrendering soldiers would be allowed to remain armed until they reached their respective state capitals where the weapons would be deposited in the state arsenals. The federal courts would be reestablished in the succeeding states, but the current state governments would be recognized until elections could be organized.[15]

The surrender terms answered political questions that were beyond the authority of any general. President Andrew Johnson sent General Grant to rectify the situation. In the end, Johnston signed a treaty almost identical to the one signed by Lee, which dealt solely with the forces immediately under Johnston's control.[16] This could have been an episode free of controversy. General Sherman submitted a poor agreement to Washington. It was quickly refused by the government. Sherman in a letter to Grant's chief of staff, John Rawlins, claimed it was only a "memorandum" meant to advise the government in Washington. President Johnson did not accept Sherman's advice, so it never went into effect and a sympathetic Grant remained in the background while Sherman fixed his own error.[17]

This incident, however, became a major issue through the maneuvering of the secretary of war Edwin Stanton, who released the original "memorandum" signed by Sherman and Johnston and his personal comments to the press on April 23, 1865. Stanton's intention was clearly to vilify Sherman. Stanton included the charge that by moving General George Stoneman's cavalry closer to Sherman's main army, Sherman allowed Jefferson Davis to escape to Mexico or Europe with a fortune from the Confederate treasury and money looted from Richmond banks. Having read Grant's official report, which included Sherman's excuse that he believed he was following Lincoln's wishes, Stanton included an order from Lincoln to Grant stating that he did not want his generals negotiating political matters. If a newspaper printed the terms of agreement without Stanton's anti-Sherman commentary they received a reprimand from the War Department.[18]

Stanton released a firestorm of controversy over the surrender terms. Although less well known today, at the time Sherman's treaty received more newspaper coverage than any other event in the war except for Lincoln's assassination.[19] On April 24, the *New York Times*, one of the leading Radical Republican newspapers, continued Stanton's attack on Sherman. The *Times* suggested that Sherman laid "the basis of a new government based on a theory of state rights as absolute and complete as John C. Calhoun ever dreamed of." They called the agreement "military insubordination" and the "*Magna Charta* of American Slavery." As part of the paper's constant stream of anti-Sherman articles, the *Times* produced a letter that Sherman had written Braxton Bragg before he resigned his position as head of the Louisiana Seminary and Military Academy. The letter, in which Sherman told Bragg that he would not take up arms against the South, was taken by the *New York Times* to mean that Sherman's entire Civil War career had been one long charade in order to give Johnston overly favorable terms after the South had been defeated, an impressive feat for a man the same article claimed was insane. Stanton ordered all commanders of the Military Department of Mississippi to disregard any orders given by Sherman and to pursue the fleeing Jefferson Davis, believed to be escaping to Mexico or Europe with between twelve thousand and twenty-five thousand pounds of gold. This order was released to Northern newspapers in a very public insult to Sherman.[20]

By mid-May, the Sherman/Johnston agreement had ceased to become the major story. Some newspapers even admitted they had gone overboard in their coverage of the issue. The *New York Times* issued a partial apology in a plea to General Sherman's junior officers and men not to call for Stanton's dismissal. The paper feared that the men of the Western armies would make some type of public display during the grand review to embarrass Stanton.[21] In the end, Sherman's refusal to shake Stanton's hand on the reviewing stand was the only rebuke the secretary of war received.

Sherman's "surrender to Johnston," as some Northern newspapers dubbed it, was almost unbelievable not because of Sherman's modern reputation as a fierce warrior and a destroyer but because he had so completely misread the political situation in April 1865. Throughout the war, Sherman had tried to avoid controversy, even shunning commands. Although his father-in-law and brother had a great deal of political pull in Washington, Sherman refused a command position. Both Congressman Sherman and his father-in-law and foster father, Thomas Ewing (a former senator and judge), held a great deal of sway in political circles.[22]

When Sherman was promoted to brigadier general, he asked Lincoln not to give him an independent command. Later in the war, Sherman accepted a position under Grant, who had less seniority. When Grant was promoted to lieutenant general and commander in chief of the army, Sherman, the new commander of the Military Department of the Mississippi, tried to convince Grant to stay in the West instead of going east to take control of the armies in Virginia. After the March to the Sea, he was disappointed when Grant changed his mind about moving Sherman's army from Savannah to Virginia. Sherman did not want to be in a position where a bad decision could ruin his career.[23] It is because of this record of avoiding responsibility that his stepping beyond his role in the negotiations with Johnston seems so strange.

Sherman would argue in his memoirs that he was only following President Lincoln's wishes. Lincoln, Sherman, Grant, and Admiral David Dixon Porter met at City Point, Virginia, on board the steamer *River Queen*. This meeting was made famous by George Healy's painting *The Peacemakers* in which Sherman, characteristically, appears to be doing all the talking. Lincoln believed the war was all but over when the four men met on March 28, 1865. According to his memoirs, both Sherman and Grant believed that there was at least one more major battle to be fought. Lincoln wanted to avoid this if possible, telling Sherman and Grant that he wanted the Confederate soldiers back on their farms as soon as possible. Sherman also wrote that Lincoln hinted he would prefer if Jefferson Davis were allowed to escape so that he could avoid the politically charged question as to what to do with his Southern counterpart. Sherman related a very Lincoln-like story in which the president tells of a man who has sworn off alcohol and tells his friend that he would not mind some brandy in his lemonade as long as he did not know about it.[24]

In his memoirs Sherman included a letter from Admiral David Dixon Porter supporting Sherman's view that Lincoln would give major concessions short of independence in order to end the war and would not be unhappy if Davis was able to escape. It was common practice for a commander sitting down to write his memoirs to ask junior officers, contemporaries, and even foes for their papers or memories on the subjects to be covered. Sherman believed that the charge was important enough and Admiral Porter's response so convincing that he included it word for word.[25]

The other witness, Grant, supported Sherman's view of this meeting. He wrote in his 1885 memoirs that Sherman thought "he was carrying out the wishes of the President of the United States." Grant labeled as "preposterous" any claim that Sherman was disloyal.[26]

This was not the first time that the secretary of war had attempted politically to destroy General Sherman. While Sherman and his army were in Savannah,

Stanton came to investigate claims that Sherman and his officers had mis-treated black refugees, namely, by not aiding them in following the army to Savannah. In his memoirs Sherman printed a letter from Halleck warning him that Stanton was coming to Savannah in order to demonstrate Sherman's dis-loyalty to the president.[27] This attack was not nearly as successful as the one over the Johnston surrender. Stanton found that the freed slaves of Savannah had nothing but praise for General Sherman.[28]

It was while Sherman was in Savannah that Sherman took action that, like the Johnston agreement, far exceeded his authority. Sherman's famous Field Orders Number 15 gave freed slaves land in large sections along the Georgia, Florida, and South Carolina coast. Sherman received heavy criticism from all sides for this controversial issue. Freed slaves and their abolitionist allies would complain that the order was short-lived while others would complain that he had no right to give away land and might set a dangerous precedent. Sherman might have been trying to address these complaints by bringing up Stanton's trip to Savannah. He used that episode to claim that he was pressured by Halleck and Stanton to issue Field Order Number 15 and that Stanton read and approved it before it was issued.[29]

Sherman's reputation at the end of the war was mixed. While thousands lined the street to see the Western army march through the streets of Washington, questions arose about his willingness to carry out the government's postwar policies. What Sherman needed in 1865 were memoirs and histories that por-trayed him as harsh on the Southern people during the war. Books like that of the journalist-turned-soldier Nichols and his *Story of the Great March* were very helpful in changing Sherman's image into that of the brutal warrior. So too were histories of the war written by Southern journalists, which were heavily critical of Sherman and everything Northern.

In 1867 Edward Pollard published his history of the war, *The Lost Cause*. Like most books before and after the war, this was printed in New York City. He is credited with originating the term "the lost cause" in referring to Southern independence. Edward Pollard was the editor of the *Daily Richmond Examiner* from 1861 until 1867. During part of the war, he was imprisoned at Fort Monroe. He had been captured onboard a blockade runner on his way to Europe to market his book about the first year of the war. Before the war, he was a noted author and defender of slavery. His book *Black Diamonds* called for a slave empire that would circle the Gulf of Mexico and the Caribbean Sea.[30]

The Lost Cause is one of the first general histories of the Civil War. His work could be the catechism for groups like the United Daughters of the Confederacy and the Sons of Confederate Veterans. Extremely pro-Southern in his writing, he blamed the war on the election of Abraham Lincoln. Pollard claimed the

South's defeat was due only to overwhelming numbers and the Union's inability to play by the rules of civilized warfare. He even blames the prisoners for the thousands of deaths at Andersonville.[31]

According to Pollard, Sherman was not only a villain who waged war on women and children; he was a charlatan who had no real effect on the outcome of the war. There was no military danger facing the Union army, so the March to the Sea was nothing but a pleasurable stroll. What Pollard failed to realize or admit was that the reason there was no strong opposition in the army's way was because of Sherman's well-thought-out strategy. By moving close to Macon and then Augusta, he ensured that those two cities were heavily garrisoned and consequently those men would not be opposing him in the field. Pollard repeated all the atrocities that his and other Southern newspapers attributed to Sherman and his army during the war. He claimed that Union soldiers stole everything of value that they could get their hands on and that pretty young slave women dressed in their former mistresses' finest garments accompanied every unit. Pollard admitted that Sherman did not order fires set. He claimed the burning was done by stragglers. He made no mention of the damage done by Wheeler's cavalry or the convicts released by the governor of Georgia.[32] Pollard predicted that Sherman would be considered insignificant to professional military men and all but lost to history.[33] Ironically Pollard's harsh statements were exactly what Sherman needed in 1867. Anyone who could produce such hatred among Richmond editors must have played a crucial part in their defeat. If Pollard had wanted Sherman forgotten by history, he would have done better to praise him for the terms he offered Johnston.

Although there was a great demand for Civil War material by the reading public, the first wartime memoirs of any of the war's leading figures did not come out for nearly a decade after the end of the war. Magazine and newspaper articles about individual battles and campaigns appeared throughout these years, but it was not until 1874 that Sherman's adversary Confederate general Joseph E. Johnston published his massive six-hundred-page *Narrative of Military Operations Directed During the Late War Between the States*. If Johnston's memoir had been a sign of what was to come, it would not bode well for Civil War literature. Published by the New York–based D. Appleton and Company, which would publish the majority of Civil War memoirs over the next three decades, Johnston's *Narrative* was nothing but a defense of his own wartime actions. From lost letters to conspiracies, no loss was ever Johnston's fault. Johnston's friends and those former Confederate colleagues whom he contacted to help him with his research warned the general not to go ahead with the project. Wade Hampton of South Carolina, who wrote to ask Johnston for a reference letter for a position in the Egyptian army, asked him to hold off publishing his memoirs because he argued the South needed unity in that trying time.[34]

The major theme of Johnston's *Narrative of Military Operations* was that the South lost because of mismanagement by their leadership. President Jefferson Davis and General Braxton Bragg received his harshest criticism. According to Johnston, the strength of the Confederacy was in the individual soldiers who could have won the war if not sabotaged by the political leadership. Davis's biggest mistake was removing Johnston from command and promoting John Bell Hood. Johnston also argued that he had retreated no further into Georgia than Lee had into Virginia. While the Johnston/Lee comparison is technically accurate, it does not really portray what happened in those two campaigns.[35]

Johnston was offended at the charge that he was using a Fabian strategy against Sherman. He claimed it was Sherman who had avoided the major battles. This was an argument like many in his *Narrative* that a person could only accept if they had very little knowledge of the war. Johnston wrote that he had been winning when he had been removed because the Union had suffered more total casualties during the Atlanta campaign. He is silent on his opinion of Sherman as a general or as a man. He did not mention the march through Georgia because he did not have a command during that time. He did, however, commend the behavior of Union troops during the occupation of South Carolina.[36]

Johnston was a well-respected military professional at the beginning of the war. He was educated at West Point and a veteran of the Mexican war. Had General Sherman been the first modern general or had he changed the nature of warfare as later historians will claim, it seems unlikely that Johnston would not have noticed or would not have commented on that fact in his memoirs.

Johnston discussed at length the surrender terms between himself and Sherman, although the controversy had died down by the time of the book's publication. Sherman argued that he had only followed Lincoln's wishes. The secretary of war accused Sherman of treason. Johnston took a third position, which was that he tricked Sherman into granting such favorable terms by appealing to Sherman's vanity. Johnston described his conversation with Sherman, whom he compared to Napoleon who when victorious over Austria entered negotiations with his Austrian counterpart, the Archduke Charles, for a permanent peace treaty that went well beyond their powers as generals. Johnston quoted Napoleon to Sherman when he said, "the civic crown earned by preserving the life of one citizen confers truer glory than the highest achievement merely military."[37]

It seems thoroughly unlikely that, had Sherman been the ogre that Pollard and later Southern historians described, Johnston would have used the argument of preserving life to persuade him. If Sherman's motive had been to punish the South, as it is sometimes argued, than he would have avoided any agreement with Johnston and would have pushed on to Virginia, destroying everything in his path until he reached Richmond. Instead, Johnston respected Sherman and the two became friends after the war, meeting more than once to discuss wartime strategy. Johnston even served as an honorary pallbearer at Sherman's funeral.[38]

Both Grant and Sherman praised Johnston's memoirs, which after all criticized neither one of them. The public was not so generous. Johnston's *Narrative* was very unpopular. Far from being a best seller, the book lost money. The Southern people wanted to believe that they had lost because of overwhelming numbers. They did not want to hear blame cast on any Confederate leader, especially Jefferson Davis, who was extremely popular at the time because of his imprisonment during the previous decade. Johnston was not successful in his attempt to bolster his reputation. By attacking Davis he would become, next to James Longstreet, the most unpopular Confederate general in the postwar period.[39] His memoirs do show that Sherman was not hated by the South at the end of the war and during the decade that followed.

In 1875 General Sherman added his own voice to the shaping of his legacy when he published his simply titled *Memoirs of General William T. Sherman*. The D. Appleton Company of New York published his memoirs in two volumes and marketed the books aggressively, sending excerpts to newspapers around the country. The initial reviews were positive. The *Milwaukee Daily Sentinel* in its review thanked Sherman for his "valuable contribution to the history of the country" and for "furnishing a work of intense interest to the ordinary reader."[40] This reviewer was correct. Sherman's *Memoirs* were a best seller, and they have been in constant publication ever since.

Sherman may have succeeded in alienating more people with his memoirs than he did with his campaigns, however. The main criticism involved how he treated his fellow officers. Sherman appeared blameless while he charged fellow officers with everything from incompetence to cowardice. He blamed Don Carlos Buell for the near defeat of the Union army at Shiloh, and James McPherson for the failure to capture the Confederate army at Resaca, and he portrays George Thomas as an overly cautious leader whom he had to bypass to get things done.[41] Even the *Georgia Weekly Telegraph* in its review of Sherman's *Memoirs* criticized him for his attacks on other Union officers rather than for what he had to say about the March to the Sea or the fire in Columbia.[42]

The memoirs of William T. Sherman and Ulysses S. Grant are generally considered the best memoirs to come out of the war. Both are extremely well written. They are valuable to professionals and enjoyable for the general reader. Although there is a great deal of defensiveness and self-aggrandizement in

Sherman's memoirs, he appeared honest, and many of his shortcomings come to light in his writings. He discussed his failures as a businessman and admitted to the great deal of assistance he got from relatives in military and civilian life.[43]

Although it reads like a general narrative of his war experiences, Sherman devoted the majority of the pages to defending himself against the charges and controversies that emerged during or right after the war and defending what he considered his greatest achievements, his participation in the Vicksburg campaign, the capture of Atlanta, and the subsequent March to the Sea. He began his narrative as a young lieutenant stationed in California. This would have been a more appropriate starting point had it been the start of his professional career. Sherman was a graduate of the US Military Academy and a veteran of the Second Seminole War and served in South Carolina and North Georgia before he was sent to California during the United States–Mexican War. As the superintendent of the Louisiana State Seminary of Learning and Military Academy, he enthralled the students with stories of California during the Gold Rush.[44] He may have included the chapter on California just for its entertainment value.

Sherman discussed at length the charge of insanity made against him by the *Cincinnati Commercial* and repeated by other newspapers and critics. The image of Sherman as the insane general would haunt him. Twentieth-century historians who wished to paint Sherman as the brutal inventor of total war would often quote that article. To the modern reader the term "insane" often creates the image of a homicidal maniac. While the reporter did not portray Sherman as a danger to small children and animals, he did refer to him as "stark mad."[45] The writer portrayed the general as someone who was ready for the asylum as opposed to a man under a great deal of stress.

Sherman makes a very good case that this oft-repeated charge was unfair. The *Cincinnati Commercial* published the "Sherman is Insane" article on December 11, 1861, after Sherman had been replaced as the commander of the Department of the Cumberland by Don Carlos Buell. Sherman wrote that he was surprised to read copies of that article in the New York papers because he assumed his removal from command had just meant that Lincoln was respecting his own wishes. After the battle of Bull Run, Sherman expected to be dismissed. Instead, he was granted his second meeting with Lincoln and was promoted to brigadier general and sent to Kentucky. During the second interview, Sherman asked not to be given an overall command. He believed that Lincoln was simply living up to their agreement by having him replaced.[46]

A general concerned about his long-term career would not have wanted the Department of the Cumberland. It was in an important strategic position, and as was the case in many places, there were not enough men, money, or supplies.

The stress became too much for its original commander, Major General Robert Anderson, who requested to be removed from command.[47] This gave Sherman exactly what he did not want, a senior command early in the war.

The stress that had driven Anderson from Kentucky now belonged to Sherman. Within days of taking over this troubled department, Sherman was informed that the secretary of war, Simon Cameron, wanted to meet him in Louisville. Sherman, Cameron, and the secretary's entourage met in General Sherman's hotel room. When asked about the situation in Kentucky, Sherman responded by painting a very bleak picture of his circumstances. He told Cameron that he needed sixty thousand men to defend Kentucky and two hundred thousand men for offensive action. According to Sherman, Cameron was shocked by his request, claiming that his information from the Kentucky congressional delegation was that Kentucky had enough men.[48] Cameron was convinced by Sherman of the need for more men and weapons in Kentucky and began sending orders to Washington to have the situation rectified. Cameron and his party were concerned for Sherman's health. They spoke among themselves that Sherman seemed to be suffering from depression and exhaustion, which he probably was. The rumor, however, began circulating at the War Department that Sherman was "touched in the head."[49]

The stories of Sherman's mental instability had two major sources— Sherman's request for two hundred thousand men and his physical bearing. The request for that many men in 1861 seemed so outrageous it suggested he was not in touch with reality. The request showed that Sherman had more of a sense of what this war was to become than did most of his seniors. In a war that would soon see battles with more than ten thousand casualties, sixty thousand men to defend a key state and two hundred thousand men for offensive action into Tennessee was in fact very reasonable. Had the Confederate army in Tennessee taken more aggressive action, Sherman's predictions of disaster very well might have come true.

Those who met General Sherman, especially during the war, described him as a ball of nervous energy, constantly fidgeting, fooling with his hair, beard, and uniform. He paced, unable to sit for very long. His spoke quickly and jumped from subject to subject. He spoke whatever thought came to his mind when a more cautious man would have remained silent.[50] One can only imagine a depressed Sherman telling Secretary of War Cameron the terrible state of affairs in Kentucky while he fidgeted about the room. It should be no surprise that rumors of his mental instability began to spread.

Sherman wrote in his memoirs that the accusation of mental instability would follow him until he redeemed himself at the battle of Shiloh. Although many Sherman critics blame him for the near disaster at the battle of Shiloh, he viewed it as one of his finest hours. This was a view shared by Generals Halleck and Grant. In his request that Sherman be promoted to major general, Halleck wrote that Sherman "saved the fortune of the day on the sixth" and "contributed largely to the glorious victory on the seventh." Grant in his report of the battle wrote that Sherman showed "great judgment and skill in the management of his men."[51]

Initial newspaper accounts of the battle blamed Generals Grant and Sherman for the massive amount of casualties suffered on the first day of fighting. According to the newspapers, versions repeated by future historians, Grant was drunk and Sherman and his men were caught unaware. Reports of Sherman's men bayoneted in their tents filled Northern newspapers, whose readers were looking for an explanation behind the unbelievable high number of casualties.[52] More men died at Shiloh than all the earlier American wars combined. In the very egalitarian Midwest, West Point–trained officers were much better targets for censure than the amateur soldiers and officers from the reporters' own communities. After the battle, there were a large number of civilians who visited the battlefield. Reporters, civilian doctors, and representatives of state sanitary commissions flocked to the battlefield. According to Sherman, these civilians who repeated camp stories to their local papers were responsible for the false reports. There were also many invented accounts of the battle that reached Northern newspapers. The term "Cairo Correspondent" became popular to describe reporters who came no closer to the battlefield than Cairo, Illinois.[53]

Sherman, in his memoirs, claimed that his men were not caught unaware. Not only were they awake and out of bed, but they were in line of battle. Prior to the main attack on April 6, there had been two days of cavalry attacks; it seems highly unlikely that the men of the Union army would not have been alert on the morning of April 6. Sherman also wrote that Grant was in control of the situation. He argued that at the end of the first day's fighting the Union army, even without Don Carlos Buell's reinforcements, was ready to move forward at sunrise on April 7.[54]

Sherman criticized Buell, claiming that he was confused and did not want to move forward on the second day. He disagreed with the version of Shiloh that Buell and his army turned the defeat of the first day into victory on the second. Buell was angered enough by Sherman to write the newspapers in 1875 and say that he looked forward to the accounts that would show the great number of inaccuracies in Sherman's memoirs.[55] To Buell's credit, he did not point out that he had successfully taken over the command that had driven Sherman "insane." Although he was at the center of several controversies during the war, Buell never defended himself with his own memoirs.

While Grant took attacks upon his professional abilities with stoic silence, Sherman wrote to several papers defending himself against charges that he was caught unprepared at Shiloh. Sherman's forces had not fortified their position. By the time of Sherman's Atlanta campaign and Grant's advance to Richmond, soldiers felled trees, dug rifle pits, and cleared a killing zone in front of their positions whenever the army stopped. However, this was not common practice at the beginning of the war. Instead, officers believed that if a position was fortified, soldiers would not advance and if driven from that position they would not stop their retreat until they reached a similarly fortified line. Sherman wrote that if he had fortified his position at Shiloh it would have invited attack by showing the weakness of his position. After the first day of fighting, Sherman ordered his lines to be fortified.[56]

Sherman's argument against fortifying a position was more than just an excuse or an anachronism from earlier military theory. The Union soldiers who fought at Shiloh were volunteers with little training. If they had spent the night of April 5 fortifying a position, it would have been a severe blow to march away from them on April 6, as was the plan. That he ordered fortifications to be built after the first day supports his argument that this was an action performed by armies in a weak position. The order, however, contrasts his argument that he and Grant were in a position to advance on the second day of fighting with or without Buell's reinforcements.

Sherman's critics would argue that in his memoirs when he claimed victories often he had been beaten, when he admitted defeat he always blamed others, and when he was truly victorious all of the credit belonged to him. During Grant's Vicksburg campaign, Sherman led an assault of over forty thousand men in an attempt to move up the Yazoo River and get behind the city. The position Sherman decided to attack turned out to be a very poor choice. His soldiers had to be moved through a swamp known as Chickasaw Bayou and assault the fortified cliffs beyond. Rear Admiral David D. Porter tried to convince Sherman to use the navy to land his forces at a more hospitable position. Porter believed that Sherman wanted to win without assistance.[57]

The soldiers took two days to cross the bayou. Fog and heavy rain slowed their progress. When they reached the cliffs they were beaten back, with heavy losses, by Confederate artillery. When the Yazoo River began to flood, Sherman was forced to call off the attack. In his official report and his correspondence following the repulse, Sherman wrote, "I assume all the responsibility and blame no one." In his memoirs, however, Sherman blamed his commander in the field, General George W. Morgan.[58]

Although he was forced out of West Point because of his poor grades, Sherman's fellow Ohioan Morgan had more military experience. He had enlisted in the Texas army during the revolution against Mexico. He rose to the rank of captain in the Texas army before returning to the United States to attend West Point. While Sherman was assigned to garrison duty in California during the war with Mexico, Morgan had been a colonel of a company of Ohio volunteers. When General Winfield Scott led his invasion of Mexico, he transferred Morgan to colonelcy of the Fifteenth US Infantry. To deal with the problem of guerrilla attacks on American troops, Morgan ordered prominent Mexican citizens to be held as hostages. The plan worked, and Morgan was given the field promotion of brigadier general. After the war, Morgan served as ambassador to France and later Portugal. At the onset of war, he returned to the United States and to uniform. After the failure at Chickasaw Bayou, he was transferred to Arkansas where his health began to deteriorate and he resigned from the army. Although there were two other commanders under Sherman at Chickasaw, Sherman singled out Morgan for the blame. Morgan's postwar career probably had a lot more to do with this than his actions on the Yazoo River. He was an active Democrat who campaigned for McClellan in Ohio. He was defeated by one of Sherman's strongest defenders, General Jacob D. Cox, for governor of Ohio. He also served as one of the Ohio representatives in the US Congress until 1873. He was a staunch opponent of the Radical Republicans. Morgan, as a Democrat on the House Armed Services Committee, and Sherman, as commanding general of the army, would have clashed many times before the 1875 publication of Sherman's memoirs.[59]

Sherman, in his *Memoirs*, was not above rewriting the battle plans of others in order to share credit for the victory. The battle of Missionary Ridge along with the battle of Lookout Mountain formed part of Grant's plan to break the Confederate siege of Chattanooga. The plan was simple. On the right, General Joe Hooker would make a demonstration against the enemy on the face of Lookout Mountain. In the center, General George Thomas with the Army of the Cumberland would attack the Confederate forces on Missionary Ridge. On the left, Sherman's Army of the Tennessee would strike. Grant intended for Hooker to hold the enemy on the mountain and for Thomas to force the enemy to concentrate on his force and give any assistance to Sherman as he might need, while Sherman's Army of the Tennessee made the breakthrough of the Confederate lines that would bring the Union victory.[60]

It is the general consensus among historians that, although the Union achieved victory, the day did not go as Grant has planned. Hooker was not content with a mere holding action; he fought aggressively. He saw this as an opportunity to repair his reputation as the inept commander at the battle of Chancellorsville. On the second day of the battle, in what came to be known as the "Battle above the Clouds," Hooker's men cleared the face of Lookout

Mountain and forced the Confederates to abandon their position on the mountain's summit. The Army of the Tennessee would have much less success. Slowed by harsh terrain and fierce resistance, they were moving forward very slowly, when at all. At the end of the second day, Sherman halted well short of his intended target, believing he had reached the northernmost point of Missionary Ridge.[61]

On the third day, Grant supposed Sherman to be in place to strike against Bragg's right and turn the Confederate army. Sherman faced heavy fighting and made little progress throughout the morning and early afternoon. According to Grant's original plan, Thomas's Army of the Cumberland was to strike the center of Bragg's line as soon as Sherman had turned the Confederate army. As it became obvious that Sherman was stalled, Grant suggested to Thomas that he move forward and capture the rifle pits at the foot of Missionary Ridge in order to relieve some of the pressure at Sherman's front. Thomas felt that attacking the enemy's center before one of his flanks had been turned would be a disaster and he had to be given a direct order to move forward. The Union soldiers went well beyond Grant's orders and charged up the steep ridge into the teeth of the Confederate army. Bragg had made a number of serious mistakes in his disposition of troops. By placing men at the bottom of the ridge and on the crest he gave up his advantage of holding the high ground. Bragg had assumed that the center of his line would not be attacked. In what some veterans would call the miracle at Missionary Ridge, the Army of the Cumberland drove the Confederates from their fortified position at the base of Missionary Ridge, and by pursuing them closely, they made the retreating Confederates a shield against those on the crest and thus broke the Confederate line. Sherman not only did not take a leading role in the victory, he did not even know about it until he received orders during the night to pursue the fleeing enemy after sunrise.[62]

This is not, however, the version of events that would make it into Sherman's memoirs. According to Sherman, Grant's original plan of battle had been for Sherman and Hooker to make demonstrations to draw forces away from the Confederate center so that Thomas and the Army of the Cumberland would have a better chance to break through. In Sherman's version, he was successful; he distracted Bragg's Confederate army long enough for Thomas and his men to succeed.[63]

There are a number of glaring flaws in Sherman's version of events. According to Sherman's own memoirs, Grant told Sherman that he wanted the Army of the Tennessee to attack first, because "Thomas's army had been so demoralized by the battle of Chickamauga that he feared they could not be got out of their trenches."[64] It seems highly unlikely that Grant would have given the most important part of his battle to a force he feared he could not depend on. The Army of the Cumberland was ordered forward only after it became apparent that Sherman's Army of the Tennessee was being stopped. Even then Grant did not expect them to have nearly the success that they did.

Four divisions of the Army of the Cumberland, nearly twenty-three thousand men, advanced along a two-mile front. The ground that had to be crossed offered no concealment and was steeper and more rugged than the famous Cemetery Ridge at Gettysburg. The Confederates had spent two months preparing the defenses that the Union troops would have to face. As it turned out, the Confederates had done a very poor job fortifying and their morale was atrocious, but Grant had no way of knowing this when preparing his battle plan. Had his plan been what Sherman suggested, success would have hinged on troops Grant did not trust to fight on terrain that was the most difficult of the war.

Of the three commanders who served under Grant at Chattanooga, only Sherman did not achieve his objective at the battle that cemented Grant's promotion to overall command of all Union armies. Yet it was Sherman who was chosen to succeed Grant as head of the Military Department of the Mississippi. Many historians credit Sherman and Grant's friendship for this. That he had become a trusted lieutenant during the Mississippi River campaign may also have vaulted Sherman over his fellow commanders. Many factors probably went into Grant's decision, but in the end, unless he wanted to bring a general from the East, politically Sherman was the only possible choice. George Thomas had been passed over many times for higher command because he was a Southerner. Even though he had proved himself a loyal and competent general, it was unlikely that the president or Congress would have reversed themselves. Hooker had been given his opportunity at high command but had failed miserably at the battle of Chancellorsville and been sent west. It is unlikely that Lincoln would want to deal with him again. Thus, beginning on March 18, 1864, Sherman commanded all Union forces between the Mississippi River and the Appalachian Mountains, arguably the most important theater of the war. It is this command that would be the most scrutinized by the press, the political leadership of the United States, and future historians.[65]

Customers who bought the two leather-bound volumes titled *Memoirs of General William T. Sherman* were probably the most interested in his campaign for Atlanta and his subsequent march through Georgia and the Carolinas. They would not be disappointed. Sherman went into great detail on those subjects and caused much controversy.

Sherman's portrayal of the campaign for Atlanta, beginning in Chattanooga in May 1864 and ending with the successful entry into Atlanta on September 1,

1864, is the most generally accepted view of this campaign. As Sherman moved south along the railroad, he drove General Joseph Johnston and his Army of Tennessee closer to Atlanta. Johnston would stop in a very defensible position such as Dalton or Resaca. While one of Sherman's three armies, usually the Cumberland, held Johnston's front, one of the other two or both would try to get behind or turn the Army of Tennessee. Military strategists refer to this as envelopment or, in the case of forces coming from two sides, double envelopment. It is a tactic as old as organized warfare.[66]

Although he received a great deal of criticism for it, General Johnston never allowed his army to be surrounded. Whenever his supply line and flanks were threatened, Johnston retreated south to another defensible position. The hardest maneuver for an army to execute is an orderly retreat. In a tactic as old as envelopment, a general would allow his outnumbered opponent an avenue of escape with the idea of falling upon him when the retreat became panicked.[67] To Johnston's credit, the Army of Tennessee conducted orderly retreats.

Although Johnston a year earlier had complained of Sherman's depiction of this campaign in his *Narrative of Military Operations*, Sherman did not back away from his portrayal of Johnston as a master of the Fabian strategy. Johnston's argument that he was heavily bleeding the Union army would not persuade future historians.[68] The main weakness of Johnston's argument was that he did not seem to understand what Fabian strategy was. A leader who successfully instituted this strategy would indeed heavily bleed his enemy.

Sherman would, however, claim in his memoirs that he had wanted to trap and destroy the Army of Tennessee very early in the campaign. He blamed his failure to do so on General James B. McPherson, commander of the Army of the Tennessee. According to Sherman, had McPherson acted more aggressively Sherman would have been able to trap Johnston in Resaca.[69] This criticism of McPherson seems out of place considering the amount of praise Sherman had given him on other occasions. This was the only time Sherman criticized the Army of the Tennessee. Critics of Sherman would point out that had Sherman planned on trapping Johnston at Resaca, he would not have sent the smallest of his three armies to block Johnston's retreat. While he did not destroy the Army of Tennessee, Sherman did capture Atlanta, so it is difficult to criticize him for his Atlanta campaign. His victory there weakened the enemy army and allowed the Union to claim the important city of Atlanta. Northern newspapers, including the *New York Tribune*, hailed the capture of Atlanta as one of the most important victories of the war.[70]

The next stage of Sherman's military operations—his now infamous March to the Sea and through South Carolina—would cause a great deal of controversy and would become the campaign for which Sherman is most identified. The general's own voice added an important perspective to the national dialog. In 1875, however, the controversy was not Sherman's treatment of Southerners and their property. Even the Augusta-based *Georgia Weekly* in its review did not mention the March to the Sea. Instead the paper accused Sherman of disparaging his fellow Union generals in order to bolster his own reputation. The *Georgia Weekly* was, however, satisfied with Sherman's treatment of General Johnston, although it claimed his praise was intended only to add "new laurels to his own crown."[71]

The initial controversies were over the importance of the March to the Sea and who originated the idea. In the fall of 1864, the drama of the Civil War was being played out on three main stages. Ulysses Grant, with the Army of the Potomac, was pushing south against Robert E. Lee and his Army of Northern Virginia. The Military Department of the Mississippi was split into two major parts. Major General George Thomas, with scattered forces as far afield as Missouri, would confront Confederate General John Bell Hood's invasion of Tennessee, while Sherman, with over ninety thousand men, would take Savannah and move north all the way to North Carolina. The commanding generals and their subordinates would argue for many years after the end of the war about which of these three theaters was the most important in bringing about the end of the war. It is on this subject that Sherman would provoke the most initial debate. His claims that his campaign through Georgia broke the will of the Confederacy more than did the crushing defeats at Franklin and Nashville and that the Army of Tennessee was a broken force before it even left Georgia greatly upset men such as Generals George Thomas and John Schofield whose reputations depended on the battles Sherman was belittling.[72]

When Sherman abandoned Atlanta, General Hood and his force of nearly thirty thousand men, mostly made up of the Army of Tennessee, was the major loose end of the Atlanta campaign. Neither Sherman nor any of his superiors knew what Hood would do next. General Grant approved Sherman's move southward only after he had been sufficiently assured that Thomas had enough men to deal with Hood. In this Sherman may have slightly misled Grant, because (as the Duke of Wellington supposedly said about the battle of Waterloo) the battles of Franklin and Nashville were a close-run thing. Union veterans of these battles would argue that without their victories over Hood, Sherman's March to the Sea and capture of Savannah would have meant little.[73]

The great controversy at the time of Sherman's memoirs was his claim that the March to the Sea was his concept, and his alone. Sherman had to have known that this claim would be a controversial one because he dedicated almost an entire chapter to the argument that he alone planned it. He included letters and telegrams that supported this argument, including his infamous telegram in which he claims he will make "Georgia howl."[74] The correspondence Sherman

selected to include was intended to show that he made sure Thomas had sufficient men to defeat Hood in Tennessee or Alabama and that Sherman had to
convince Grant to allow him to cut loose from his supply line and move toward
Savannah.[75] Grant would tell Sherman after reading the *Memoirs* that this
chapter had been unnecessary. Sherman not only took credit for mastermind-
ing the March to the Sea; he concluded that his campaign through Georgia and
the Carolinas was the death blow to the Confederacy.[76]

Sherman continued his feud with the former secretary of war Edwin Stanton
in his *Memoirs*. Not only did he accuse Stanton of trying to destroy his reputation for political reasons, he claimed that Stanton was complicit in fraudulent
claims against the US Treasury for cotton captured at Savannah by ordering that
identifying marks be removed.[77] Sherman got the last word in the feud, because
he wrote his memoirs six years after Stanton's death, and today Sherman is one
of the more prominent figures from the Civil War while Stanton is by far a sec-
ondary figure in the literature.

The last chapter of Sherman's *Memoirs* is titled "Military Lessons of the War."
Sherman's lessons are not grand strategic lessons but very practical ones dealing with issues as varied as the size of military divisions, recruitment, the load
a soldier should be expected to carry, and the duties of chaplains.[78] This last
chapter was obviously intended for professional military men.

Sherman also made predictions about the effects of new technology on warfare, and these were accurate predictions, for the most part. He saw that the
technological advance that would most change warfare was the improved rifles
carried by the infantry. He wrote that, as the infantrymen's weapon improved,
so their lines would thin, high-ranking officers would be further separated
from their men, and because of that frontline soldiers would have to be better
trained.[79] These are all predictions that proved accurate.

It would be very unlike Sherman to write an entire chapter without eliciting
some controversy. The last paragraph of Sherman's more than eight hundred
pages is an attack on the press. He included a recommendation that they be
kept as far away from an army as possible.[80]

Sherman was serving as the general of the army in 1875 when his *Memoirs*
were published. In this position, he won praise for the reforms he implemented.
Many of his improvements—like the command schools and war colleges—are
very much a part of modern military education. Sherman was still fighting for the
reform he wanted most, a Prussian style staff system, when he wrote his memoirs.[81]

The US Army in the nineteenth century, as were most modern armies, was
based on the French system, in which the army was split into two major divisions. The first under the command of the general of the army was the actual
field troops. The second group was made up of the staff officers. The majority

of staff officers dealt with supplies, legal matters, intelligence, recruiting, and training. These staff officers answered to the secretary of war and were independent from the commanding general. A captain stationed in Arizona who needed more equipment or supplies for his men would have to send his request through his chain of command to the commanding general in Washington. The request would then be sent all the way down through the Logistics Corps to the local supply officer. In small isolated posts, the captain and the supply officer were sometimes the same man.[82]

This was not a very efficient way to run an army. Sherman wanted a system based on the Prussian army, where the commanding general had complete control of the entire army. He believed that by adopting a more unified system the army would be more efficient and both field officers and staff would work better together in time of war as opposed to the rivalry that then existed.[83]

Sherman had served both as a field officer and as a staff officer. He wrote from experience, not because of petty differences with current and former politicians. Sherman's "military lessons" were not just from the American Civil War. In his 1872 trip to Europe, he had toured battlefields from the Franco-Prussian War. The French after that war had laid part of the blame for their defeat on their staff system, which the United States copied.[84]

The first book-length critique of Sherman's *Memoirs* reached the market in December 1875, less than six months after Sherman's work was published. It was authored by Henry Van Ness Boynton, the Washington correspondent for the *Cincinnati Gazette*. Sherman and the *Gazette* had a long history. The *Gazette* had been one of Sherman's main detractors throughout the war. It had been one of the first papers to report his insanity, and with the exception of the evacuation of Atlanta, they editorialized against every one of his wartime decisions. His wife, Ellen, had even tried to convince him to sue the paper.[85]

Boynton's work had been serialized in Northern newspapers before it ever appeared in book form as *Sherman's Historical Raid; The Memoirs in Light of the Record*. Boynton's book can be considered no less than an attack on Sherman. The general believed that Boynton was hired by Orville Babcock, Grant's personal secretary, to respond in print to Sherman's *Memoirs*. Boynton received six hundred dollars from the US Treasury and, more important, special access to the then unpublished *Official Records of the War of Rebellion*.[86]

The Vermont-born Babcock had served as Grant's aide-de-camp during the last year of the war. He had the honor of escorting Robert E. Lee to his meeting with Grant at Appomattox Courthouse. He continued his service to Grant into the White House. Babcock was involved in the infamous Whiskey Ring in which 110 federal employees were convicted of defrauding the government. He escaped conviction because Grant interceded on his behalf.[87]

Babcock was loyal to Grant. Grant was the type of leader who instilled loyalty in the men around him. Men like Babcock had an added cause to defend Grant's reputation, as their position in history depended on Grant's reputation as president and general. As a member of Grant's presidential administration Babcock may have seen Sherman's book as attacking some of the president's policies, especially those dealing with the military. Sherman had also spent the last decade questioning the Republican Party's Reconstruction policies. He was especially outspoken against the Ku Klux Klan Act, which Grant considered one of the crowning achievements of his presidency. Sherman believed that Babcock had initiated this attack piece, but his only evidence was that Babcock had helped Boynton by getting him access to the *Official Records* and procuring him a stipend to help him with expenses in order to speed the writing process.[88]

It seems a lot more probable that Boynton launched the project out of personal reasons and enlisted the aid of members of the Grant administration in order to have access to government records. Boynton had first approached President Grant. As his own memoirs would later prove, Grant was above this type of public credit grabbing. The president admitted, in a letter to Sherman, that he had been upset by what he had been told about the *Memoirs*, but when he read the book himself, he felt that Sherman had treated him justly.[89]

Boynton had plenty of his own reasons for writing a critical piece on Sherman and his *Memoirs*. Boynton was employed for a newspaper that was traditionally anti-Sherman. In itself that was enough of a reason to attack Sherman in a series of articles. Journalism was a second career for Boynton; he had been a professional soldier. A graduate of the Kentucky Military Institute, Boynton joined the Union army at the onset of the war. He began the war as a major of Ohio volunteers and by 1865 was a lieutenant colonel with the brevet rank of brigadier general. Boynton served heroically at the battles of Chickamauga and Missionary Ridge. As part of George Thomas's Army of the Cumberland, Boynton felt that they had been treated unfairly in Sherman's *Memoirs*.[90]

Sherman constantly praised the role of the Army of the Tennessee, at the expense of the Army of the Cumberland. At Missionary Ridge, an action that earned Boynton the Congressional Medal of Honor, Sherman wrote that it was his Army of the Tennessee that had faced the bulk of the Confederate force, drawing them away from the Army of the Cumberland. He also portrayed Boynton's fellow soldiers as dispirited from Chickamauga. He criticized its commander, George Thomas, for not taking more decisive action against Hood in Tennessee.[91]

Although Boynton may have felt that Sherman had dishonored his former commander and his own contribution to the Union victory and he knew there would be financial rewards, his real motivation was a great deal more personal. It had to do with a dispute between Boynton's father, Dr. Charles Brandon

Boynton, and Oliver Otis Howard, one of Sherman's most trusted subordinates. As Grant looked to Sherman for someone with whom to confer, Sherman did the same with Howard. Ten years younger than Sherman, the Maine native was a West Point graduate and had lost an arm at the battle of Seven Pines. After the death of General James McPherson (a favorite of Sherman and Grant), Sherman put Howard in charge of the Army of the Tennessee. This was a controversial decision, for Sherman passed over several more senior officers in promoting Howard. For Joseph Hooker, still bitter over being passed over by Sherman after Chattanooga, this was the last straw. He asked to be relieved. From Hooker's point of view there could not have been a more insulting choice. He blamed Howard for his loss at Chancellorsville. His request was approved, and Hooker spent the rest of the war as a departmental commander headquartered in Cincinnati. Sherman was pleased to be rid of him; Hooker had been a difficult subordinate.[92]

General John A. Logan, who took command immediately after McPherson's death, felt as if he had been demoted when he was not allowed to retain command. In an attempt to soothe hurt feelings, Sherman allowed Logan to ride at the head of the Army of the Tennessee during the grand review in Washington. This gesture was obviously not enough, however. In 1870, as a member of the House of Representatives and the chairman of the House Military Affairs Committee, Logan introduced a bill that would dismantle the regular army altogether. He also pushed for General Sherman's salary to be substantially cut. In the end the army survived, and only its budget was cut, including a great reduction in the general's pay. Sherman responded in 1875 with harsh criticism of Logan in his *Memoirs*, calling Logan a political general who did not have the trust of his fellow officers. Sherman had made powerful enemies with his support of Howard. In the case of Logan, it cost him financially.[93]

At the end of the war, Howard was assigned to command the newly formed Freedmen's Bureau. Sherman tried to dissuade Howard from taking this position, because he disliked military officers' doing what he saw as civilian work and he was by no means the strongest supporter of the Freedmen's Bureau.[94] It was while stationed in Washington, DC, that Howard met Charles Boynton, Henry Van Ness Boynton's father.

A devoutly religious man, Howard joined the First Congregationalist Church of Washington. The first minister of the newly formed church was Dr. Charles Boynton. He had moved to Washington from Ohio at the end of the war in order to write a naval history of the Civil War. The two men worked together to fund the building of a church to accommodate the congregation that had been meeting previously in the homes of parishioners. The two were also cofounders of Howard University. Boynton served as the university's first president.[95]

The elder Boynton and Howard became the heads of opposing factions within the First Congregationalist Church. The issue that divided the church was black membership. Howard had actively recruited blacks into the church's Sunday school program to prepare them for membership. Boynton had made it clear through his sermons that he strongly believed in the separation of the races. Although a strong opponent of slavery, Boynton believed that blacks were different from whites and should have a different fate.[96]

In a bitter contest between the minister and his followers and the church's leading fund-raiser and his followers, Howard won. Blacks were admitted to the church, and Boynton lost both his posts as minister and as president of Howard University. Boynton's son, however, would do his best to avenge his father. Henry Van Ness Boynton published a series of stories accusing Howard of dishonesty in his management of the Freedmen's Bureau.[97]

There was no truth to these allegations, but Democratic congressmen who were already opposed to the bureau used the opportunity presented by Boynton to attack the Republican Party through the Freedmen's Bureau. New York representative Fernando Wood was the leader of the Democratic opposition to Howard. Based on Boynton's articles, Wood pushed for congressional hearings and eventually a court of military inquiry. Howard was accused of misappropriating bureau funds to support Howard University, the First Congregationalist Church, and the Washington YMCA. After hearing from witnesses, the Republican-controlled Congress dismissed the charges against Howard. The committee found there was no evidence against Howard and suggested that General Boynton had been the instigator of the charges, not Wood. Although Howard was vindicated, Boynton and Wood were successful in giving the public an impression of corruption within the bureau, which unfortunately has survived.[98]

Wood and Boynton persevered, and in 1874 a military court of inquiry was called to look into Howard and the financial dealings of the Freedmen's Bureau. As with the congressional hearings, those in charge did not believe the charges but because of the seriousness of the accusations felt that they had to be heard. President Grant put Sherman in charge of the court of inquiry. With Sherman as its head, the findings of the court were all but predetermined. Howard was cleared of all charges.[99]

Within a year, Sherman had published his *Memoirs*, and Boynton had written a scathing book-length review. *Sherman's Historical Raid: The Memoirs in the Light of the Record, A Review Based Upon the Compilations From the Files of the War Office* was a point-by-point attack on Sherman. According to Boynton, his purpose was to keep the future historian from "perpetuating the error and injustice which pervade both volumes of the work."[100]

Even the title is a subtle jab at Sherman. By calling Sherman's March to the Sea a raid Boynton greatly diminished its importance. By definition, a raid is a quick, sudden attack that has a high probability of success. In military terms it is the exact opposite of a campaign. Of the 276 pages, Boynton wrote very little. Most of it is taken directly from Sherman's *Memoirs* and from the *Official Records*. He wrote only to connect the long quotes and make conclusions that often are gross exaggerations of the quoted material. The majority of the work constituted accusations that Sherman blamed other generals for his failures and took credit for the success of others. In the first chapter, Boynton accused Sherman of taking credit for Grant's capture of Forts Henry and Donelson. Boynton quoted Sherman describing a conversation between Henry Halleck and himself in which he advised Halleck to strike at the center of his front, which would be the general area of the Tennessee River. As a former officer, Boynton should have known that there is a great deal of difference between suggesting a movement as vague as moving southward near the Tennessee River and planning and carrying out an operation as successful as Grant's capture of Fort Henry and Fort Donelson.[101]

Much of Boynton's work is simply a rehash of controversies that had been fought out in the newspapers during the war and immediately after. He accused Sherman of being unprepared at Shiloh and repeated much of what was written about the Sherman/Johnston surrender terms. He presented the exact terms of the surrender to allow the readers to judge for themselves, giving the impression that they had never been made public in their entirety.[102] Anyone who had picked up a paper in April 1865 would have known this to be false.

Any commander who was criticized by Sherman in his *Memoirs* was defended by Boynton, regardless of how minor or how justified the criticism. Boynton accused Sherman of unfairly blaming General Sooy Smith for the failure to destroy Polk's army. Sherman was to march from Vicksburg to Meridian, Mississippi, where he was to rendezvous with Smith and his seven-thousand-man cavalry. The next move was at Sherman's discretion—Polk's army, Selma, and Mobile were all targets mentioned. Smith was stopped at the very important but little-known battle of Okolona by Confederate cavalry. Without cavalry support, Sherman returned to Vicksburg. Boynton claimed that Sherman should have marched on without cavalry.[103] No Civil War general would move into enemy territory without a cavalry force to scout and screen him from enemy forces. Sherman's criticism of Smith was justified. Even if Smith had been able to defeat Forrest, he was so far behind schedule he would have arrived too late to have been any use.

Boynton's most controversial attack on Sherman concerned the planning of the March to the Sea. Sherman in his *Memoirs* unapologetically claimed that he—and he alone—planned the campaign. He printed several letters that supported this claim. Boynton's main evidence disputing Sherman's claim was his original orders from Grant, who ordered Sherman "to break up" Johnston's army and "get into the interior of the enemy's country."[104] Here, according to Boynton, lies the origin of the March to the Sea. When the letters from Grant to Sherman appear as if Grant is approving a plan originated by Sherman, he referred to moving south before breaking up the Confederate army. This is a dubious argument. Sherman's letters to Grant between the fall of Atlanta and the beginning of the March to the Sea showed the emergence of the plan. Each successive letter in the series would answer Grant's concerns as the plan evolved in Sherman's mind. Although Boynton and Grant's many supporters would attempt to give Grant credit for planning that operation, Grant never did. In his autobiography he gave Sherman full credit for the plan.[105]

Boynton's *Historical Raid* received glowing reviews from newspapers that were already anti-Sherman. The *New York Times* praised Boynton for his professional training and military experience, always referring to him as General Boynton. Even newspapers that had traditionally been friendly toward Sherman could not bring themselves to side with him over another journalist.[106] Boynton's work sums up almost all of the criticism of Sherman in the decade following the war. While he did not paint a flattering picture of the general, Boynton's attacks on Sherman do not accuse Sherman of brutality or making war on women and children.

Sherman's *Memoirs* were well accepted by the general public. They sold more than ten thousand copies in the first month. The general's highly readable style is still praised. The immediate criticism of the *Memoirs* came from the same group that had been criticizing Sherman since the end of the war, his fellow officers. This was further proof to Southern writers at the turn of the century that Northerners had monopolized the writing of Civil War history during the first decades that followed the end of the war. They had also dominated the criticism of Sherman. Southern newspapers that were critical of Sherman followed the same lines as his Northern critics. As late as 1886, Sherman was accused by some in the Northern press of having tried to grant slavery to the South.[107]

For Southerners, in these first two decades after the war, it seemed a lot more likely that Sherman would be remembered for his "memorandum" with Johnston and his infighting with other Union generals than he would be for his March to the Sea. Sherman's views on Reconstruction and racial equality made him more of an ally for Southerners than an enemy. It was the first postwar generation of Southerners, revisiting the work of Edward Pollard, who would turn General Sherman into the evil monster and destroyer of states.

CHAPTER 4

The War of the Memoirs

T he public's perception of General William T. Sherman from the end of the Civil War until his death in 1891 would change repeatedly. The accusations that General Sherman and all Union generals were brutal destroyers appeared in the Southern press before the end of the war, but these accusations had quickly been overshadowed by the twin evils of Radical Republican politicians and carpetbaggers as the perceived enemy of the South. Sherman visited the South many times during his tenure as general of the army and was always warmly greeted. While Sherman's reputation in the South was at its high point, he was the center of controversies in the North largely because of his treatment of Union generals and politicians during the war and in his writings. As those controversies and accusations of leniency were beginning to be forgotten in the North, Sherman, however, managed to stir new controversies in his attempt to ensure that history would favor the Union cause. This would have the twin effects of boosting Sherman's favorable perception in the North and inviting hostility from the South.

Accusations of Sherman's brutality would start to emerge again after the publication of his memoirs. Most of these claims would come from Northern men who felt they had been wronged by Sherman in his memoirs or as head of the army during peacetime. In an interview with the *Milwaukee Sentinel* given in 1875, just after the publication of Sherman's memoirs, General Joseph "Fighting Joe" Hooker became one of the first to claim that Sherman prosecuted the war "like a brigand" who had forgotten that he was "making war on his own countrymen." Hooker would say in this same interview that Sherman's destructive way of war was why Grant's administration had distanced itself from him. Hooker must have chosen to forget that Grant promoted Sherman to general of the army in 1869. Although there was a great deal of friction between Grant and Sherman when Hooker made this statement (Sherman had even moved his office from Washington, DC, to St. Louis), this was because of political issues such as the reorganization of the War Department and the admittance of African Americans to West Point. Hooker's statements can only be seen as lashing out against a junior officer whose career greatly bypassed his own. It was Sherman's promotion of Oliver Otis Howard to command of the Army of the Tennessee that had finally driven Hooker to resign his command. By the time Hooker made his statements he was well on his way to being remembered as the great bungler at Chancellorsville.[1]

Hooker echoed the wartime Richmond press when he accused Sherman of leaving a "black streak in his rear" and that eventually his actions would be "considered disgraceful by the great Christian world." Although comments like these would be used also by twentieth-century historians, this was not the commonly held view of Sherman during his lifetime. The accusations of Sherman as a traitor to the Union cause had never taken hold, and the North viewed him as one of the great heroes of the war. Southerners still approved of Sherman and reveled in his supposed break with the Grant administration.[2]

Southern generals who published their memoirs during this period disagreed with Sherman on aspects of the war, mostly on questions of strategy and the ratings of certain generals. Even the most critical of memoirs stopped well short of accusing Sherman of outright brutality as Hooker had done. One of the more critical of Sherman was General John Bell Hood's memoir titled *Advance and Retreat*. It was published in 1880, a year after Hood, his wife, and their oldest daughter died in a yellow fever epidemic in New Orleans. General P. G. T. Beauregard had the memoir published. The proceeds went to support Hood's ten surviving children, the youngest born just weeks before the death of her mother and father.[3] Hood, however, would have taken at least a little comfort from the fact that his tragic death made it difficult for Johnston, Sherman, or anyone for more than a generation to criticize him or his memoirs without appearing heartless.

Hood began preparing to write his memoirs almost as soon as the war was over. It was the continuation of the battle to clear his name and blame others for his defeats that had begun before the war was over. Hood collected official reports and wrote subordinates looking for material to use to place blame on Joseph Johnston for the loss of Atlanta in 1864. He even wrote Sherman asking for information about the number of prisoners, stragglers, and deserters during the Atlanta campaign. One of his subordinates, Stephen Dill Lee of Mississippi, gave him the good advice to wait—because the South was not ready for its generals to battle each other.[4]

Whether Hood took Lee's advice or the everyday struggle of providing for such a large family kept him from finishing his work for over a decade cannot be known. When Joseph Johnston published his book blaming Hood's leadership for the Confederate loss in the West, and thus the entire war, Hood began preparing a written response to Johnston. When Sherman published his memoirs, which agreed with Johnston's on many points, Hood broadened the scope of his project to respond to Sherman as well.[5]

Hood could not be as critical of Sherman as he might have wished in his memoirs. Hood did not want to criticize someone in a position to help him. Like other former opponents, John Bell Hood visited Sherman in his New York home after the war. Hood, like most Confederate officers, had fallen on hard times after the war. Hood met with Sherman hoping that the commanding general of the army could help him sell his papers.[6] Hood probably had a less utilitarian reason as well. He would not want to make an enemy out of someone who had the power to damage his reputation further. If Sherman decided to respond in print to Hood's work it could prove fatal to his reputation.

Unlike Johnston, however, Hood could not leave Sherman's version of the war unchallenged. He blamed Johnston for the Confederate defeat in the Western Theater. According to Hood, Johnston had instilled a sense of defeat in the Army of Tennessee that not only caused the loss of Atlanta but also led to his defeats at Franklin and Nashville. Hood not only blamed Johnston for the downfall of Atlanta; he downplayed the importance of the city. He denied that Atlanta was a manufacturing center and claimed it was only Northern propaganda that turned it into one.[7] By minimizing his failure, he also diminished Sherman's achievement. By arguing that Atlanta was not such as important target and that Sherman's burning of Atlanta was not justified, and completely unexpected, Hood tried to make the point that he did not seriously hurt the Confederate cause by abandoning Atlanta.

Hood criticized Sherman for destroying Atlanta but did not even mention his March to the Sea. Either Hood saw the burning of Atlanta and the evacuation of its citizens as worse than any suffering Sherman caused in middle and south Georgia or he did not mention it because he could not justify abandoning Georgia to a Union army. Hood was fortunate enough that, in the first decade that followed the war, the blame for an undefended Georgia fell on President Jefferson Davis.[8]

Regardless of what Sherman and Hood may have written about one another in their books and articles, there was obviously some degree of professional regard between the two men. When Hood experienced financial hardships during his final years, probably from ignoring his insurance business to concentrate on *Advance and Retreat*, he attempted to sell the records he had collected during his research to the federal government. Sherman acted as Hood's advocate. Hood was dismayed when Congress offered him a little more than half of what he was asking. The night before he was to leave Washington and return to his home in New Orleans, Hood visited Sherman and left his military papers with the general. Sherman did not just hold the papers for Hood; he actively campaigned for his old foe, lobbying the House and Senate to purchase Hood's papers and to pay more than their appraised value in order to compensate Hood for collecting them. As someone who had faced financial difficulties himself, Sherman was obviously sympathetic to Hood's plight. He was unsuccessful in his attempt to sell Hood's papers, however. After Hood's death, Sherman handed the papers over to the Louisiana representative Randall Gibson. Eventually the papers would make their way to the National Archives.[9]

Like his predecessor Joseph Johnston, Hood had reached out to Sherman after the war. Although there may have been some harsh words in their writings, both generals had pleasant postwar relations with General Sherman. This was not an unusual situation, especially for those who did not become active in politics after the war. Had Sherman been the "Merchant of Terror" as later historians portray him, it seems unlikely that his wartime antagonists would have sought him out for friendship or help.

General Hood, however, was not the only Confederate general to criticize Sherman for the forced evacuation of Atlanta and then fail to mention the march through Georgia and the Carolinas. General Richard "Dick" Taylor of Louisiana, son of former president Zachary Taylor, had many of the same complaints as Hood. Taylor had a varied and successful career during the war. He led troops at the battle of Manassas, served under "Stonewall" Jackson during his Valley campaign and defeated General Nathaniel Banks during his disastrous Red River campaign. Taylor replaced Hood as the commander of the Army of Tennessee after the battle of Nashville. He had the dubious distinction of surrendering the last army east of the Mississippi River.[10]

What Taylor found offensive about Sherman's behavior was the forced evacuation of Atlanta, not his March to the Sea. Like Hood, Taylor did not even mention Sherman's actions after Atlanta.[11] Unlike Hood, however, General Taylor could not be blamed for abandoning Georgia to Sherman. Yet in attempting to portray Sherman in the most negative light, Taylor also discussed the evacuation of Atlanta instead of the March to the Sea. He must not have viewed the latter as out of the ordinary in nineteenth-century warfare.

Taylor's memoirs are the first truly negative representation of Union soldiers written by a Confederate veteran. Memoir writers on both sides treated their former enemies as fellow professionals and reserved their venom for the political leadership. Taylor was different from the majority of Civil War generals in that he was not trained at West Point. He was educated at Harvard as the haughty language of his memoirs painfully attempted to show. Taylor lost everything in the war; the Louisiana sugar plantation he inherited from his father was looted by Union troops.[12]

More than just having been an unreconstructed Rebel, unhappy with his financial losses because of the war and the Thirteenth Amendment, Taylor was a close personal friend of Confederate president Jefferson Davis, and Taylor's sister was Davis's first wife. Davis used his position as president to help Taylor's military career, and Taylor used his contacts with former Whigs to make Davis's confinement more bearable. When Union officers, like Sherman, blamed Davis for the war and the Confederate defeat, Taylor lashed out, attacking Sherman's inhumane treatment of Atlanta's citizens.[13]

In the last three decades of the nineteenth century, the generals and senior officers who wrote their memoirs heavily influenced the public's perceptions of the war's leaders. Because the Southern generals who faced Sherman portrayed Sherman as a professional, the people of the South mostly accepted Sherman as their former generals had. More important than wartime accomplishments to most Southerners was a general's postwar politics, as most Southerners would fight the peace much more aggressively than they fought the war.

Sherman's postwar relationship with the South was nearly as positive as his prewar relationship. In his position as general of the army, Sherman made several tours of the South. His first visit was to Louisiana in 1869. During this inspection tour, Sherman went to the Louisiana Academy, later to become Louisiana State University. He was given a tour of the new campus by the academy's superintendent, David F. Boyd. Sherman had been the school's first leader when it was founded just before the war, and Boyd had been the school's professor of ancient languages. After the general's death, Boyd would become one of Sherman's most dedicated defenders. Boyd's credentials as a Southern loyalist were firm; he served as a major under General Stonewall Jackson in Virginia. When he wrote articles for newspapers across the country, he would identify himself as a "professor under Sherman and a major under Jackson."[14]

In a much reprinted article, Boyd described Sherman's visit to the school. The general was a former superintendent and still financially supported the institution, and his portrait hung in a place of honor in the school's administrative building. He received a more than friendly greeting from the faculty and students. Sherman had been warned by the Reconstruction government in New Orleans that it was not safe for him to travel into the country to visit former students. According to Boyd, Sherman responded "that he was going, and that instead of being in any danger, he felt that everybody along the road would be glad to see him; but that as for him and the rest of the carpet-baggers he wouldn't blame the people much if they did kill him."[15]

While in Louisiana, Sherman was named the duke of Mardi Gras, an institution still very much controlled by the locals, and was invited to visit Jackson and Canton, Mississippi, both of which had suffered at the hands of the Union army under Sherman's command. He did not accept this invitation because of his heavy schedule, but while he was still in Louisiana, Sherman met with former Confederate generals James Longstreet and Jeff "the Missouri Swamp Fox" Thompson. The meetings were reported as friendly and social in nature and could only have bolstered Sherman's reputation with Southerners. Longstreet was still looked on favorably as "Lee's Old War Horse." He had not yet alienated most Southerners by leaving the Episcopal Church to become a Catholic, leaving the Democratic Party to become a Republican, leading African American troops to put down a riot in New Orleans, and worst of all, criticizing Robert E. Lee.[16]

As he had been before the war, Sherman had a very favorable impression of the South and most Southerners. In a letter that must have dismayed his brother the Republican senator John Sherman, the general wrote that the young veterans of the Confederate army should be given political power. In his opinion, he wrote, "they are a better class than the adventurers who have gone South purely for office."[17]

E. P. Howell, the editor of the *Atlanta Constitution*, wrote to Sherman just days after he had left Atlanta, asking him to write about the advantages of the Atlanta area for industry and immigration. Sherman wrote back in a letter widely published in Northern and Southern newspapers that there was no better area for settlement than the northern parts of Georgia and Alabama and east Tennessee. Southern papers that paraphrased and editorialized about the letter seemed proud that Sherman held the South in such high regard. Hard-line Confederates may have felt more malice toward him for siding with New South supporters than anything he may have done during the war.[18]

In 1879 General Phil Sheridan and Sherman were invited to a reunion of Confederate and Union troops in North Carolina. Sheridan declined the invitation, citing other engagements. Sherman, however, wrote that he would not attend an event that gave the impression "that Confederate and Union men were alike worthy of a celebration for the terrible history of 1861 and 1865." He did consent to attending any event that celebrated North Carolina's Revolutionary past.[19] While Sherman was extremely friendly to Southerners, he never wavered from his belief that the Union cause was just.

At nearly the same time Sherman was making his last tour of the South in 1881, another Sherman was also in that region. Then secretary of the Treasury,

John Sherman, the general's brother and closest confidant, was in the South stumping for the Republican Party. As a Radical Republican and a prewar abolitionist, he was not greeted nearly as kindly as his brother. He was blamed for what Southern newspapers called the "fraud of '76" and the "shameless thieves" appointed to party positions in the South.[20]

Throughout most of their lives, John Sherman was the more disliked of the two brothers. Before the war, this was because John Sherman was the more famous brother. When William T. Sherman was the head of the Louisiana State Military Academy, being the brother of an abolitionist, "the most horrible of all monsters," caused a great deal of friction with the leaders of that state. After the war, Southerners identified John Sherman with Reconstruction and what they saw as the tyranny of the federal government.[21]

During his visits to the South, General Sherman gave speeches that must have pleased his Southern audience. He defended the terms he offered Johnston, arguing that if peace had been left to the army instead of the politicians there would not have been nearly as many problems. He disparaged most of the Reconstruction acts, especially the Ku Klux Klan Act, and under President Andrew Johnson pushed for the immediate admittance of the former Confederate states.[22]

What most accurately shows the low level of animosity toward Sherman was the strong belief that he could be elected president of the United States. Sherman had publicly stated that he had no intention of running for president. At least one editor of a Southern paper believed this statement was an invention of the Radical Republicans because they were afraid he would run as a Democrat. Rumors spread before the 1868 presidential election that if the Republicans nominated Ulysses S. Grant then the Democrats would nominate William T. Sherman. There was never a serious effort to nominate Sherman, but this was due to Sherman's fierce resistance to holding political office of any kind. Politicians had no job security. There was resistance among Democrats to a Sherman nomination, but it was mostly from those Northern newspapers that resented the election of any Union veteran.[23]

While it was possible for a Republican to win with no Southern support, a Democrat had to carry every Southern state and at least a few in the North or far West.[24] The Democratic Party believed that it needed a candidate who had proved loyalty to the Union on the battlefield but was not so controversial as to drive away any Southern votes. That there was any talk at all of Sherman as a candidate shows that the public perception of Sherman could not have been of the monster that later historians portrayed.

With Reconstruction over and relative political quiet returning to this country, the war's twentieth anniversary brought heightened interest to the Civil

War. The vast majority of memoirs were published during the 1880s. The reading public apparently could not get enough. In 1884, the *Century Magazine* announced that it would begin publishing a series entitled "Battles and Leaders of the Civil War." The articles, published monthly, would be written by the most prominent veterans of the war, North and South. Post offices around the country were packed with subscribers waiting for the next issue.[25]

The "Century War Series" dealt with many controversies. Readers expected the writings of the leaders themselves to put most of the issues to rest. This was a misplaced hope, however, as the magazines only really created a forum for officers not warranting a national newspaper interview to put forward their grievances and for the more famous leaders to repeat arguments they had made already. Authors ranged from second lieutenants to General Grant himself.[26] Many articles were lifted from memoirs that had already been published, as was the case with General Hood, and the majority would eventually end up in the memoirs of their authors. They are mostly of a very technical nature and are obviously written for other soldiers. The argument over whether Hood, Johnston, or Davis was responsible for the fall of Georgia reemerges in its pages, as well as descriptions of Sherman's March to the Sea that differed very little from those written by George Ward Nichols twenty years earlier.[27]

The March to the Sea was treated by these military writers as a means to an end. Captain Daniel Oakly of the Second Massachusetts wrote that "fast marching was the order of the day." The goal was for the army to reach Savannah and the coast, not to wage war on the civilian population. Even Wade Hampton agreed with this view, writing in his article that Sherman's goal was clearly to meet up with Grant, and it "was evident to everyone who had given a thought to the subject."[28]

The paramount achievement of the "Century War Series" was that it led directly to publication of Ulysses S. Grant's memoirs. On learning that Grant planned to write a handful of articles only about key battles, Mark Twain convinced Grant to write a complete memoir and allow Twain to publish it. It was a bonanza for both men. Any belief that Grant harbored any ill will toward Sherman—either for anything the latter had written in his memoirs or for any actions he took while Grant was president—was put to rest when *The Personal Memoirs of Ulysses S. Grant* were published in 1885. General Grant's memoirs were very well received by the public in the North and in Europe. The story of a near penniless General Grant racing against death to finish his memoirs in order to provide for his family gave the volumes a sense of being his last testament and beyond reproach.[29]

Grant agreed with and defended Sherman on every point of controversy during the war years. On some issues, certainly, it was in Grant's best interest to back

Sherman. Grant claimed that Sherman was not caught unprepared at the battle of Shiloh. Of course, if the accusations against Sherman at Shiloh were correct, then Grant also was guilty of incompetence. Sherman's and Grant's critics accused them of not being ready for the Confederate attack on the first day of the battle. Both Grant and Sherman wrote that they had been prepared for the Southern onslaught and that the first day of fighting had not been a rout. The most often-cited evidence to the contrary was that Sherman had not ordered his soldiers to entrench on the night of April 5, 1862. Sherman offered several reasons in his memoirs for not preparing defensive positions. He argued that untrained soldiers would not advance from a fortified line and would not stop running if driven from one, and that a prepared position invited attack. Grant not only supported Sherman's claims; he offered a much better reason for not fortifying than did Sherman. Grant simply argued that with the raw recruits who made up the Union force at Shiloh time was better spent in drilling than in digging. The Union armies of the last years of the war that dug in whenever the army stopped were veterans who would have gotten little use from additional training.[30]

Grant defended Sherman's actions at Vicksburg and at Chattanooga. Any failure that Sherman encountered either was an intended diversion or was beyond the control of any general. Grant supported the surrender terms that Sherman offered to General Johnston. According to Grant, Sherman submitted articles of capitulation that were refused by the government and then he submitted a more acceptable set of terms, with no real harm done. Grant defended the non-pursuit of Jefferson Davis as a case of Sherman's implementing the implied wishes of Abraham Lincoln.[31]

Sherman's critics such as Henry Boynton accused him of unfairly taking from Grant the credit for devising the March to the Sea. Boynton and other critics would argue that Sherman's orders had been to defeat Johnston's Confederate army and move into the interior. This was exactly what Sherman did, and it cut the Confederacy in half once again as Grant had done with his capture of Vicksburg. There are serious flaws with the argument that Grant was the mastermind behind the March to the Sea. In his memoirs, Grant wrote that Sherman—and Sherman alone—was the author of the March to the Sea. Regardless of what others may have written, Sherman would not have written that he came up with the plan had he not. Had he made a false claim, with Grant as its victim, he had to have known that if a question had come down to Sherman's word versus Grant's, Grant would have been the victor and Sherman's reputation would have been seriously wounded. Sherman also knew that when the *Official Records* were eventually published, his correspondence with Grant would show that the March to the Sea was his idea. Also, Lincoln should have the final word on the issue, and when the *Official Records* were published, there was a letter of congratulation from the president to Sherman. "The honor is all yours; for I believe none of us went further than to acquiesce."[32]

Grant would also defend the actions of the Union army during the March to the Sea. He wrote that most of the stories were more fiction than fact. By no means claiming that the Union army was completely innocent, he wrote that "there was much unwarrantable pillaging." This phrasing meant that there was some. He blamed "the worst acts that were attributed to Sherman's army" on the Georgians themselves. He did not mention General Wheeler and his cavalry or other Confederate units operating in Georgia. Grant wrote that the convicts released by the state of Georgia and those Georgians "who took advantage of their country being invaded" were the most responsible for the suffering of Georgia's civilian population.[33]

Despite modern historians' portrayal of Grant as mired in controversy from his scandal-plagued presidency, Grant was still wildly popular at the time his memoirs were published. The popularity of his memoirs was helped by his highly readable style. He rose above the prevailing style of the day, which was to include numerous letters and reports to shore up arguments. Grant abandoned the majority of the ones that he could have used. He only included quotes when someone else's words were significant. The success of his memoirs and wartime reputation combined to make Grant's view of the war one that would carry a great deal of weight, at least with Northerners.[34]

In 1886 Senator John A. Logan wrote his history of the Civil War, *The Great Conspiracy*. Logan had a long and distinguished résumé by then. He had served in the House of Representatives and had been one of the leaders of the Johnson impeachment. Previously he had been a general in the Union army and the Republican candidate for vice president. Logan had been one of Sherman's most bitter enemies. His "pay bill" had slashed the salaries of Sherman and other generals. Sherman was convinced that this was a personal attack on him because Sherman had replaced Logan in command of the Army of the Tennessee with Howard, after the death of McPherson.[35]

Sherman had been critical of Logan in his own memoirs. He wrote that Logan was more interested in "personal fame and glory" as a way to further his political ambition.[36] Logan's *Great Conspiracy* would have been a perfect opportunity for him to strike back at Sherman in print. To Logan's credit, however, he did not. Logan presented Sherman as one of the great generals of the war who was responsible for its successful conclusion. The only issue he took with Sherman was a very minor point over who deserved credit for the discovery of a river crossing during the battle of Manassas.[37]

The fact that Logan did not attack Sherman in his *Great Conspiracy* or his posthumously published *The Volunteer Soldier of America* makes it seem that any ill will Logan may have held during the war did not consume him during the postwar years. If he had spared Sherman more biting criticism in an attempt to further his own reputation, he was more than a decade too late. Logan had already borne the brunt of Sherman's attacks in his 1875 memoirs. Had he simply just wanted to avoid a conflict with Sherman, he would not have attacked the general's beloved professional army.

Sherman was probably wrong in his belief that Logan's pay bill and his other legislation aimed at disbanding the professional core of the army were personal. Logan's 696-page book *The Volunteer Soldier of America* was nothing but a very long argument for an all-volunteer militia-style army and the disbanding of the US Military Academy.[38] Logan obviously felt passionate about this issue. The second book was written after Sherman had retired and the two men were on friendly terms.[39]

Sherman and Logan had put their personal difficulties behind them. Logan had made the first move by praising the general at a dinner held in honor of his sixty-third birthday. The next day, Sherman wrote Logan explaining, for the first time, why he had replaced him with Howard, after the battle of Atlanta. Sherman told Logan that George Thomas had convinced him to choose Howard. Thomas had died in 1870, he was in no position to deny Sherman's claim. Logan responded with a confession of his own. He had been secretly ordered to the rear by President Lincoln to campaign for the Republicans, a plausible claim considering the importance of the 1864 election. Sherman's belief that Logan had returned home for his own political gain was something Sherman held against Logan since the war.[40]

Sherman was openly critical of what he called the political generals. Although West Point was mainly an engineering school that taught little grand strategy, Sherman did not trust officers with high commands if they had not attended the academy. Regardless of this, Sherman's strongest literary and political supporter, next to his brother John and Ulysses S. Grant, was Jacob D. Cox, the epitome of the political general. The first time Cox put on a military uniform was as a brigadier general. He had been an Ohio state senator and was given command of Ohio's volunteers. While Cox would not make the list of America's greatest generals, he did prove competent in leading troops at Antietam, Atlanta, and Franklin. After the war, Cox served as governor of Ohio and in Grant's cabinet.[41]

Cox could have had issues with Sherman. Sherman was highly critical of officers who had not been part of the prewar army. Cox served in Tennessee against Hood. Franklin and Nashville were two of the fiercest battles of the war. They were also two of the most clear-cut Union victories of the war. Many of the general officers of the Union army who served in that campaign felt they had been slighted. General George Thomas, the Union commander at Nashville, and General John Schofield, the Union commander at Franklin, felt they had finished the war in the West and that these battles were a great deal more important than Sherman's March to the Sea. It was the Georgia campaign, however, that caught the public's attention while Franklin and Nashville were pushed to the periphery.[42]

Cox wrote a series of books about the war for Charles Scribner's Sons of New York as part of their series *Campaigns of the Civil War*. He described events that he participated in and others that he had to relate secondhand. Although he was at Nashville and Franklin, Cox glorified the March to the Sea. Cox, as the book reviewer for *The Nation*, also strongly defended Sherman's memoirs against those who questioned Sherman's accuracy.[43]

General Cox had several very good reasons for siding with Sherman. The two men held many of the same postwar political views. They were both against allowing African Americans to vote. Cox went so far as to call for the forced colonization of former slaves to Africa. Moreover, both Cox and Sherman had their difficulties with the Grant administration. Sherman argued with Grant over the organization of the US Army. Cox criticized Grant for not doing enough to stop Radical Reconstruction and grew frustrated with the corruption in the administration.[44]

Cox also sided with Sherman against the other generals in Tennessee because they were his rivals for fame. Cox claimed in his writings and in his political campaigns that he had commanded the fortified line at Franklin that took the brunt of the Confederate attack. Thomas and Schofield both charged Cox with vastly exaggerating his service record. Another general at Franklin, David Stanley, called Cox "a reckless inventor of lies."[45] Cox's motivation was to repay the men who had denied him the credit he felt he deserved. Even though Cox was not a military man by profession, his writings were of a very technical nature. He discussed regimental strengths and movements with no emotion. He offered no answer to the charges of brutality made against Sherman's army. He only wrote that the scavengers made the perfect picket line for the army since no enemy force could get near the army without crossing their path.[46]

Another one of Sherman's subordinates who wrote of his experiences during the war was William B. Hazen, a general who served in Sherman's Atlanta campaign and the March to the Sea. Hazen had more in common with Sherman than with Cox. A fellow Ohioan, Hazen served in the army from his graduation from West Point in 1855 until his death in 1887. In 1885 Hazen published his *A Narrative of Military Service*. In his introduction Hazen stated that he would stay away from the controversies "which buzz and sting for long years after kindly nature has repaired the battlefields." Hazen would only include what was necessary to tell his story. What controversies he excluded are unknown since he discussed all of the ones that he would have had any knowledge about.[47]

Hazen was a strong supporter of General Sherman. Although he never rated Sherman, or any other leader, his description of many of the events of the war revealed a clear bias toward his fellow Ohioan. One glaring example was his description of the battle of Kennesaw Mountain. Hazen disagreed with the almost universal view that the order to attack that fortified position directly during the Atlanta campaign was a major mistake on the part of Sherman. According to Hazen, the overall strategy was more than sound; it was just not carried out effectively by Sherman's junior officers.

When Hazen wrote his memoirs, Grant had not yet published his memoirs giving credit to Sherman for the March to the Sea and ending that particular controversy. Hazen addressed the issue directly. He wrote that it did not matter who originated the idea, for "the plan was in the mind of thousands, but only one adopted and executed it."[48] According to Hazen the March to the Sea was a "grand picnic." He dismissed the idea of the march being anything but a strategic movement in order to bring the army to bear against Lee and the Army of Northern Virginia. In his chapter "Lessons of the War," Hazen dedicated only a few paragraphs to the issue of foragers. He called the duty "legitimate, necessary and honorable." He lamented the term *bummer* because it gave a negative connotation to that duty. According to Hazen, the foragers were carefully selected and some of the best men of the army. Hazen admitted that there were "bad characters in the army," as would be natural in such a large force, and it was those men who were responsible for the anecdotal evidence against Sherman. General Oliver O. Howard, Hazen's superior, gave orders against men leaving the ranks and committing robbery. There were court-martials, but the senior officers were hesitant to convict since that verdict meant a firing squad. According to Hazen, "the actual amount of lawlessness was exceedingly small," and there was not one "well authenticated case of the violation of women."[49]

Hazen spent more words arguing for the replacement of the cartridge box with a bandoleer and the retiring of the bayonet than he did the issue of foragers.[50] This made a strong argument that the army's conduct in Georgia did not need to be defended. Hazen must have mistakenly believed that the record would speak for itself.

As a witness to the Union occupation of Columbia, South Carolina, Hazen wrote that a battery under Hazen's command and Sherman's direction fired six shots into the unfinished state courthouse. He very accurately wrote that the damage would "be pointed out for generations."[51] Hazen blamed the destruction of Columbia on the common soldier, Confederate and Union, and cleared the high command of both sides. Union sources generally blamed Confederate general Wade Hampton's order to set fire to bales of cotton that lined the city's main thoroughfare. The burning cotton was supposedly blown through the city, spreading the fire.[52] Hazen defended Hampton, writing that the cotton fire was easily, quickly, and completely put out by Union soldiers when they first entered Columbia. According to Hazen, the Confederates were not blameless. They had looted most of the city's stores before evacuating in front of advancing Union soldiers. Hazen did not downplay the destruction in Columbia. He wrote that the city was "turned to ashes." He was sure that the city was purposely "set on fire in more than a hundred places," but said that this had not been ordered and that it could not have been stopped.[53]

As a professional soldier, Hazen was a disciple of Sherman. He praised the formation of the War College and other professional military schools. Hazen, like Sherman, called for the formation of a Prussian-style staff system. He believed that, with a proper staff, disasters like Chancellorsville and Chickamauga could have been avoided. Hazen also shared Sherman's opinion of the press. While Sherman's complaints about the press came across as personal, Hazen made reasonable arguments that the press had too much access to the front. According to Hazen, the press inadvertently gave information to the enemy because of its lack of knowledge of military affairs. Hazen was not for a total ban on the press. His command had been accompanied by a reporter from the *New York Tribune*. The reporter and Hazen had become friends. Hazen did argue that the press should be assigned to the headquarters and closely regulated.[54]

Hazen did, however, take issue with Sherman and his memoirs over his failure to mention the battle of Pickett's Mill. Hazen described it as the "most fierce, bloody and persistent assault by our troops in the Atlanta campaign."[55] His willingness to criticize Sherman in this instance shows that Hazen did not follow Sherman's leadership blindly. Even though it was only a relatively minor point, he obviously felt free to challenge Sherman. The fact that, in general, he did not shows that Hazen truly believed what he wrote.

Hazen's *A Narrative of Military Service* was representative of works by the majority of Sherman's officers who put pen to paper in the 1880s. Although they may have disagreed with their commander on minor issues, the overall story was the same. Even political enemies such as John Logan praised Sherman's wartime accomplishments. By the end of the decade, Sherman mostly had been forgiven by the Northern population. Wartime and Reconstruction controversies had been largely forgotten. The exact opposite occurred in the South. During the last fifteen years of his life, Sherman would stir controversies that made the Southern population forget his politics and Southern sympathies.

Wartime portrait of Sherman, a rare image of
the general standing (courtesy of the Library of
Congress).

Ellen Ewing Sherman (courtesy of the Notre Dame Archives).

Sherman and his son Thomas (courtesy of the Notre Dame Archives).

Sherman family gravesite, Calvary Cemetery, St. Louis. Sherman's gravestone (center) is very plain compared to those of other Civil War leaders. Buried at the far right, next to Ellen Sherman, is the Shermans' eldest son, Willie, who was only nine years old when he died in 1863. The decoration on his gravestone reflects his "adoption" as a mascot by the Thirteenth U.S. Infantry after the Vicksburg campaign (courtesy of the Catholic Archdiocese of St. Louis).

Sherman (front row, center) at a veteran's reunion. He was a common sight at these reunions (courtesy of the Library of Congress).

The controversial Sherman statue in Washington, D.C. (courtesy of the Library of Congress).

Statue of Sherman in Central Park, New York, and (detail) the hind
hoof of Sherman's horse crushing a pinecone, symbolic of the "March
to the Sea" (courtesy of the Library of Congress; detail courtesy of
the author).

John Sherman, the most controversial of the brothers and always his brother's advocate (courtesy of the Library of Congress).

Sherman and his staff taken just after the fall of Atlanta (left to right): Oliver Otis Howard, John A. Logan, William B. Hazen, Sherman, Jefferson C. Davis, Henry Slocum, Joseph A. Mower (courtesy of the Library of Congress).

Sherman's men destroying Georgia railroad (courtesy of the Library of Congress).

Henry Van Ness Boynton, Sherman's harshest Northern critic. The former general had a professional and personal grudge against Sherman (courtesy of the Library of Congress).

John Schofield, a leading general of the postwar army. His autobiography contained the most damaging accusations against Sherman (courtesy of the Library of Congress).

Jefferson Davis, 1885, at the time his memoirs were released and he and Sherman began their war of words (courtesy of the Library of Congress).

CHAPTER 5

Sherman's Last Years

William T. Sherman's reputation in the American South had been very positive in the first fifteen years that followed the Civil War. During Reconstruction he was the political ally of the South, from his surrender terms to Johnston to his stand against the Ku Klux Klan Acts and his less than lukewarm acceptance of African Americans in the army. This, of course, would not last, however. As the generation that fought the war aged and their children became adults, Southerners began to look at their war in a different way. The antebellum period was romanticized as were the men who fought to preserve that way of life. This view of the Confederacy became so strong it became almost a secular religion. The trinity of this religion were Thomas "Stonewall" Jackson, Robert E. Lee, and Jefferson Davis.[1] Of the three, Sherman criticized two of them severely. Heresy was Sherman's real crime.

In 1881 the D. Appleton Company of New York published Jefferson Davis's history of the Civil War, *The Rise and Fall of the Confederate Government*. In it Davis defended the righteousness of the Confederate cause. The two-volume set blamed the war on the North and accused the Union army of violating the laws of civilized warfare. His work was not one of reconciliation.[2]

On June 8, 1881, Sherman attended a reunion of the Army of the Potomac in Hartford, Connecticut. Among the speakers were the novelist Mark Twain, the secretary of war Robert Todd Lincoln, the governors of Pennsylvania and Rhode Island, and several senators and former generals. Although Lincoln received the standing ovation, it was General Sherman's speech that received the most attention in the press.[3]

Sherman began his speech by praising the current soldiers of the volunteer US Army, but the majority of his speech dealt with Jefferson Davis's recently published book. Sherman's first objection to Davis was his treatment of Grant.

Davis had argued that Grant's Virginia campaign had been an unnecessary waste of life. To Sherman, "a certain amount of killing had to be done" and that was as good a place as anywhere.[4]

In that speech Sherman also defended his friend Confederate general Joseph Johnston, who in his memoirs blamed Davis for the Confederate defeat. Davis returned the favor in his writings and accused Johnston of not following orders in the opening days of Sherman's Atlanta campaign. According to Davis, Johnston had been ordered to attack Sherman as he moved south from Chattanooga, not to use the Fabian strategy that he adopted. Sherman argued, as did Grant, that Johnston adopted the best possible strategy for the situation.[5]

The majority of Sherman's speech was a defense of his own actions that had been attacked in *The Rise and Fall of the Confederacy*. Sherman felt he needed to defend himself against two charges: his forced evacuation of Atlanta and the burning of Columbia. According to Davis, the nearly seventeen hundred Atlanta residents sent south out of the city were severely mistreated and robbed of their few positions. Sherman was offended by this accusation. He told the audience of veterans and dignitaries that it was "simply absurd" to make such a claim. He felt it was important for him to refute this claim, and he read a report written by Major William Clare, who had been appointed by Hood to handle the evacuation. One can only imagine the level of excitement among the thousands of veterans gathered to hear Sherman speak as he read from an official report written by a Confederate major involving the transfer of civilians. But if Sherman lost his audience while reading from the official records, he most likely regained it in the fiery language he used to defend himself against the accusation that he was responsible for the burning of Columbia, South Carolina.[6]

According to Davis there were "hundreds of unimpeachable witnesses" who "testified that the burning of Columbia was" a "deliberate act, . . . permitted, if not ordered by the commanding general." He compared Sherman's actions to that of the infamous Albrecht von Wallenstein during the Thirty Years' War (who, ironically, may also have been the victim of propaganda and politics).[7] Sherman blamed the burning of Columbia on General Wade Hampton and his cavalry. This was the position he had taken in his memoirs and in his official report written in 1865. In that report, sent to Halleck, Sherman wrote, "without hesitation I charge General Wade Hampton with having burned his own city of Columbia, not with malicious intent, or as the manifestation of a silly 'Roman stoicism,' but from folly and want of sense." In the 1881 speech, Sherman also correctly pointed out that the same destruction occurred in Richmond as the Confederates withdrew. Sherman also downplayed the destruction of Columbia. The strongest argument he offered was that he and his officers set up their separate headquarters inside the city.[8] This would have been an unlikely action had he ordered the entire city put to the torch.

His denial of responsibility offers an interesting question; why would General Sherman deny responsibility for burning Columbia? If, as many writers have claimed, Sherman destroyed Columbia as punishment for the war, and if he was attempting to make South Carolina howl, he would have defended his destruction of Columbia, not placed the blame on the Confederates. When Sherman was being accused of sympathizing with the Southern cause at the end of the war, why did he not claim the destruction of Columbia as proof against such claims? The only reasonable answer is that the facts did not support such a claim. When Sherman made his defense against Jefferson Davis, he was speaking to a large crowd of Union veterans. Had he taken credit for Columbia, it is most likely he would have received as many cheers as he did for calling the president of the former Confederacy a "pompous" liar.[9]

Sherman was concerned about how future generations of Americans and Europeans would view the war. He accurately predicted how Southern historians such as Douglas Southhall Freeman would write about the war. Sherman believed that, unless the North wrote its own history of the war, Southerners would convince future generations that the Union "conquered not by courage, skill and patriotic devotion, but by brute force and by cruelty." The truth, according to Sherman, was the exact opposite. "We never could work up our men to the terrible earnestness of the Southern forces. Their murdering of Union fugitives, burning of Lawrence, Paducah, &c., were all right in their eyes, and if we burned down an old cotton gin or shed it was barbarism. I am tired of such perversion, and will resist it always."[10]

Sherman summed up this section of his speech by addressing Davis's claim that General Johnston had disobeyed orders, once again, when he refused to retreat toward the Trans-Mississippi instead of surrendering to Sherman. According to Sherman, if this were true then all people "North or South" should "feel a debt a gratitude to General Johnston for his good sense and humanity in stopping the war." In his last words about Davis, Sherman called any attempt to prolong the war after April 1865 "an unpardonable crime against humanity."[11] There were no stronger words Sherman could have used in condemning the former president of the Confederacy.

Jefferson Davis responded to Sherman's criticism in the press. In an interview given to the *Chicago Times*, a Democratic newspaper that had been very critical of the Union war effort, Davis lashed out at Sherman over his remarks in Connecticut. He called Sherman "a vain man" who suffered from the "hallucination that he is a great general." He argued that if Stonewall Jackson, instead of Johnston, had faced Sherman in Georgia the outcome would have been much different. Davis also addressed the march to Savannah, calling Sherman's men, "an organized gang of plunderers."[12]

Davis also fell upon one of his staunchest supporters, blaming General Hood for not stopping the March to the Sea. He called the invasion of Tennessee "the wildest of wild goose chases" and "the folly of the hot-headed Hood."[13] In this assessment, Davis agreed with Sherman and most Northern historians, who had little respect for Hood. It does, however, tarnish Davis's credibility considering he approved of Hood's invasion of Tennessee before it took place.[14]

The reporter for the *Chicago Times* was by no means a supporter of Jefferson Davis, referring to him as "the relic of the Confederacy." The writer also predicted that this episode would "restore his waning popularity."[15] This unnamed journalist's prediction would prove to be extremely accurate. Sherman's harsh words against Jefferson Davis at the moment Davis was reaching the peak of his popularity would help make General Sherman the embodiment of the evil Yankee for the first postwar Southern generation.

In 1881, within months of his exchange with Davis, Sherman was invited to Atlanta, for the International Cotton Exposition. Newspapers claimed that public furor was over and the exposition proposed a "Sherman day" in Georgia. From South Carolina, Columbians came by train to Atlanta to protest. There were even threats of burning the general in effigy.[16] Although the general's visit to Atlanta was relatively uneventful, the large number of negative stories written about General Sherman had not occurred on his earlier visits to the South except for his 1864–1865 military campaign.[17]

Southerners might be able to forgive Sherman for criticizing Davis, but his next action would prove unforgivable. In 1887 Sherman began another feud over the character of a leading Confederate. In March, *Macmillan's Magazine* published an article written by Lord Garnet Wolseley, a senior officer in the British army. As a young officer, Wolseley was sent to Canada as part of Great Britain's military buildup during the diplomatic crisis known as the *Trent* Affair. Wolseley traveled to Virginia to witness the war firsthand. He was not one of the many official foreign observers who traveled with the Union and Confederate armies in the East. He took a leave of absence and paid his own way from Canada to the camp of the Army of Northern Virginia.[18]

Wolseley was very pro-Confederate in his sentiments. In the articles he published during the war, he called for British recognition of the Confederacy and diplomatic intervention to force the Union to accept an independent South. By 1887 Wolseley was a well-respected military critic, a scholar, and a prolific contributor to British magazines and newspapers. His article praising Robert E. Lee published in *Macmillan's Magazine* bordered on worship. Wolseley rated Lee as the greatest general of the war.[19] This would not necessarily have

drawn Sherman's attention and critical pen. Wolseley and Sherman held similar views on many issues, including their criticism of Jefferson Davis. They
were also both professional military men who supported an organized staff
system under a commanding general and were extremely skeptical of amateur
soldiers.[20]

Wolseley drew Sherman's ire by disparaging the recently deceased Ulysses
S. Grant in order to make the argument that Lee was the greatest general of
the war. Wolseley gave international credibility to the argument of Jefferson
Davis and Confederate historians that Grant was a butcher. In their opinion,
it was only by throwing the overwhelming Union numbers into the fray that
Grant could overcome the superior generalship of Lee.[21] Sherman was angered
by any criticism of his old friend, whom Sherman considered the greatest gen-
eral of the war. Sherman wrote a reply to Wolseley that was published in the
North American Review. In his May 1887 article, titled simply "Grant, Thomas,
Lee," Sherman ranked those three generals in that order.[22] Both Wolseley's and
Sherman's articles appeared at a time when Southerners were turning Lee into
one of the nation's greatest heroes.[23]

Sherman wrote that Grant was superior to Lee because he had the ability to
see the entire situation. According to Sherman, Lee "never rose to the grand
problem which involved a continent and future generations."[24] While Sherman
probably would have upset many Southerners by arguing that Grant was the
superior general, his position probably would have been viewed by most as an
act of loyalty to his commander and friend. However, his rating of Thomas as
a superior commander was galling to Southerners. George Thomas, like Lee,
was a Virginian from a semi-aristocratic family. He was trained at West Point
and, like Lee, had served continuously in the army from the time of his graduation. Unlike Lee, he was viewed as a traitor to his state, and even his own
family never forgave him.[25] Sherman's argument was a simple one. Thomas had
destroyed an entire army, namely Hood's army at the battle of Nashville. Lee
had not had that type of success. The logic of the argument did not matter;
comparing the symbol of Southern nobility to a traitor to the Old Dominion
was too much to bear.

Sherman also took aim at Wolseley himself. As a personal barb against the
man and his pro-Confederate leanings, Sherman concluded his article by stating that Ireland had much more cause to revolt in 1887 than the South had in
1861. He challenged Wolseley's military experience, calling him the "quasi hero
of the Sudan," who "covered himself with glory by bombarding a seventeenth-
rate town and fortress in Egypt."[26]

In 1883, Sherman retired from the US Army. He was succeeded by Philip
Sheridan as general of the army. He favored a mandatory retirement age so that

his friend and subordinate could have his turn as general of the army. Sherman spent his retirement years attending the theater and dinner parties in New York and, unfortunately for his future reputation, writing for magazines and speaking to reporters and at veterans' meetings.[27]

For a few years, the general outlived his wife of thirty-eight years. Ellen Ewing Sherman died of heart trouble at their home in New York City on November 18, 1888. Unlike most of their married life, Sherman was at her side when she passed away, along with most of their children.[28]

On February 4, 1891, General Sherman attended the theater near his home despite the bad weather. By the next morning he had developed what seemed like a cold. He ignored the warnings of his daughters and went out again the next night. His condition grew worse. On February 8, the general's seventy-first birthday, he was unable to get out of bed and sent for his doctor. The condition complicated his streptococcal infection and his chronic asthma. His doctor brought in a specialist and called the family.[29]

Word spread quickly that Sherman was fighting his last battle. The press and the public crowded the streets outside of Sherman's New York home waiting for any word. The death watch lasted nearly a week. Sherman died on February 14 at approximately 1:50 in the afternoon. His death was the headline in almost every paper in the United States and in Europe. President Benjamin Harrison proclaimed in his message to Congress that "no living American was so loved and venerated as he." Railroad companies offered half-price tickets to St. Louis for Sherman's funeral.[30]

It would have been uncharacteristic of Sherman to have died without being the subject of at least a minor controversy. The Ewings, Sherman's adopted family, were devout Catholics, and once a month a priest would visit the Ewing home to instruct the children. No pressure was put on Sherman to convert to Catholicism because, although Maria Ewing was a staunch Catholic, her husband believed that denomination did not matter, a viewpoint Sherman adopted as his own as an adult. Sherman was, however, baptized into the Catholic Church.[31] Rumors spread through the press that the general had converted to Catholicism on his deathbed. The rumors were fueled by the fact that a priest had been one of the last visitors to his home. When General Sherman's son, Thomas Ewing Sherman, was asked by reporters about his father's faith, he disagreed completely with his uncle John Sherman who had denied the general's conversion to the press. According to Thomas Sherman, a young Jesuit priest in training, Sherman had been baptized into the Catholic Church and had attended services regularly until the war. Thomas Sherman told the press that his father had told him, "if there is any true religion, it is the Catholic religion." He stated that Sherman had received the sacraments of absolution and extreme unction, last rites, and the fact that his father was unconscious at the time "had no bearing."[32]

Newspapers citing Catholic sources argued that, even if Sherman had received last rites, because he had not expressed a desire to become Catholic and had not been baptized into the church that the sacrament was "a mistake." These newspapers made the assumption that Sherman had not expressed a desire to become Catholic or was not already Catholic. In an interview published throughout the country, Sister Mary Anthony of the Sisters of Charity declared that Sherman was a Catholic.[33]

A native of Ireland, Sister Anthony (as she was commonly called) started an orphanage in Cincinnati, Ohio, in 1837. During the war, Sister Anthony and her fellow nuns volunteered as nurses. She earned the reputation as a friend of all soldiers, Union and Confederate, and was sometimes called "the Florence Nightingale of America." Sister Anthony was a close friend of Ellen Sherman. Before Sherman left Ohio for Washington, Mrs. Sherman asked the sister to watch her children because "the colonel was about to be baptized by Archbishop Purcell and that she wanted to devote the whole day to him." General Sherman never mentioned this incident in any of his writings and never identified himself as a Catholic. The old nun's memory was perhaps a little hazy about an event that had happened thirty years earlier. Sherman had probably been either confirmed or received first communion instead of being baptized. It is very likely that whatever sacrament Sherman entered into that day was a way of humoring his very religious wife as he went off to war. Ellen Sherman had the distinction of being the only American woman at that time to be decorated by the pope for her missionary work. It is unlikely she would have allowed her husband to go into war without his soul prepared.[34]

The question of Sherman's religion was one invented by the press. Sherman was baptized into the Catholic faith when he was nine years old and living with the Ewings after his father's death. The Ewings were Catholic and Sherman received a basic Catholic education. His children were raised in the Roman Catholic Church. Had the question been whether Sherman was a Lutheran or a Baptist, it would have been a trivial matter limited to the back pages and church newsletters. Hatred of the Catholic Church was at its peak at the time of his death. Groups such as the American Protective Association called for removal of all Catholics from elected or appointed government positions. Immigrants from Ireland and southern and eastern Europe were almost all Catholic. Catholics were identified with crime and corruption in the cities. The growing public school movement was anti-Catholic in nature.[35]

Sherman's religion was a complicated issue. Those groups who bore ill will toward him who were anti-Catholic supported the story that he had converted to Catholicism. In their view it showed the general in a negative light. His defenders who were anti-Catholics argued vehemently that he had not converted and that any action by a Catholic priest on Sherman's deathbed was not permissible according to the Church's own rules. Then there were those Catholics who wanted to claim Sherman because they believed he was a hero, and his membership, even if only at the very end, would help the image of the Church. There were also Catholics who felt Sherman's conversion would cast a negative light on the Church.

Sherman never took religion seriously. He was Catholic only because it pleased those around him. He was baptized as a young boy because it made his foster mother happy; he allowed his children to be raised Catholic because this was what his wife wanted. When his son decided to become a priest Sherman was upset, but this was more because of his belief that Thomas had abandoned his responsibilities to the family when the general felt he needed his son the most than because of any ill will toward the Catholic Church. Even though he felt betrayed, the general eventually accepted his son's decision.[36] Sherman's illness and death were the major news story of February 1891. It took the demise of the general to knock the most hated of the Sherman family off the front page of the nation's papers, namely, Senator John Sherman. He was pushing for a canal to be dug through Nicaragua and arguing against that populist idée fixe, the free coinage of silver. Papers throughout the South gleefully reported John Sherman's altercation with fellow Republican Senator Henry Teller of Colorado over the silver issue.[37]

Northern newspapers praised General Sherman in the articles reporting his death. He was proclaimed a hero of the war. Poetic headlines such as "death vanquishes the veteran hero and leads the way across the dark river" or about joining "the reunion of the blue and the gray under the shade of the trees" were common. Little was said of his wartime achievements in these obituaries, because his accomplishments were "so thoroughly known by every man, woman and child in this country, that it is unnecessary to make extended mention of them."[38]

Southern newspapers were mixed in their sympathies for Sherman. All were respectful. Some newspapers downplayed his wartime achievements while praising his postwar activities. The *News and Observer* of Raleigh, North Carolina, praised General Sherman's campaign against Joseph Johnston. It argued that had the original Sherman/Johnston treaty been accepted in 1865 it "would have spared the South many evils." Under a headline "Cold in Death," the *Galveston Daily News* reported Sherman's death with only praise for the general. The *Daily Mississippian* called Sherman "a brave soldier and a great commander" and wrote that "the South" "joins in patriotic regret for the death of a distinguished citizen and erring patriot." Overall, Southern newspapers reported relatively little about the death of Sherman.[39]

In a series of articles, the *Daily Inter Ocean* criticized the Southern newspapers. The Chicago-based paper claimed they had not been sympathetic enough in Sherman's obituary. According to the articles, the vast majority were very respectful. The paper singled out the *Columbus Sun* and the *Charleston News and Courier* for their negative articles. The *Daily Inter Ocean* accused these papers of being irrational, considering how lenient Sherman had been during the peace process.[40]

A week after the general's death, the *Galveston Daily News* reported that "happiness over the privilege of a day's rest when a big government official dies is mistaken for sorrow and regret." It argued that the majority of the public was too young to be saddened by deaths of Civil War leaders. On the same page the newspaper printed an article reporting that the island of Cuba was breaking in two and would sink into the ocean before the end of the century.[41]

Some of the harshest criticism in the days following Sherman's demise came from an unlikely source, the *Morning Oregonian*. The Portland paper was upset with Sherman, not for his actions during the war but for daring to criticize General Robert E. Lee. It accused Sherman of being "temperamentally prone to mix truth and exaggeration in his utterances." The paper was greatly bothered by Sherman's comparison of Lee to General George Thomas.[42]

It took nearly four months for General Sherman to be replaced in the pages of the newspapers by local crime, baseball, and politics (especially the issue as to whether John Sherman would retire or run for the Senate again), and not all Union generals were treated as respectfully by the Southern press on their passing. When General Benjamin Butler died in January 1893, for example, the *Daily American* of Nashville, Tennessee, announced Butler's death with the headline "The Beast is Dead." The article stated that he had lived too long and was bound for Hell.[43]

There was a great deal of similarity between the coverage of the deaths of Sherman and General and former President Ulysses S. Grant, who dominated the papers only a few more months than Sherman. Both men had reporters and well-wishers camped outside their New York homes waiting for any news. Their last hours and funerals were described in minute detail.[44] Northern newspaper editorials complained about the few Southern papers that were not sufficiently respectful to the dead generals. While there was controversy over Sherman's religion, for Grant there was equal controversy over his final resting place. As with Sherman, biographies of General Grant flooded the market, but his recently finished memoirs dominated public interest.[45]

After Sherman's death there was a rush to bring to market biographies of the general. Several appeared within months, including one that was claimed to be cowritten by Oliver Otis Howard. The Curtis Company of Cincinnati, Ohio, asked General Howard to review and write an introduction to the biography it was preparing. Howard agreed and wrote an introduction praising the book as entertaining but no replacement for Sherman's own writings. Even though Howard stated in his introduction that he only reviewed the book for accuracy and wrote the short introduction, the Curtis Company advertised the book as being cowritten by Howard and Willis Fletcher Johnson, a company man who also wrote histories of Sitting Bull and the Johnstown flood. Howard, not wanting to mislead the public, issued a statement to the press denying authorship of the book except for his introduction and his wartime reports that were quoted.[46]

The Globe Bible Publishing Company of Philadelphia rushed to print *Life and Deeds of General Sherman*, so that it would appear as soon after the general's death as possible. Its author, Henry Davenport Northrop, was a very prolific writer in the late nineteenth and early twentieth centuries.[47] His works varied from children's books to biographies of famous military men such as Admiral George Dewey, to international topics such as the Boer War and the Armenian genocide, even to a guide to self-education for African Americans. Although very popular in his day, little is known of Northrop today except his writings.

Northrop's *Life and Deeds* was a tribute to Sherman. "Superbly embellished with striking illustrations," the work portrayed Sherman in the best possible light. The more exciting parts of Sherman's memoirs were published along with humorous anecdotes about the deceased general. What is unique about *Life and Deeds* was the hour-by-hour coverage of Sherman's last days and his funeral services. The work included letters from Congress and President Benjamin Harrison among other dignitaries who offered the family their condolences. Northrop described the funeral services in detail. He named all of the veteran groups that marched in the procession and recounted by name the enlisted men who drove the caisson bearing Sherman's body to the cemetery. Members of the Sons of Confederate Veterans might find it fitting that these men were not only veterans of the massacre of Wounded Knee Creek but also worked the Hotchkiss gun, which caused the most casualties among the Sioux. It is tradition in a military funeral that a saddled horse, with no rider and with boots turned backward in the stirrups, follow a military officer ranked colonel or higher. Although Northrop did not identify the horse by name, he did record what cavalry troop the horse belonged to—Troop D, Seventh Cavalry from Fort Riley, Kansas.[48]

Northrop portrayed Sherman as the ultimate American hero. Being at the peak of the Gilded Age, he presented Sherman as a Horatio Alger–type hero who had risen from "poverty and obscurity . . . to the highest pinnacle of fame." In 1891 this would have increased Sherman's popularity with the general public. It was, however, far from an accurate description of an officer who first saw combat in a uniform tailored by Brooks Brothers.[49]

Biographies of Sherman published right after his death differed very little from popular accounts of the general published at the end of the Civil War. Writers such as Northrop and Reverend Faunt Le Roy Senour, in his 1865, *Major General William T. Sherman, and his Campaigns*, had only one intention, to glorify General Sherman.[50] By the time of his death, however, General William Tecumseh Sherman was becoming a very controversial figure. While he had mostly been forgiven by Union generals for his memoirs and by Republicans for his postwar political leanings, he had spent the last years of his life angering Southerners who were in the beginning stages of constructing the Lost Cause mythology. As the generation that had fought in the Civil War died off at the turn of the end of the nineteenth century, their children would seize upon these controversies and turn Sherman into something he had never been.

CHAPTER 6

Sherman versus the Lost Cause

The death of General William Tecumseh Sherman on Saint Valentine's Day 1891 was the news story of the year. The great Prussian general Helmuth von Moltke died the same year, but this was a much bigger story in Europe than in the United States. John Holland built the first practical submarine that same year, but its significance would not be realized until the next century. The world was changing, but the scars of the Civil War were fresh in many minds, and those too young to remember the horrors of war were raised on the romantic stories of fathers and older relatives. Sherman's generation—the officers of the old army—were vanishing. The closeness of these men before, during, and after the war has been written about extensively. Among soldiers of opposing sides of any war there is a closeness that those who have not been in combat can never understand. There was a sense of brotherhood that existed among the war's survivors that led to many reunions in the late nineteenth century.[1] As their numbers dwindled, however, this spirit vanished with them, and the image of William T. Sherman perhaps suffered the most.

After Sherman's death, his reputation as a great general was fixed in the minds of Northerners. A grateful public would build statues and write worshipful biographies of the general. However, in the decades that followed Sherman's death, Southerners would rewrite the history of the Civil War. Sherman would become the major target of Southern historians' new version of the American Civil War. His March to the Sea and the events surrounding the Union occupation of Columbia, South Carolina, would give them plenty of material to use in portraying Sherman and the Union army as monsters.

General Sherman dominated the newspapers for months after his death. There were gossipy stories about the state of the family's finances and about the general's religion, humorous stories about his dealing with Southerners, and tributes to the "old hero."[2] It was not until midsummer of 1891 that General Sherman began to fall from the pages of the nation's newspapers. As it was before the war, stories about Senator John Sherman, his battles with political newcomer William McKinley and his stance on the monetary policies of the day, became the major stories in the newspapers.[3]

Although Southern newspapers had remained quiet during his final illness, death, and their aftermath, the general gushing over Sherman and his genius became too much for some Southern journalists. When former president and Union veteran Rutherford B. Hayes claimed that Sherman was superior to their beloved Robert E. Lee, the silence had to be broken. While counterfactual history about the Civil War had become a pastime by 1891 (and has remained so ever since), when Hayes suggested that had Sherman been in Lee's strategic position he would have captured Washington, DC, and ended the war, the *News and Observer* of Raleigh, North Carolina, declared not only that Hayes was manifestly wrong but that such speculation was useless. The *News and Observer* included a not-so-veiled insult directed toward Hayes about the contested election of 1876.[4] These types of news articles were very minor in their criticism compared to what would be written in the first years of the twentieth century.

In the early months after the general's death, the public, at least in the North, had completely forgotten about the rumors of treachery that emerged at the end of the Civil War. Many citizens showed their support for Sherman with their pocketbooks. Two separate subscriptions were raised in the general's memory. The first was designed to raise money to build a statue, the second was intended to raise money to support Sherman's family.[5]

A group of prominent New York businessmen met within a month of the general's death to begin work on a monument. They personally contributed six thousand dollars toward the project, which they predicted would cost nearly thirty-five thousand. Among the contributors were Jacob H. Schiff, a prominent banker and philanthropist; Cornelius Bliss, the dry goods magnate and prominent member of the Republican Party; and Abram Stevens Hewitt, industrialist and former chairman of the Democratic Party. A ten-man committee was chosen to manage the project. It was made up of the most respected men of New York. Among its members were Samuel D. Babcock, the president of the New York City Chamber of Commerce; Chauncey M. Depew, the president of the New York Central Railroad; and Charles S. Smith, one of the city's most prominent bankers. One of its members, William Dodge, was the president of Phelp's, Dodge and Company, one of the world's largest mining corporations. Dodge was an outspoken opponent of the US Army's policy toward Native Americans, a policy authored by Sherman. Dodge was also heavily invested in the rebuilding of Georgia's railroad system and profited greatly from the Union army's work in that state during the war.[6]

The only military man on the committee was Horace Porter. In 1891 Porter was a vice president of the Pullman Company, but during the war he had been aide-de-camp to General Grant. Like so many officers, Porter would publish a book about his wartime experiences. Although his *Campaigning With Grant* was mostly about the commanding general, he did discuss Sherman. Porter had acted as a confidential messenger between Sherman and Grant after the capture of Atlanta. Because in 1897 the number of surviving senior officers from the war was steadily falling, Porter wrote with the air of a man who had the final word on all of the military controversies of his day. Porter followed the lead of his chief and dismissed any criticisms of Sherman and any suggestions of tension between the two leaders.[7]

The New York statue of Sherman was intended to be unveiled on the first anniversary of his death and would be given the place of honor at the entrance of Central Park. Any excess money raised would be used to support the Sherman family. This was done at the suggestion of Amos R. Eno, the eighty-one-year-old legend of the New York banking and real estate industry. He promised a thousand dollars toward the statue and more than twice that if the surplus was promised to the family. The Sherman family through its spokesman, the general's son Philemon Tecumseh Sherman, refused to accept any money. General Sherman had left them in a good financial situation regardless of what the newspapers printed.[8]

Within a month, the committee raised nearly twice as much as was needed. Some newspapers, while praising the generosity of the public, lamented the fact that, even though Grant had been dead for over six years, there had not been enough money raised to build him a monument. Southern newspapers such as the *New Orleans Times Picayune* found Grant's fund-raising troubles quite humorous.[9] If asked, General Grant probably would have preferred to see a statue of his most successful subordinate rather than himself.

The committee for the New York statue chose Augustus St. Gaudens as the sculptor. Born in Ireland, raised in the United States, and educated in his craft in Europe, St. Gaudens had produced a famous bust of Sherman, which Sherman had sat for. He was well-known in 1891. Today he is best-known for his statue of Abraham Lincoln in Lincoln Park in Chicago, the Robert Gould Shaw Memorial in Boston, and the statue of the Irish nationalist Charles Parnell in Dublin.[10]

While the St. Gaudens statue to be built in New York was moving ahead with little difficulty another proposal, for a statue of General Sherman in Washington, DC, was not making similar progress. While most Southern congressmen were satisfied or at least resigned to the fact that Sherman would indeed have a statue in Washington, DC, Representative Buck Kilgore of Texas attempted to block any spending on the project. Kilgore claimed his objections were on a purely technical basis, the legislation not being introduced at the proper time. Kilgore praised Sherman for his honor and bravery but still refused to withdraw his objections to the statue. It was not until Representative Tom Watson of Georgia was able to push through a sub-treasury bill, for purely technical reasons, that the fifty thousand dollars was approved for Sherman's Washington statue, the same cost as the statues of John Logan and Winfield Scott Hancock already in Washington, DC.[11]

Two committees were formed. One was made up of leading men from the Society of the Army of the Tennessee, which had led the way in private fund-raising for the second statue, and from the government, which had put forward a considerable sum of money. Former General Grenville Dodge was head of the committee. General of the Army Nelson Miles and Secretary of War Daniel Lamont also served. A second committee was formed of eminent sculptors and architects including Augustus St. Gaudens. Between private donations and government funds, a fund of over ninety thousand dollars was raised for the statue. Even after expenses it would be an impressive payday for the artist. With that and the prominence of the project, over twenty-six designs were submitted. The committee of artists would then choose four designs from which Dodge's committee would choose the winning artist.[12]

Dodge's committee chose a statue designed by Carl Rohl-Smith. He was a favorite of the old soldiers of the Society of the Army of the Tennessee, having been commissioned to build Civil War monuments throughout the North. The problem, however, was that Rohl-Smith's submission was not one of the four chosen by the committee of sculptors. The membership of this committee felt they had been insulted and wronged. They complained to the National Sculpture Society, which sparked a war of words between that society and the Society of the Army of the Tennessee.[13]

The National Sculpture Society and the Fine Arts Federation of New York criticized the winning statue and asked the secretary of war to overturn the decision. The *New Orleans Times Picayune* seemed to delight in reporting that Rohl-Smith took offense at the statement made by those two groups. He was a member in good standing of both. They quickly backtracked and claimed it was only the system they were upset with and not his art, forgetting that earlier they had called his statue "inartistic and ridiculous."[14]

Senator Edward Wolcott, a Republican from Colorado, put forward the motion in the Senate that there should be an investigation and that the building of the statue should be suspended until the inquiry was completed. It was the two senators from Texas who led the opposition to Wolcott's motion and helped to defeat it.[15] The Texans were probably more upset over the snobbery of New York City artists than the possibility that Sherman would not get his statue in the capital.

The Society of the Army of the Tennessee still carried enough political weight at the end of the century that Rohl-Smith kept the contract and began work on the bronze statue that would be located in Lafayette Square in Washington, DC. Unfortunately, the artist did not live long enough to complete it. His widow had to go to the press to find other artists willing to finish her husband's work.[16] Consulting with the secretary of war, Elihu Root, Mrs. Carl Rohl-Smith chose two artists to complete the statue. Both men had originally submitted designs for the statue in 1896. There were still, however, grumblings about the artistic quality of the statue and the *New York Times* hoped that the participation of Secretary Root would ensure the quality of the statue.[17]

Although the New York statue faced much fewer roadblocks than did its Washington, DC, counterpart, it was unveiled only a few months earlier. The New York committee did not have to deal with groups of angry artists, government bureaucracy, politics, or the death of the artist. What they did have was an artist who wanted to produce a great piece of art and was not concerned with the time it took, nearly eleven years from when it was commissioned until it was ready for public viewing, well past the one-year unveiling that had originally been hoped for. The unveiling was quite an impressive spectacle with ten thousand veterans marching through the city and Secretary of War Elihu Root giving the address.[18]

While the Washington, DC, statue was criticized for being of dubious artistic value, there would be no such remarks made about the New York statue by Augustus St. Gaudens. Artist and art historian Kenyon Cox called it "one of the half-dozen masterpieces of its kind in the world." The gilded bronze statue is mounted on a charger led by the Greek goddess of victory; an astute observer might notice the pine branch, symbolic of Georgia, being crushed under the right rear hoof of the animal. At the time of the unveiling, the St. Gaudens's statue had won the Grand Prix at the Paris Expo in 1900, one of the greatest honors an artist could receive.[19]

The difference between the receptions of the New York and Washington, DC, statues by the European and the New York art communities had more to do with General Sherman's horse than anything else. Sherman's mount in New York was a massive muscular beast suitable to a conqueror. It would have been equally at home under an armored European king such as Charlemagne or Richard the Lionhearted. Critics at the time approvingly pointed out the similarities between it and the statue of Emperor Wilhelm I in Berlin. The Washington statue, while grand, was more American. Rohl-Smith had attempted a sculpture that was more realistic, a snapshot of General Sherman in subdued bronze. Nowhere is this more evident than in the horse Rohl-Smith chose for his statue. The animal was a very practical beast, just the sort of animal Sherman or any other Civil War general would have chosen for his mount. While on campaign, a general spent the majority of his day in the saddle. This was especially true for Sherman who liked to keep his armies on the move. A horse with a great deal of stamina and an easygoing nature would be of much more use to the manager of war, and this was the type of horse Rohl-Smith portrayed, an easygoing mount, not the fire-breathing beast of war that St. Gaudens chose for New York. The Washington, DC, statue was a practical Sherman, and no one who knew Sherman or had served in the war ever complained about it.[20]

The Washington, DC, statue was officially unveiled on October 15, 1903. General Sherman's children were all present for the unveiling. Two of his daughters had to travel from Europe; one daughter was married to the US ambassador to France. Present also, of course, was General Dodge and the widow of the artist. Giving the keynote address at the unveiling was President Theodore Roosevelt, the first president of the post–Civil War generation, the same generation as the general's children.[21] Even though Roosevelt was a native New Yorker, he had Southern roots as well. His mother was from an old Georgia family, and he had two uncles who had been officers in the Confederate navy. One had fired the last shot from the CSS *Alabama* before she was sunk off the coast of France.[22]

Roosevelt's speech, while it paid great tribute to the old soldier, tells us a great deal more about the speaker and his strong sense of nationalism than it does his subject. Roosevelt paid homage to Lincoln by alluding to the Gettysburg Address in his speech and lamenting that there was not yet a statue of Lincoln in the city. He praised the character and energy of the men who fought the war, both common themes in Roosevelt's speeches. He also told his listeners that the best tribute that could be paid to Sherman and the heroes of the war was to support the current army and navy. Roosevelt avoided anything controversial in his speech. There were no accusations of cruelty or references to wanton destruction nor was there any mention of the necessity of the war.[23]

The controversy over Sherman's statues kept his name in the newspapers for a while after his death—but after the initial fights, only occasionally. The newspapers being mostly about what was happening at the moment, Senator John Sherman's actions appeared in the papers much more than any references to the deceased general. When a veteran who had served with Sherman died, stories of their joint experiences and an occasional humorous anecdote would appear in the newspapers. General Sherman's children were still newsworthy.

When a daughter married or Father Thomas Sherman, SJ, was assigned to a new parish, the newspapers felt obligated to run the story, perhaps along with a mention of Sherman's war record.[24]

Sherman was generally well thought of in the South up until his death. While Southern newspapers and journals might have enjoyed picking at his legacy or his memoirs, he was held in high regard. In his politics he had remained a Whig even though there was no party to claim that banner. Southerners had not forgotten his defense of their rights in the Reconstruction era. He had been well received when he traveled throughout the South and was seen as a speaker for the New South.[25] This began to change after his death.

The postwar philosophy of the defeated Confederacy, generally referred to as the Lost Cause, evolved in three large stages. The first occurred during the period of Reconstruction. This first era was controlled by the group many historians have termed the diehards. They were led by men like the Virginia newspaper editor Edward Pollard, former general and future governor of Georgia John B. Gordon, and of course, Confederate president Jefferson Davis. The diehards were most concerned with resisting Reconstruction, justifying the war, slavery, and the South's right of secession. These men were not nearly as concerned with rewriting military history as later Southerners would be, but the generals among their ranks were concerned about explaining their defeats. The reputations of most Union generals remained fixed in the half century that followed the war because when Southerners began to rewrite the history of the war, they first concentrated their literary hatchets on one another.[26]

The first target of this postwar revision was Lieutenant General James Longstreet, CSA. He was given the blame for Lee's mistakes and defeats, especially Gettysburg, which the diehards identified as the major turning point of the war. Longstreet was given the honor of being the South's postwar whipping boy because he had committed three great sins. He had become a Republican, he had converted from the Episcopal Church to the Catholic Church, and he had dared to criticize Robert E. Lee.[27] These traitorous sins were worse than anything a Union general could have done.

The Southern press took joy in the discovery that William T. Sherman also held a negative view of Longstreet. While he had nothing against Longstreet personally, Sherman had refused to recommend him for an ambassador's post with the new administration of Benjamin Harrison because he believed no former Confederates should hold high office in the State or War Departments. Sherman was not alone in this view. President Grant's appointment of Longstreet as surveyor of the Port of New Orleans, a lucrative patronage position, rankled many.[28] While Southerners could have taken offense at that slight and being kept out of high office, they so enjoyed any insult aimed at Longstreet they overlooked the insult aimed at all former Confederates.[29] Hatred of their own who, they felt, had betrayed them outweighed any bitterness they felt toward old enemies.

The second phase of the postwar philosophy is commonly called the period of reconciliation. Beginning at the end of Reconstruction, the reconciliation movement was marked by the building of monuments across the country. Soldiers' reunions at battlefield sites and the efforts to preserve battlefields began during this time as well. The national reunion that occurred during this time was on Southern terms.[30] It is no coincidence that the first national battlefield park was Chickamauga, a Confederate victory. During the era of reconciliation, Lost Cause spokesmen such as the former general and Robert E. Lee's nephew Fitzhugh Lee were most concerned with showing the righteousness of the Southern cause. This, of course, was masked in patriotism for the United States. Lee, after praising his former foes on a trip to Brooklyn in 1883, told his audience he now realized that perhaps secession was the wrong way to confront the South's very legitimate "ills we complained of" and that now he would "promote the glory and welfare of our country." He received great applause for these statements, which summed up the reconciliation period very nicely.[31] Attacks on former foes would not have been consistent with the goals of this era of reconciliation. If Fitzhugh Lee, speaking in Brooklyn, or any other former Confederate general speaking in front of large crowds of Union veterans and their descendants had attacked or disparaged wartime Northern leadership, he at the very least would not have been able to get his subtle message across.

In the late 1890s, the third phase of the Lost Cause philosophy would begin. It would be controlled by two major groups and one publication. The United Confederate Veterans (UCV) was formed in New Orleans in 1889 from smaller local veterans groups. The first leader of the UCV was John B. Gordon, then governor of Georgia. The UCV would eventually be replaced by the Sons of Confederate Veterans (SCV) formed originally as an auxiliary to the UCV. The United Daughters of the Confederacy (UDC) was founded in 1894. According to their official history, decided upon during the second annual convention held in Atlanta in 1895, the UDC was founded independently by Caroline Meriwether Goodlett of Tennessee and Anna Mitchell Davenport of Georgia.[32]

The UDC was an active and powerful organization. By the First World War it had more than a hundred thousand members in more than four hundred chapters across the South and the occasional Northern state. The UCV never reached more than eighty-five thousand members. The UDC was responsible for many of the Confederate memorials that dot the South. They offered college scholarships to the descendants of veterans and ran essay contests dealing with Southern history.[33]

In 1893, Sumner Archibald Cunningham founded the monthly magazine *Confederate Veteran*. The Tennessee native was a Confederate veteran. He fought in the battle of Franklin but deserted before the disastrous battle of Nashville. After working in several professions after the war, Cunningham unsuccessfully attempted to publish his own newspaper. He owned three newspapers that failed, including one in New York. In 1884, Cunningham took a position as a reporter for the *Nashville American*. When Jefferson Davis died in New Orleans, Cunningham was put in charge of raising funds for a statue of the former president. A newsletter to keep donors informed of its progress evolved into the *Confederate Veteran*. By the turn of the century, Cunningham's magazine would have more subscribers than any other publication in the South, with more than twelve thousand paying the one-dollar subscription. By 1900, it was the official publication of both the UDC and UCV. He would edit the monthly magazine until his death, at his desk, at the age of seventy in 1913.[34]

In 1893, Cunningham hired a nineteen-year-old college graduate named Edith Drake Pope. Although she was originally hired as a secretary, Pope's responsibilities grew, and she would take over editing duties of the *Confederate Veteran* when Cunningham died. It is very likely that by the last decade or more of his life he was only a figurehead. She would run the paper until its final printing in 1932.[35]

The defense of Confederate honor was central to men like Cunningham who served and the younger generation like Pope whose parents fought the war. They erected monuments in almost every Southern town square and giant monuments to men like Jefferson Davis and Robert E. Lee. How future generations viewed Confederate history was extremely important to them. The education of those born after the war was a priority. In the last decade of the nineteenth century there were still textbooks blaming Wade Hampton for burning Columbia or even presenting a positive image of Sherman. Kate Kleer of Houston, Texas, in a representative letter to the editor of the *Confederate Veteran*, for example, wrote to complain that her children were being taught from a history book that presented a positive image of Sherman and that "the South not only claims the duty to teach her own youth the truth, but she owes a duty to the misinformed children of the North."[36]

Rewriting the Civil War was the stated goal of these organizations. Even the name of the conflict had to be changed. The name "War Between the States" was a creation of the UDC, because the "War of the Rebellion" sounded as if the Southern states did not have the right to secede.[37] Education was very important to Southerners who wanted to defend their way of life and their view of history. This predates the UDC, the SCV, and other defenders of the Lost Cause mythology and even the war. Southerners in the 1850s complained that their children's textbooks were filled with "the poison of anti-slavery dogma." This coincided with the movements to train more Southern teachers and to build universities in the South.[38]

According to Southern writers of the late nineteenth and early twentieth centuries, the war—whatever it was called—was purely the fault of the abolitionist government of the North. Ironically, even though this was a war started by rabid antislavery forces, according to this view, the war had nothing to do with slavery. The South fought only to repel invasion and there would have been no war if the Lincoln government had not invaded the South. Confederate forces fired on Fort Sumter, but there was no war until the North retaliated.[39] Abraham Lincoln, of course, was one of the major victims of this rewriting of history. Not only was he the cause of the war, but in pursuing his unjust war, he "virtually abrogated the Constitution" and "violated every law of humanity."[40]

Ulysses S. Grant was another major target. In the Lost Cause philosophy, Grant was a butcher. This had to be the case, because it was the only explanation for Grant's defeat of Robert E. Lee that did not suggest the Union general might be superior to his Confederate counterpart. Grant won simply by throwing overwhelming numbers at the Confederate army, and had there been anything close to equal numbers, Lee would have defeated Grant.[41] Almost as many pages have been written to explain Grant's defeat of Lee and to compare the skills of these two generals as have been written about the Confederate defeat at Gettysburg. The overall public consensus that Lee was the superior general shows how successful the post–Civil War South has been in rewriting history.

Of course, the biggest victim of Lost Cause mythology was William Tecumseh Sherman. While Grant was portrayed as a poor general with no regard for the lives of his own men, Sherman is portrayed as much worse. An 1899 story sent in by Mary Barnett, whose husband had been a minor official for the state of Georgia, summed up the *Confederate Veteran*'s view of General Sherman the best, stating that his "name was but another for murder, theft, fire and the sword."[42] Sherman was a natural target for the main publication of the Lost Cause. Based out of Nashville, the *Confederate Veteran* magazine mostly ignored the Eastern Theater of the war. It served as a response to the *Southern Historical Society Papers*, which concentrated on the campaigns involving the Army of Northern Virginia.[43] As the premier general of the Western Theater (at least after Grant was brought east), Sherman received more coverage in the *Confederate Veteran* than any other Union general. Leaders such as Phillip Sheridan, whose Shenandoah Valley campaign was more destructive than Sherman's Georgia campaign, were ignored.

The Lost Cause mythology argued that, despite its military loss, the South was culturally superior to the North. Being industrialized and having a much larger population gave the North a serious advantage in war, but these did not make the North better, an argument that would easily find a home in postcolonial thought. Three major themes were put forward to prove this. Man to man, the Confederate soldier was superior to his Union counterpart in both fighting skills and morals, especially with respect for private property. The Southern woman was virtuous and strong. The slaves had been treated better than Northern wage earners and were loyal to their masters.[44]

Sherman was a perfect tool for those writing Lost Cause mythology. The comparison between Sherman's March to the Sea and Robert E. Lee's invasion of Maryland and Pennsylvania was natural when discussing issues of private property. Sherman moved his army across more miles of Confederate territory than any other Union general. In 1903 Thaddeus Oglesby, an Alabama journalist, wrote what he termed "a vindication of the South against the Encyclopedia Britannica." In *Some Truths of History*, Oglesby argued that the destruction of private property was the policy of the US government and that the policy of the Confederate government was the exact opposite, and that Sherman and Lee were the perfect examples of these policies. Mildred Lewis Rutherford was the longtime historian general of the United Daughters of the Confederacy, and in her 1920 book (also titled *Truths of History*) she made the same argument that the policy of the Union army was the destruction of personal property while the policy of the Confederate army was to save it.[45]

John S. Mosby, the famous Confederate raider and outspoken critic of the Lost Cause mythology, ridiculed these arguments. He wrote that Lee's Army of Northern Virginia took what it needed when it invaded the North. As did Sherman, Lee organized special commissaries to seize the necessary supplies. Any orders Lee gave respecting civilian property, according to Mosby, was in order to maintain discipline. He was amazed that Sherman was denounced more for the destruction of material goods than for the Confederate soldiers killed by his army.[46]

What better way to show the strength and virtue of Southern womanhood than in the path of an unchecked invading army? It could be argued that no women suffered more than those women who with husbands and fathers far away found themselves under the control of an enemy force. The *Confederate Veteran* was filled with stories of these brave Southern women. As late as 1932, firsthand accounts of Southern women in the path of Sherman appeared in its pages. Eighty-four-year-old Bettie Thomas Sampson—living in Tampa, Florida, but formerly of Marlboro County, South Carolina—wrote of her wartime experience for her grandchildren. An excerpt was printed in the November 1932 issue. Mrs. Sampson's story, while highly negative in its tone, did not differ from any of the other accounts printed in the *Confederate Veteran* or any of the many women's journals published in the latter half of the twentieth century. She was very scared because of the reports she had read and heard about atrocities committed by Sherman's army. These proved not to be what happened when the hated Yankees reached her home. The first soldiers were professional, and in many cases, including Sampson's, guards were posted at their homes.[47]

Dolly Lunt Burge in her diary, first published in 1918, told a story very similar to Sampson's. Burge was unfortunate enough to have not only Sherman's scroungers pass through but also one of the main columns of the army. Guards were placed to ensure her home was not disturbed. A captain came to the house whom she described as a gentleman and a friend. Before the army arrived, she had heard that Sherman was destroying everything in his path and that her house would be burned down, she would be left to starve, and the soldiers would desecrate the family cemetery in search of valuables. Although some of the outbuildings were destroyed, the house was left standing. Food and livestock were taken, but Burge was left with thirty bushels of wheat, fifteen bushels of corn, a few gallons of syrup, several hogs, sheep, and a few cattle. Her cemetery was also left undisturbed. Burge's experience with the Union army did not live up to the rumors she had heard. She was not happy because her slaves were taken from her, but she did not suffer the utter destruction she was expecting.[48]

In fact, the amount of destruction or theft did not matter. The fact that Union soldiers entered their homes, regardless of the military necessity or the laws of war, was seen as enough of a violation of Southern womanhood. Benjamin Butler earned the nickname "the beast" for simply disrespecting loyal Confederate women in New Orleans. After the main army passed, there was a second wave of men who were a lot more destructive. The women in their path assumed these men were with Sherman's army. Some modern historians have given Sherman some benefit of the doubt and described these men as stragglers from the Union army. The truth is that there is no way to tell exactly who these men were. The Confederate and Georgia governments fled in front of the Union forces. Since Sherman was not occupying territory, he left complete lawlessness in his wake. There were, more than likely, Union stragglers who would commit offenses against Southerners with no means of defense, but Sherman's army would have fewer men prone to straggling than other Civil War armies. The shirkers would probably have headed back North with the wounded, the sick, and the noncombatants when Atlanta was abandoned for what they must have assumed was less dangerous duty in Tennessee. There was also the danger of Confederate cavalry and Georgia militia. A Union soldier would not want to be too far away from the main body of his army. If a Union soldier fell behind Grant's army he was in Union-held territory, but if he fell behind

Sherman's army he was deep within enemy territory. The vast majority of these soldiers described by Sampson and other Southern women were more than likely Southern draft dodgers and deserters. Bands of these men were causing havoc throughout the South, and their havoc would have been much worse in the wake of lawlessness left behind by Sherman's army.[49]

The difference between a Massachusetts soldier and one from South Carolina would have been obvious to a south Georgia women, but it is unlikely she could have told the difference between an east Tennessean and a west Tennessean. Abraham Lincoln and Jefferson Davis were both Kentuckians by birth, a state that had sent many men into both armies. It would only be natural for these women to assume the men stealing from them or worse were with the invading army. It also made a better postwar story to have been victimized by the Union rather than by fellow Southerners.

The slaves, according to these narratives, were carried away against their will by the army. The idea of the loyal slave was a common theme in the *Confederate Veteran*. Sampson's narrative tells of how their house slave only left because he was forced to and that he returned after the war. In letters to the editor readers urged Cunningham to show that slaves were happy with their situation and that many remained loyal in the face of the enemy. The magazine also published the winners from UDC essay contests, in which the loyal slave was a common theme.[50]

Once again Sherman was a natural fit for the point the *Confederate Veteran* was attempting to make. If slaves had remained loyal, what better way to portray this than in the path of Sherman's March to the Sea? Most other places during the war, slaves and civilians were evacuated in the face of advancing armies. Although there were stories in the *Confederate Veteran* of slaves who saved their owners on the battlefield or of slaves who returned after they had been taken away by the Union army, the most common form these stories took was of the slave who protected the mistress of the plantation and her valuables from the "thieving Yankees."[51]

In most of these stories, Yankee looters were looking for either valuables or an important government official. Working together, the flower of Southern womanhood and the loyal negro slave would easily be able to outsmart the soldiers. These stories not only showed the alleged loyalty of the slaves but were also an insult to the invaders, showing that even the slaves were smarter than the Yankees. In one of these stories, Alexander Stephens himself was saved from the Yankees by the quick thinking of his slaves. This story, an obvious fabrication, is also an insult to the vice president of the Confederacy. Stephens did not run from the advancing enemy but waited bravely and calmly in his Georgia home for whatever fate might await him.[52]

Within the pages of the *Confederate Veteran*, even as they portrayed Sherman in the most negative light, were the same humorous stories that appeared in newspapers during the general's lifetime. One such story tells about a speech contest in which a young man became flustered when he discovered that the general was one of the judges. Having forgotten his speech, he told the audience about his experience in the path of General Sherman's army as it marched through Georgia. The speaker, only a small boy at the time, had attempted to prevent his prize pony from being taken by a Union soldier by telling the soldier that he would tell General Sherman on him. The punch line to the story was that the speaker, addressing only Sherman, said, "I am here today to inform you, that that soldier took my horse."[53] Unlike their Northern counterparts, the stories in the *Confederate Veteran*, although humorous, always presented Sherman and his men as destroyers and looters.

To the credit of the *Confederate Veteran*, its editors did allow debate, and there were some positive articles written about Sherman. The blasphemous claim that Confederate cavalry under the command of General Joseph Wheeler was as responsible, if not more so, for the destruction and theft that took place between Atlanta and Savannah even found itself into the pages of the *Confederate Veteran*.[54] John Bell Hood and later Braxton Bragg ordered Wheeler to destroy everything that could be of use in front of Sherman.[55] Wheeler would be strongly defended against these charges by Lost Cause historians. He had to be. If Wheeler's men, along with Confederate conscription agents, had been responsible for many of the things that Sherman's men were blamed for, it would be a serious blow to Lost Cause mythology.

To trace over the map of Georgia, to determine who was responsible for what, would be a nearly impossible task. However, there are letters to the editors of Southern newspapers that predate Sherman's March to the Sea complaining of "Wheeler's Men." According to an article in the *Fayetteville Observer* during the war, General Wheeler was so distressed about the poor reputation his command was receiving that he sent a detachment to the rear of Sherman's army to "apprehend the marauders." According to the report, these men were Confederate deserters and convicts from the state prison at Milledgeville. No mention was made of stragglers from the Union army.[56] Colonel Ben Lane Posey of Hood's Army of Tennessee was a part-time correspondent for the *Mobile Registrar*. Posey after leaving Hood's army wrote an article for his paper claiming:

> The track of an army is an utter desolation. They steal your houses, they
> kill your hogs and cattle, they burn your fences, they rob you of corn, fod-
> der, potatoes, indeed everything, and leave you to starve or abandon your

home a wandering refugee. It is a common remark of people along the line of march, that it matters little whether the Yankee army or ours visits them. The result is the same—they are ruined.[57]

There were also the kinds of debates that one would expect to find in a magazine for veterans, ones dealing with strategic and tactical issues. They resemble the ones found in the "Century War Series" more than those in the bitter writings of Lost Causers. Discussions concerning the position of Confederate and Union troops at certain battles or of who was responsible for which victory, or which defeat, pepper the magazine in its early years.[58]

One question debated often among the readers of the *Confederate Veteran* was why Sherman and his army twice bypassed Augusta, Georgia. It was an important city. It was linked by river and railroad to other parts of the Confederacy and held one of the last munitions plants in the South. One theory suggested that Sherman had been stationed in Augusta before the war and that he had a son buried in the city. If the author of this theory had picked up one of the many biographies of Sherman available at the turn of the century he would have known both of these theories to be untrue. One of the wilder claims was that Abraham Lincoln had a personal friend, a General J. W. Singleton, who was heavily invested in the city and Sherman had been ordered to bypass it.[59] Singleton was a friend of Lincoln. He had served as a brigadier general of volunteers during the 1844 Mormon War in Illinois, but he refused a commission in the Civil War. He was a Peace Democrat who met with Confederate agents in Canada and even traveled into Virginia during the war. There were rumors that with Lincoln's permission he was preparing a scheme to trade with the Confederates and had met with Robert E. Lee and Jefferson Davis.[60] Regardless of whatever conspiracy theories might swirl around Lincoln and his relationship with Singleton, however, there is no record that Sherman was ordered by Lincoln to bypass Augusta. It is also unlikely that, if Sherman had been given specific orders dealing with Augusta, he would not have reprinted them in his memoirs.

In 1888 an Augusta attorney, P. A. Stovell, in order to settle the issue of why Sherman bypassed Augusta, wrote the aging general to ask him why he had not destroyed the town. There was more than intellectual curiosity behind the letter. Augusta sits almost halfway between Atlanta, Savannah, and Columbia, South Carolina, three cities visited by the Union army under Sherman. Civic pride was on the line. Why was Augusta not valued enough to warrant being a target of the Union army? Sherman wrote back a friendly letter to Stovell, which was printed in the *Augusta Chronicle* and later reprinted in the *Confederate Veteran*, explaining the military reasons for bypassing Augusta,

Columbus, and Macon. According to Sherman, by his passing close to these cities but not attacking them, the Confederate army was forced to use men to garrison those cities instead of trying to block his path. He concluded with proof that, at sixty-eight years old, he still had a sense of humor. He wrote that "if the people of Augusta think I slighted them in the winter of 1864–65, let them say so, and with the President's consent I think I can send a detachment of a hundred thousand or so of Sherman's bummers and their descendants who will finish up the job." Edith Pope, however, did not have a sense of humor, and in the editor's note following the reprint of Stovell's and Sherman's letters she all but challenged a man who had been dead for more than twenty years to refight the Georgia campaign now that all the Georgians were not occupied fighting Generals Grant and Thomas. Of course, the most applauded theory printed in the *Confederate Veteran* for Sherman's neglect of Augusta was that Wheeler and his cavalry stopped him.[61]

One issue that was discussed but not debated, nor was it ever allowed to be treated with humor, was the destruction in Columbia, South Carolina. According to the *Confederate Veteran*, the burning of Columbia showed Sherman and his army at their worst. They "wantonly destroyed the beautiful capital of the hated Palmetto state."[62] Evidence of this is given from the letters of Confederate veterans who stated that when their units left Columbia the city was not on fire. If one was not satisfied with the evidence offered within the pages of the magazine, one could mail order a copy of the book *Who Burned Columbia* by J. G. Gibbs. The proceeds from the sale of the book went toward building the Wade Hampton monument on the grounds of the state capital in Columbia. Unfortunately for the reader, the advertisement gave away the ending; it was Sherman. The amount of space given to the question of Columbia showed that there was disagreement over this issue, even if the *Confederate Veteran* only published one side. Sherman and his generals denied they were responsible, both in their memoirs and to the newspapers during a time when they would have been applauded for destroying the city.[63]

Beyond the debates in autobiographies, an Anglo-American commission weighed in. The joint British and American Commission was formed by the Treaty of Washington to adjudicate claims made against each of the two nations by the citizens of the other, with the exception of claims dealing with Confederate privateers. The commission began its hearing in Washington, DC, on September 26, 1871, and ended exactly three years later in Newport, Rhode Island. It was charged with examining 478 claims against both the US and the Confederate States governments totaling more than ninety-five million dollars. The commission examined massive amounts of paperwork and interviewed numerous witnesses, including General Sherman.[64]

The commission collected evidence about the burning of Columbia. British cotton and other property were destroyed. In his memoirs and in his testimony to the commission, Sherman stated that large parts of the city had been burnt before his troops entered it, and the fires of the night of February 17, 1865, were simply the reigniting of the flames his soldiers had put out that afternoon. The questioning of Sherman by the commission, as it was reported by the *New York Times*, tried to portray the events at Columbia as a case where the forward elements of Sherman's army were undisciplined and out of control. This would have allowed Sherman to admit to burning the city without having to take personal responsibility. Sherman, however, refused to accept this and defended his soldiers, especially the Fifteenth Corps, which was the first to enter the city. Sherman made the very good argument that he "would not have been able to do what we did unless we had kept them under good discipline."[65]

Sherman denied responsibility for burning Columbia. He testified to the commission that if there had been a military reason to put Columbia to the torch he would have done so. Not only was there no military reason to destroy the city, it was a great inconvenience. Sherman and all of his general officers set up their individual headquarters within the city limits on the night of February 17.[66] Had Sherman set the city on fire it would have made the most sense to do so as his forces moved out of the city.

Wade Hampton also testified to the commission. His argument was that Columbia had been burned in retribution for secession. The commission, however, found against the Confederate general. They dismissed the claim that the Union army was responsible for the damage in Columbia.[67] Contributors to the *Confederate Veteran* and later Lost Cause historians simply ignored the commission and its findings. It was obvious to them that Sherman and his officers lied in order to disparage the name of General Wade Hampton. The proof they offer for this is one much quoted line from Sherman's *Memoirs*. Sherman wrote that he believed the fire spread from the cotton and the warehouse filled with sacks of grain that the Confederates had set to fire before abandoning the city. These fires had been put out when the Union army entered the city but still smoldered in places. When a strong wind arose, it fanned the embers and the fire spread. Sherman wrote that he did not know whether the original fires were started on Hampton's orders or not, but he "distinctly charged it to General Wade Hampton, and confess, I did so pointedly to shake the faith of his people in him."[68] To a future generation of Southerners, this was an admission that Sherman had purposely destroyed Columbia and then lied about it to damage Hampton's reputation.[69] This was a distortion of Sherman's meaning. Nothing in his statement says that Hampton was not guilty or that Sherman was; he just stressed the point for military and political reasons.

In the end, Ulysses S. Grant perhaps best summed up the issue of Columbia. In his memoirs he wrote that he did not know who set the fires in Columbia, but he did know that the Union troops put them out. He added that, even if the Union army did set Columbia on fire, this in no way compared to the Confederate burning of Chambersburg, Pennsylvania.[70]

In a sense, Sherman benefited from the attacks of the *Confederate Veteran*. He was given complete credit by Lost Causers for the March to the Sea. The old debate between Union veterans over whether the campaign was indeed Sherman's idea was put to rest as the Lost Cause mythology became more accepted by the American public. Grant was presented as the professional soldier who would have been able to march his army through Georgia and the Carolinas with no destruction.[71]

The Lost Cause historians have shaped how this country views its Civil War. Sherman's reputation will be changed completely by champions of this mythology through the writings of organizations such as the Daughters of the Confederacy, Sons of the Confederacy, and in the pages of the *Confederate Veteran*. It is in those pages that the brutal, destructive Sherman emerges.

CHAPTER 7

Embracing the Lost Cause

Sherman benefited from the Lost Cause. As the old cliché goes, no press is bad press. The Lost Cause may have demonized Sherman but they never downplayed his importance. The criticism in the *Confederate Veteran* helped Sherman overcome what might have been the most devastating attack on his legacy, that of his former subordinate John M. Schofield, whose *Forty-Six Years in the Army* was by far more critical of Sherman than any other autobiography written about the war. Published after Sherman's death and after Lost Cause mythology had taken hold, Schofield leveled a charge about the March to the Sea that was worse than any accusation of barbarism that would come from Lost Causers or their descendents. Schofield accused Sherman of inventing the idea of destroying Southern morale in order to hide the fact that he did not play a major role in the final Union victory.[1]

Forty-Six Years in the Army was published six years after General Sherman's death, making it impossible for Sherman and most other senior Civil War generals to reply. It was also written after Schofield had retired. He had served both as commanding general of the army and as secretary of war. Schofield was one of the most important figures in late nineteenth century American military history. He was in command during a time when the US Army had to deal with Native American resistance as well as the growing problem of violent labor unrest.[2] Schofield bridged the gap between the old army and the twentieth-century army that would serve around the world. He attended West Point while Robert E. Lee was superintendent. He served as an advisor to William McKinley during the war with Spain and had John Pershing as a junior officer. As commander of the Department of the Pacific, he led campaigns against Native Americans and identified the importance of Pearl Harbor as a strategic position.[3]

Publishing his book in 1897 after his retirement, Schofield's motivation for writing his memoirs cannot be attributed to politics or promotion. Either he wanted to shape how future generations remembered him, defend the reforms he had made in the army, or as he claimed, write for the benefit of future historians "a truthful history of our times."[4] Although this was a cliché among Civil War memoirs, it is very likely that someone who spent the majority of his military career working to improve the education of officers would write an autobiography for the purpose of improving the understanding of the Civil War. His question and discussion style of writing takes the tone of a professor leading students to his own conclusions.

According to General Schofield, Sherman's purpose in abandoning Atlanta for Savannah could not have been the reasons stated by Sherman in his letters or his *Memoirs*. Hood's army was the main target of the campaign. The original idea was a change of base. By moving his army to the coast, it could be easily supplied by the US Navy, and Sherman would not have to use men to defend the single railroad running from Atlanta to Chattanooga. It was because of this that Confederate newspapers compared the March to the Sea to Napoleon's retreat from Moscow.[5] Because antebellum Americans were familiar with classical history, they compared Sherman to Xenophon, the ancient Greek mercenary who led his defeated army across the modern nation of Georgia (ironically), to reach safety on the shores of the Black Sea.[6]

When Hood abandoned Georgia, moved into northern Alabama, and began moving toward Tennessee, the idea of changing position to fight Hood should have been abandoned, according to Schofield. He also argued that had Sherman meant to show the Confederate people and the governments of Europe that the South could no longer defend itself, he could have done so with just a cavalry raid.[7] This was later proved by General James H. Wilson's raid into Alabama and Georgia. One could easily argue that Wilson's cavalry raid was more successful than Sherman's march. Wilson, with less than half the force of Sherman, captured Montgomery in Alabama and Columbus and Macon in Georgia. Wilson's forces were also responsible for the capture of Jefferson Davis.[8]

Schofield wrote that anyone who knew Sherman also knew that "it is not possible that he could have preferred a manifestation of the power of the nation by destroying Southern property rather than by destroying a Southern army." Schofield's argument was that the purpose of the March to the Sea was exactly what Sherman subsequently did; move north toward Virginia and the army of Robert E. Lee. According to Schofield, the reason that Sherman chose Lee over the much closer and weaker Hood was a much publicized speech given by Jefferson Davis at Palmetto, Georgia. Davis pledged that Sherman would be driven out of Georgia and the rest of the state would be saved. As Hood moved into Alabama toward Tennessee, Schofield argued, Sherman believed following him would prove Davis right.[9]

According to Schofield, it was Sherman's concern for his reputation and place in history that kept him from being more forthcoming about his plans to march north against Lee. If Grant defeated Lee and ended the war before Sherman reached Savannah, the march would look like a fool's errand. If the situation in Georgia changed and Sherman found it necessary to emerge at Pensacola or Mobile instead of Savannah, he would look foolish if he had proclaimed earlier that his intentions were to attack Lee. Sherman, Schofield argued, needed "a sufficient logical reason for the preliminary operation, if that finally had to stand alone."[10]

Of course, Sherman would not reach Virginia in time and would take no part in the campaign against Lee. The March to the Sea would have to stand alone, and so it was claimed that the point of the march was to take the war to the civilians, to destroy the ability of Georgia to supply the Confederate armies. If this had been the sole purpose, it seems unlikely that three major Georgia cities with important factories and river access to the rest of the Confederacy would have been bypassed. There are historians who argue that the morale of the Confederacy was already broken by the time Sherman left Atlanta.[11] Confederate papers would exaggerate the destructiveness of the March to the Sea in order to rally the troops.[12] If Sherman's strategy was to break the morale of the Southern people, the utter destruction of Hood's army would have been more effective, and it would not have been terribly difficult to capture the first capital of the Confederacy in the process. Every statement that Sherman made during and after the war regarding the nature of warfare or bringing war to civilians has to be considered in light of Schofield's accusations that Sherman was simply trying to bolster his reputation, since he did not reach Lee's army in time. Schofield would attack Sherman on other points, also. For example, he claimed Sherman was wrong in his treatment of Joseph Hooker during the Atlanta campaign, but all of these are minor attacks compared to the accusation that, after Atlanta, Sherman did not play a major role in ending the war.

The *New York Times*, when it chose *Forty-Six Years in the Army* as its "book of the week" for the week of December 18, 1897, claimed that Schofield's motivations were not to malign his "brother commanders in the field."[13] Schofield, however, was not as innocent as he and the *New York Times* claimed, for he was attempting to aggrandize his own role during the Civil War. Schofield was a hero of the war. He commanded the Union army at the battle of Franklin, one of the bloodiest battles of the war. He was also second in command at the battle of Nashville.[14]

Schofield asked a legitimate question. How would Sherman have been remembered if Hood had managed his invasion of Tennessee better? If Hood had reached Kentucky, or even Ohio, would anyone remember Sherman's Christmas gift to Lincoln and the nation?[15] Schofield was trying to make the case that the defeat of General Hood and the Army of Tennessee was more important than Sherman's operations in South Georgia and the Carolinas. This was a self-serving argument since Schofield is mostly associated with the operations in Tennessee. Schofield hid his self-aggrandizing argument by praising George Thomas, which had an added benefit, for Schofield had often been criticized for scheming to have Thomas replaced before the battle of Nashville. Most of Thomas's strongest supporters, such as Henry Vann Ness Boynton, were also strongly anti-Sherman.[16] Schofield may have believed that if in his autobiography he was highly critical of Sherman and praised Thomas Schofield's wartime attacks on Thomas might be forgotten and his place in history become more favorable.

Schofield and Sherman agreed on the need for reform in military education and the command structure.[17] As commanding general of the army, Sherman launched a series of reforms. One of these was the modernization of military education. He created the infantry and cavalry command schools in Leavenworth, Kansas, the first post–West Point military education for the army. Sherman wanted to improve the education at West Point as well and appointed Major General Schofield as its commander. Traditionally this had been a position held by a colonel but Sherman felt a high-ranking officer in command in West Point would elevate its importance. He had been inspired by Admiral David Dixon Porter who had taken command of the Naval Academy and greatly improved that institution.[18]

Events during Schofield's tenure at West Point soured the relationship between the two generals, however. In 1876 Johnson C. Whitaker became only the second African American student in West Point history. Whitaker was born into slavery in South Carolina in 1858 and had replaced the first African American cadet. As one might expect, Whitaker did not have a positive experience at the United States Military Academy. On the morning of April 6, 1880, Whitaker did not report to the morning assembly. A guard was sent to his room where Whitaker was found tied to his bed and bleeding from cuts on his ears and face. He reported that he had been assaulted by three cadets. The assault made national headlines, and Schofield quickly launched an investigation to find the culprits.[19]

The outcome of the investigation and subsequent court-martial were more controversial than the event itself. The investigation found that Whitaker, afraid of being dismissed for academic reasons, faked the attack. Not being satisfied with the results, or possibly fearing the public out, ordered a second investigation, which had the same result. A cour held, and Whitaker was dismissed from the academy. The public o in the North, cost Schofield his position. He was replaced by fel and outspoken supporter of African American higher education, Howard.[20] President Chester A. Arthur would eventually overturn the decision of the court-martial on technical grounds, but Whitaker was not allowed to return to West Point. After new public attention was called to the case by a popular made-for-television movie, President Bill Clinton posthumously commissioned Whitaker a second lieutenant in the US Army.[21]

Sherman showed uncharacteristically good political judgment by remaining silent on the subject. He dodged the controversy, but Schofield took it personally that Sherman did not stand up for him.[22] The Whitaker case and the desire to improve his own wartime reputation gave Schofield plenty of motivation to disparage Sherman's reputation after his death. Regardless of what Schofield's motivations may have been, however, some of his arguments were sound. Ironically, the fact that the attacks of the *Confederate Veteran* shielded Sherman from Schofield adds weight to Schofield's argument. The magazine, reflecting Lost Cause mythology, would accuse Sherman of almost everything—except being irrelevant.

In the first five years of its publication, the *Confederate Veteran* referred to the Civil War as the "late war" and the "great war." This changed in 1898 with the declaration of war against Spain. Modern US history textbooks often portray the Spanish American War as the event that brought Americans back together after the Civil War.[23] That is a great oversimplification, although there were both Union and Confederate veterans who fought. Fitzhugh Lee, Robert E. Lee's nephew, and Joseph Wheeler are of course the most famous former Confederates to serve in Cuba, but there were others. Sons of Civil War veterans filled the ranks of the army that invaded Cuba. The feelings of national unity, however, did not exist—at least, not in the South.[24]

Southern newspapers were concerned that General Wheeler would not be treated fairly by the US government and its army or that the Northern press would not give him the credit for single-handedly winning the war.[25] Mostly, however, the message of groups such as the UDC and the SCV was that the Southerners "were the first to rally about the stars and stripes and to carry its silken folds in triumph on every position." While the sons of the South fought bravely for the national interest, Northern schoolchildren were singing divisive songs such as "Marching through Georgia."[26]

This song, "Marching through Georgia," was written by a twenty-three-year-old songwriter called Henry Clay Work from Middleton, Connecticut. The song would make Work a well-known name and would launch a career that included a number of hits. He was the son of an abolitionist, Alanson Work, who served time in prison for being part of the Underground Railroad.[27] The song became wildly popular in the North. It was played by brass bands at every parade or patriotic gathering. The song was attacked by the UDC and the SCV. They claimed it memorialized the destruction and suffering that Georgia was put through. "Marching through Georgia" not only celebrated how the North had fought the Civil War; its popularity as late as the turn of the century was "a covert insinuation that they are disloyal today." At the 1902 reunion of the Sons of the Confederate Veterans, Miss Laura Talbot Galt, an elementary school student from Louisville, was honored for refusing to sing "Marching through Georgia." Miss Galt did not get much press attention outside of the pages of the *Confederate Veteran*, but she played a part in a wider movement to keep the song from becoming a patriotic one.[28]

As with many of the debates that surrounded Sherman, there were other factors involved. "Marching through Georgia" was the only one of the most popular songs about the Civil War to deal with specific issues that could be debated or complained about. More important, it is a song celebrating abolition. Its chorus exclaims "Hurrah, Hurrah we bring the Jubilee." If your argument is that the war was not fought over slavery, there can be nothing more offensive than a song that celebrates the freeing of slaves.

Sherman would have loved it had the UDC and the SCV launched their campaign against "Marching through Georgia" while he was still alive, for he had come to hate that song. It had been played for him from Europe to California. Perhaps he had just heard it too many times or maybe it had come to represent the invasions of privacy and demands upon his time by adoring crowds that had become a major part of his life. Sherman loved reunions of soldiers and was an active leader of the Grand Army of the Republic and the Societies of the Army of the Tennessee, the Ohio and the Cumberland. He commented at the 1890 GAR encampment in Boston, however, that he would never come to another GAR encampment unless the bands pledged never to play "Marching through Georgia" again.[29] This was in fact his last encampment, not because of the general's musical taste but because this was the last one held during his lifetime. It is possible that Sherman enjoyed his postwar trips to the South as much as he did because no one performed "Marching through Georgia" in his honor.

Perhaps no event better shows that the spirit of reconciliation was in the past than Father Thomas Sherman's attempted march through Georgia. One thing that emerged from General Sherman's reforms in military education was the staff ride. It is a simple but effective educational tool where officers are led over historic battlefields in order to study the strategies of the leaders. Most major

Civil War battlefields are still used today for this purpose. In 1906 a group of West Point cadets planned on traveling from Chattanooga to Atlanta to study General Sherman's 1864 campaign. The controversy erupted when President Theodore Roosevelt invited Father Sherman, SJ, to join the trip.[30]

Sherman had not approved of his son's decision to become a priest. General Sherman had a complicated relationship with the Catholic Church. He was descended from a long line of New England Puritans. When he was taken in by the Ewings on the death of his father and was raised as a Catholic, his foster father made sure he was free to choose his own faith. Sherman's wife, Ellen Ewing, was a devout Catholic, but he was really without a religion. Ellen raised their children in the Church, but he was never a practicing Catholic.[31]

The relationship was made worse when his oldest surviving son became a priest. Sherman tried hard to convince his son, Thomas, not to join the Jesuit order. General Sherman was proved right about his son's decision to join the Society of Jesus. Being the son of a legendary warrior and an extremely devout woman, it must have seemed a natural choice to join the Jesuits and become a soldier of Christ. The problem was that what the Jesuits had in mind for Father Sherman was not fighting the spiritual battles of the Church but the quiet, contemplative life of a university professor and parish priest. Father Sherman was not happy as a Jesuit and had many conflicts with the order. He was not as obedient to his general, as the head of the Jesuits is called, as William T. Sherman's soldiers were to him. The Jesuits had to handle Father Sherman gently because of the ever present threat that Father Sherman would make public his disagreements with the order. An anti-Catholic story linked to General Sherman would have been very popular with the press. Because of this, Father Sherman's demands were usually met.[32]

In 1898 Sherman decided to join the war effort as chaplain of a Missouri regiment of volunteers. He attached himself to the personal staff of Ulysses S. Grant II in Puerto Rico. Sherman, however, was not just a chaplain; he was a special observer for the War Department, a position the Jesuits would surely have frowned upon. At the unveiling of the statue of his father in Washington, DC, Father Sherman wore his uniform from the Spanish American War. Perhaps it was his presence in uniform that gave Roosevelt the idea of inviting Sherman on the staff ride through Georgia. By April 1906, Sherman, the West Point cadets, and a detachment of the Twelfth United States Cavalry were traveling through North Georgia.[33]

The reaction to this in Georgia and the rest of the South was hostile, to say the least, and shows the effectiveness of Lost Cause practitioners in destroying General Sherman's reputation. J. M. Weigle, described as a local veteran, told the *New York Herald* that it would not be unfortunate if someone killed Father

Sherman. The mayor of Savannah, James M. Dixon, threatened to have the priest hanged if he came near his city.[34]

At the same time Father Sherman was receiving death threats, Georgia's congressmen complained that their hospitality had been insulted. According to them Father Sherman could have safely traveled through the state without a cavalry escort. Others complained about the cost of what they viewed as a sightseeing tour.[35] Of course, they did not understand that the entire point was for the cadets to make the journey to learn the military lessons the war offered and Sherman was along simply as an afterthought.

It did not take long for President Roosevelt to realize that the offhand suggestion he made at a Washington, DC, reception had the real potential of costing him politically. It is surprising that Roosevelt did not realize beforehand what the reaction would be. He had been in Roswell, Georgia, the year before. He visited his mother's childhood home and gave a speech praising his Confederate ancestors. He should have known that a Sherman was not going to be welcomed. When Senator Augustus Bacon of Georgia formally protested to the War Department, Roosevelt ordered the soldiers to return to Chattanooga.[36] In interviews to the Northern press, Father Sherman explained that he had "no ill feeling toward Southern people" and he just wanted to see "the scene of my father's achievements." Southern newspapers used the opportunity to reiterate what a brutal monster Sherman had been and seemed amazed his son did not realize this. The *Confederate Veteran* suggested that Sherman should be grateful Roosevelt had the good sense to cancel the trip since it saved him "from the mortification and ridicule this folly would surely have subjected him to, the old slaves and their descendants even would have hooted at him."[37] It was truly an amazing sentiment written only two months after the Atlanta race riots, where twenty-five African Americans were killed. The difference between the receptions Father Sherman received on his short-lived trip to Georgia and those received by General Sherman when he traveled through the South after the war is striking. That Sherman was a political ally to the South following the war and was outspoken against so many Reconstruction policies had obviously been completely forgotten by the time his son visited Georgia in 1906.

Most historians who study the emergence of the Lost Cause mythology cite racial issues as the reason that Union soldiers did not resist the rewriting of history.[38] What this overlooks is that the Lost Cause myth fit with some of the arguments Union veterans had been making among themselves. If Lee was the most important man in the Confederacy, obviously the army that defeated him was the most important army in the Union. Of course, they would disagree with particular points (such as the image of Grant as a butcher), but the overall theme of the importance of the Virginia Theater was acceptable to both sides.

Sherman's followers argued that they were important in the ending of the war. If Lost Cause historians exaggerated his record of destruction, they unwittingly inflated his importance. It was difficult to argue that Sherman wreaked widespread destruction throughout the South and that those actions were of little or no consequence.

As World War I approached and the world arguably became a great deal more complicated, Sherman's reputation was at its worst in the South. The children of the Civil War's veterans in the South saw him as a monster. In the North he was seen as one of the trinity who had won the war—Lincoln, Grant, and Sherman. This view had evolved slowly from April 1865 when accusations of disloyalty flew in the North and in the South he was viewed as the Sherman brother who cared about the South. In the twentieth century, the views of North and South would combine to form the modern image of Sherman as a revolutionary in the field of war, for good or evil.

CHAPTER 8

Sherman in Film

he myth of William T. Sherman created by Southern writers in the last decade of the nineteenth century became widely accepted and disseminated during the twentieth century. Hollywood films presented the Lost Cause mythology to worldwide audiences. Professional military men and historians used the myth of Sherman to make arguments about events in the twentieth century. It is now difficult for modern historians to write about Sherman without being affected by these myths.

The United Daughters of the Confederacy would never be as influential again as they were during the last decade of the nineteenth century and the first decade of the twentieth. During that time, a UDC president had met with three sitting presidents in the White House—Roosevelt, Taft, and Wilson—to discuss how the government could aid the UDC. The organization had achieved most of its goals. By the time war broke out in Europe in 1914 the Lost Cause mythology was well entrenched. Woodrow Wilson was the first southerner to occupy the White House since Andrew Johnson and the first to be elected since Zachary Taylor in 1848. Wilson was not just a southerner by birth. His *History of the American People* was steeped in Lost Cause mythology. Pro-Confederate textbooks were common in southern public schools, and monuments to Confederate heroes could be found throughout the South.[1]

William Tecumseh Sherman's place in Lost Cause mythology was secure by the time US troops entered the Great War in 1917. Sherman was a monster whose soldiers, on his orders, burned and pillaged throughout the South. If Davis, Jackson, and Lee were the holy trinity, in this mythology, then Sherman was the devil. The *Confederate Veteran* published editorials that compared Sherman's actions with the atrocities committed by the Imperial German army in Belgium.

One of the more bitter and poetic denunciations of Sherman as being even worse than the Germans was written by Dr. Henry E. Shepard, the former superintendent of public instruction for Baltimore public schools and one of the founding members of the Modern Language Association.[2] Shepard's comparison is more fitting than he realized. German war crimes in Belgium were as much a creation of British propaganda as Sherman's were the creation of Lost Cause mythology.[3]

In the year William T. Sherman died, Thomas Edison patented the moving picture camera. The film industry would take the mythology created by nineteenth-century Southerners and cement it in the mind of the public, North and South. By 1910 there were over ten thousand movie theaters in the United States. By 1924 that number had swollen to more than twenty-two thousand. The US film industry has produced over seven hundred movies about the Civil War, the majority of these during the silent era.[4]

The first Civil War films had decidedly pro-Union story lines. The first Civil War–era film was *Uncle Tom's Cabin* in 1903. The thirteen-minute film adaptation of the famous Harriet Beecher Stowe novel was extremely successful at the box office. That pro-Union movies were making money must have convinced the filmmakers, who were mostly from New York and New Jersey, to continue on that course. They also assumed that southerners would not want to be reminded of their loss and so there would not be a southern market for Civil War films. In this they could not have been more wrong. Not only did southerners want Civil War movies, they wanted the Confederacy to win. In 1909 a Florida reader wrote *Moving Picture World*, the official organ of the Moving Picture Exhibitors Association, and asked, "Why do all the Civil War movies have the Northern army come out ahead?"[5] The purveyors of Lost Cause mythology had been successful; a generation of southerners wanted to know why the movies did not agree with what they had been taught in school.

The leaders of the movie industry at that time were strong believers in giving the customer what they wanted. So, starting in 1909, Civil War movies were predominately pro-Confederate. These films were naturally popular in the South and, surprisingly, they were also well received in the North. The underdog story has always been popular in movies and plays, and most movies had a reconciliation theme. Even D. W. Griffith's famous Lost Cause epic, *The Birth of a Nation*, had former Union soldiers fighting side by side with former Confederates against rampaging African Americans. It ended with the marriage of two mixed Northern/Southern couples.[6] The racist component of these movies may also have led to their success in the North, which was dealing with more race problems of its own. When *The Birth of a Nation* was re-released in 1922, many moviegoers in the North had to make their way through protests organized by the NAACP and carried out by African American veterans of World War I.[7]

Sherman appeared in few Civil War films. He was not alone though. Of the more than seven hundred Civil War movies, there are no biographies of Civil War generals. These types of films would have meant an examination of the causes of the war on a deeper level than the movie studios wanted to produce. Another reason that few generals appear in these movies as main characters is a lack of action. When Confederate soldiers charged Union lines at Gettysburg, Robert E. Lee sat watching on his horse. This is not unique to Civil War movies. Of the many movies about the landing at Normandy, Eisenhower is rarely shown for he was pacing back and forth in a London office as the men splashed ashore. In Civil War movies, Ulysses S. Grant and Robert E. Lee only appeared as stock characters. The Civil War general portrayed most often in the movies was Philip Sheridan. His famous ride to Winchester, Virginia, was tailor-made for the movies and his command of the army during the Indian Wars made him a character in many westerns.[8]

Sherman or an army under his command only appeared in three silent films. Unfortunately, the first two—*Hearts and Flags*, released in 1912, and *When Sherman Marched to the Sea*, released the following year—no longer exist.[9] The third film was D. W. Griffith's groundbreaking *The Birth of a Nation*, released in 1915. This was the first movie to make more than a million dollars. The three-hour film encompassed every aspect of the Lost Cause myth, but especially the notion that the war was an insidious plot by Northern abolitionists whose end goal was the equalization of the races, including biracial marriages. The mastermind of the plot was Senator Stoneman of Pennsylvania, an obvious caricature of Thaddeus Stevens, and his biracial mistress. Hostilities began only when Lincoln called for seventy-five thousand volunteers, but had Lincoln survived, the horrors of Reconstruction would not have happened. *The Birth of a Nation* only shows Southerners mourning the loss of Lincoln; the abolitionists are portrayed as seeing his death as an opportunity to gain more power. African Americans are shown as either out of control animals or loyal servants willing to live as if slavery had never ended. Southern women are, of course, symbols of virtue and chastity.[10]

Sherman is never shown or mentioned by name in *The Birth of a Nation*, but in two short scenes he is introduced by a title card reading "while the women and children weep, a great conqueror marches to the sea." In the first scene, a woman and her small children hide in the woods as an army marches through the valley beneath them. As the large unstoppable army move through, homes and barns burn in the background. The second scene showed "the torch of war against the breast of Atlanta." This nightmarish scene shows panic-stricken civilians running through the streets trying to escape with what valuables they can carry, chased by soldiers with torches.[11]

That Atlanta was evacuated long before its factories and railroads were destroyed was only one of many facts ignored by Griffith. His mischaracterizations of the Civil War are comparatively harmless compared to his portrayal of the postwar South and African Americans. Any critic writing about *The Birth of a Nation*, a film that portrayed the Ku Klux Klan in a heroic light, had more than enough to write about without discussing the few minutes of film portraying Sherman.

Griffith did not originate anything that was in his movie. All he did was present in a much more dramatic fashion what had already appeared in the pages of the *Confederate Veteran*, the speaker's podiums of countless UDC and Sons of Confederate Veterans meetings from across the South and the many literary works of Southern authors including Thomas Dixon's trilogy upon which *The Birth of a Nation* is based.[12]

Even though Sherman is rarely portrayed in film, the few occurrences are in significant works. The second great epic that does not show Sherman but obviously his campaigns in Georgia was *Gone With the Wind*, released in 1939. Like *The Birth of a Nation*, this was an epic movie that spanned the war years and Reconstruction. Costing over four million dollars, it was the most expensive movie made up to that time. Although many, including its director, believed the film would not be profitable, it made over sixty million dollars and broke most box office records.[13] Based on the best-selling novel of the same name by Margaret Mitchell, it is steeped in Lost Cause mythology. The movie portrayed an idealized South where Southerners were mostly wealthy plantation owners and their slaves were happy and loyal, remaining with their owners even after the war. Even though the attack on Fort Sumter is mentioned, the war was started by Lincoln's call for volunteers, and the North only won because of a preponderance of resources.[14]

Sherman's portrayal in *Gone With the Wind* is little different from in *The Birth of a Nation*. Although he is never actually shown, Sherman is the title character. The movie is introduced by scrolling script telling the viewers of a "land of cavaliers and cotton fields," of "knights and their ladies," that was "gone with the wind."[15] The title card introducing the section of the film in which the Union army invades Georgia reads, "and the wind swept through Georgia," and accompanied by dramatic music the next card states simply, "Sherman." Sherman's goal according the film was "to leave" the South "crippled and forever humbled."[16]

The first representation of Union forces is of random artillery falling into Atlanta. A stained-glass image of Christ is shown destroyed by Yankee cannon fire. *Gone With the Wind* portrays the siege of Atlanta exactly the same as General Hood had done fifty years earlier. In his memoir, Hood accused Sherman of breaking the laws of war by shelling the city.[17] *Gone With the Wind* also portrays this as a break from civilized warfare. What the film and Hood did not mention is that Atlanta was a fortified city and the rules of war have allowed firing on them since cannon fire brought down the first castle wall.

While the movie shows Union soldiers in a negative light, Sherman and his men are portrayed much better than they could have been. In the film, Atlanta is burned to the ground, but it is not Sherman and the Union army who set these fires. According to the film, Atlanta was set on fire by retreating Confederate forces trying to keep munitions from falling into the enemies' hands. Civilians are shown looting stores. Even the Union soldier whom Scarlett O'Hara kills to prevent his raping her was identified as a deserter. Regardless of technicalities, however, the viewer still receives the impression that Georgia was needlessly devastated by Sherman and Northern aggression. This is highlighted best by a scene that shows paroled Confederate soldiers returning home at the end of the war, half-starved and destitute, while a black carpetbagger in a nice suit and carriage rides past singing "Marching through Georgia."[18]

In order to make the movie more marketable in the North, a great deal of the bitterness and racism of the novel is removed. The derogatory term *nigger,* which appears throughout the novel, was left out of the movie. The film is still offensive in its portrayal of African Americans, however. The Ku Klux Klan was left out of the film. Ashley Wilkes and several of the other characters do become vigilantes in the film, but there are no sheets or any mention of the Klan. Even Reconstruction was shown in a positive light in some scenes.[19]

The movie also leaves out the portion of the novel in which Sherman's men visit Tara during their March to the Sea. The Union soldiers are thieves who take anything they can find of value. As was the case in most women's diaries, Scarlett's experience with the "March" was not nearly as bad as the rumors she had heard. She had been told that "Yankees raped women and ran bayonets through children's stomachs." Neither was done at Tara, and Rhett Butler, ever the realist, argued that "the Yankees aren't fiends. They haven't horns and hoofs, as you seem to think. They are pretty much like Southerners—except with worse manners and terrible accents." That the novel would agree with women's wartime diaries is not surprising since Mitchell used them as sources.[20]

Like *The Birth of a Nation, Gone With the Wind* was not original. Its portrayal of the South and Southerners had been crafted over the years by the creators of the Lost Cause mythology. *Gone With the Wind* just took the stories from the *Confederate Veteran* and showed it in beautiful Technicolor to millions of Americans.

The third epic was the 1962 Metro Goldwyn Myer film *How the West Was Won*. Although not as revolutionary as *Birth of a Nation* and *Gone With the Wind*, it was an epic all the same. Inspired by a series in *Life*, the film told the story of three generations of a pioneer family and starred Hollywood's biggest western names from James Stewart to Henry Fonda. The Oscar-winning film used three cameras simultaneously and was shown in the theaters using three projectors and three screens. The legendary John Ford directed the segment on the Civil War. The twenty-minute segment shot on a sound stage centered on Sherman and Grant after the first day of the battle of Shiloh. Sherman, played by screen hero John Wayne, was portrayed as the hero of the day. Not only did he hold the flank that prevented the Union army from being routed and driven into the river but he also convinced Grant (played by the much shorter Harry Morgan of *MASH* and *Dragnet* fame) not to resign. Whether Union forces were surprised at Shiloh was a controversy during the war and the decade that followed. Sherman, Grant, and many of the officers on the front line wrote in their memoirs that they were prepared and waiting when the Confederate attack came. The newspapers reported what has become the generally accepted version of events, and this is the version presented in *How the West Was Won*.[21]

John Wayne's Sherman was very much like many of the other characters that he played. His Sherman was identical to Colonel John Marlowe, the fictional Union cavalry officer from *The Horse Soldiers*. Although he appeared in many Civil War films, the Iowa-born Wayne never donned the Confederate gray. He often portrayed an ex-Confederate, but in films that took place during the war he never took up arms against the United States. Although the scene at Shiloh did not give him the opportunity to commit atrocities against Southern civilians, one can easily imagine the gruff cigar-chewing general laying waste to Georgia if it would help the Union win the war. Although Sherman was portrayed as a hero and the main characters were all Northerners, there was nothing in the film that Southerners could find offensive about the portrayal of the war.[22]

The movie industry has perhaps done more than any other group to cement the Lost Cause version of Sherman in popular culture. The ideas presented were not original, but they certainly reached such a wider audience. Although most of the themes of the great epics are viewed as outdated today, the Lost Cause themes and especially those dealing with General Sherman have been too easily accepted.

CHAPTER 9

Sherman and the Modern Historians

T hat so many of the major stars in *Gone With the Wind* were British is perhaps very telling. Although not intended by the movie's creators, the large number of British actors and actresses in the film reflect an interesting aspect of the creation of the Sherman myth. The modern view of Sherman is as much a product of the view of British professional military men as it of the Southern Lost Causers and Sherman's Northern political enemies.

The first British officer to write extensively about the American Civil War was Garnet Wolseley. The twenty-nine-year-old lieutenant colonel in the British army, stationed in Canada, took a leave of absence and smuggled himself into Virginia after the battle of Antietam. Wolseley then became an unofficial observer with the Confederate army. After the war he wrote about the war's leaders in British and American magazines, newspapers, and professional journals.[1]

When Wolseley joined Lee's Army of Northern Virginia, he had as much battlefield experience as any of the men he interviewed. He had seen action in the Second Burmese War, was decorated during the Crimean War and the Indian Mutiny, and had served during the Second Opium War with China. After his visit he consistently proved that he knew what he was talking about when it came to military affairs. In Britain, Wolseley earned the reputation as a professional soldier who could be depended on in the worst of situations. For his services in the countless colonial conflicts in Victorian Africa, Wolseley was promoted to commander in chief of the British army in 1894 and was given the noble title of Viscount by a grateful Parliament.[2]

Wolseley's writings were decidedly pro-Confederate. This should not be surprising since the British elite tended to favor the Confederate cause. This was due as much to anti-Union sentiment as anything else. The British elite, not knowing much about the South, created an image that was an idealized view of their own past, of noble cavaliers who took up sword to protect home and hearth. They saw the North as the culmination of the changes that had happened in Britain and were continuing to happen, such as democracy and industrialization. The British elite had created their own version of an idealized South of "moonlight and magnolias" long before Margaret Mitchell began her novel.[3] Wolseley saw Robert E. Lee and Stonewall Jackson as the great generals of the war. He blamed Lee's failures on his obedience to President Jefferson Davis and argued that his strategy at Gettysburg could have succeeded had his subordinates been more aggressive in its execution as Grant's officers had been at Chattanooga.[4]

Wolseley had high praise for Sherman. He considered Sherman to be Grant's Stonewall Jackson. When Sherman did not agree with the orders from his superiors, he still carried them out with vigor. According to Wolseley, it was this respect for the chain of command that guaranteed Union victory in the Vicksburg campaign.[5] As a commanding general, Wolseley would have greatly appreciated that trait.

He criticized Sherman for not being more aggressive against Johnston's Army of Tennessee during the Atlanta campaign and for allowing himself to be drawn deeper into Georgia. On the Joseph Johnston versus John Bell Hood debate, Wolseley agreed with Sherman that the Confederacy made a serious mistake in removing Johnston. He wrote that the March to the Sea showed the world that the South could no longer defend itself. This goal was reached by simply marching through; no destruction had to take place. Wolseley wrote nothing with which Sherman's contemporaries, North or South, would have disagreed. Even Wade Hampton agreed with Wolseley's statement that the most important aspect of the March to the Sea was that it put Sherman into position to strike at Lee.[6]

Wolseley's praise of Lee did cause a minor controversy in the North before Sherman's death. Sherman responded to Wolseley's magazine articles in the press. He wrote that "the American people will be fully prepared to select subjects" to glorify "without hint or advice from abroad." Southern newspapers attacked Sherman, as they did anyone who suggested Lee was anything less than a god.[7]

Wolseley was a romantic and, like most military men, a conservative who did not like change. The second industrial revolution was changing the face of war. He perhaps foresaw the coming of the great industrialized wars of the twentieth century and longed for the often mythical days of small professional armies led by noble officers. Wolseley saw Lee and his officers as gentlemen fighting a war against the modern age. Wolseley praised Sherman because he did voluntarily what Lee was forced to do, which was fight with a small army and not the unwieldy behemoths of the industrial age.[8]

The British writer who had the most effect on Sherman's reputation, however, was Basil Henry Liddell Hart, a decorated veteran of World War I. After the war he served in the Army Educational Corps and wrote several training manuals. He retired at the age of thirty-two after suffering two heart attacks, which may have been caused by his exposure to gas attacks during the war. He wrote for several major British newspapers before finding his niche as a writer of military history. His most popular books were biographies of great generals. Hart's strength lay in his knowledge and understanding of military strategy. He chose as subjects the great generals for whom he could explain the reasons they were victorious. His first book, subtitled *Greater than Napoleon* and published in 1926, was a biography of Scipio Africanus, the great Roman general who defeated the Carthaginians in the Second Punic War. The title alone must have helped sales in England. His best seller was his biography of Sherman, titled *Sherman: Soldier, Realist, American.*[9]

Scipio Africanus and Sherman had several things in common. Both led highly successful armies on the winning side in a war in which historians credit a general who lost as the great general. Hannibal and Robert E. Lee are considered great generals but ultimate victory belonged to their opponents. The most important similarity between the two was their use of what Hart called the "indirect method of warfare."[10] Critics of Hart would accuse him of only writing biographies of generals who practiced Hart's theory of warfare.[11] This may be true, but it does not invalidate Hart's arguments. He would have argued that these generals were successful only because they used the proper strategy.

Hart's theory of warfare and strategy was not complicated; it was the "indirect method" of striking the enemy where he least expects it. This, as Hart biographer Alex Danchev explained, was "more an attitude of mind than an arrow on the map." The aim is to strike the enemy in a way "to assure the opponent's unreadiness to meet it."[12]

Military theory is not as complicated as many writers try to make it. Hart suggested that an army strike its enemy where least expected. Sometimes this is because a position is the strongest and is the point that the enemy commander thinks the least likely to be struck. So sometimes the direct path can be the indirect path. The perfect example of this is the battle of Chattanooga. Because of the lay of the land, Lookout Mountain on the extreme right and Missionary Ridge in the center should have been the strongest points of the Confederate line. Sherman's section of the line was the natural line of approach. This was where the attack was expected, hence the rest of the line was weakened so the left could be held and the Union forces pushed through Missionary Ridge. Of course, this is not always successful. Hart argued that Sherman's attack against the fortified position at Kennesaw Mountain was another example of this. Because he had attempted to flank Joseph Johnston and the Confederate army throughout the campaign, an attack against the fortified center would not have been expected.[13] Sherman was repulsed at Kennesaw Mountain, of course, a setback he was obviously able to overcome.

Hart was controversial for his theories, and for other reasons as well. He angered many in the British military establishment by using the title of captain after his retirement, when it is only acceptable for those ranked major and above to keep their titles. This faux pas probably upset more military men than his scathing criticism of the British army in World War I. On the other hand, Hart's criticism of the British leadership during World War II bordered on treason since it was so often quoted in Nazi propaganda; there was even an investigation by British Intelligence to discover whether Hart leaked details of the Normandy invasion to the Germans.[14]

Hart could not afford to be a romantic. His intention was to use the Civil War to make arguments about military strategy, especially in World War I. Praising the defeated side would not have served this purpose. Hart's portrayal of Sherman was extremely positive. The British writer dismissed the charges of insanity leveled at Sherman during his tenure in Kentucky in 1861 as a misunderstanding that the press blew out of proportion. He gave Sherman much of the credit for the victory at Shiloh and claimed that the disorganization and panic reported by the press resulted because the journalists were unwilling to leave the safety of the rear. By using letters Sherman wrote to Grant, Hart showed how Sherman was ashamed of the theft and destruction by the enlisted men and tried to enforce discipline during the Mississippi campaign. It was during that campaign that, according to Hart, Sherman drew a rebuke from Grant for being too generous to the people of Jackson with the army's provisions.[15]

Some contemporaries and later historians criticized Sherman for his role at Chattanooga, but Hart defended him, making the commonsense argument that the Union army won the day and that Sherman's demonstration on Braxton Bragg's flank, regardless of the fact that it was meant to be the main attack, weakened the center enough for George Thomas to take Missionary Ridge. Hart had the highest praise for Sherman and his campaign for Atlanta. Any shortcomings or failures were the fault of his subordinates; it was never the plan. Hart even made the dubious claim that the setback at Kennesaw Mountain was more Grant's fault than Sherman's since his orders were to stay so close that Johnston could not detach forces. This order, according to Hart, kept Sherman from properly instituting the indirect approach.[16]

The only criticism Hart had for Sherman concerned his choice of Oliver Otis Howard, instead of John Logan or Francis Blair, to replace James McPherson. According to Hart, Howard was chosen purely because he was a West Pointer.[17] This argument probably had more to do with bitterness over his own lack of promotion within the British army than with any belief that Blair and Logan were really the more competent generals.

Hart defended Sherman's decision to evacuate the city of Atlanta. To him it was obvious that civilians would not want to remain and suffer the dangers of a second siege of Atlanta. That Hood believed this was cruel or unprecedented "confirms the witness of his place on the West Point graduation list—that his knowledge of the history of war was somewhat shallow!" Sherman's reply to complaints of his forced evacuation of Atlanta that "war is cruelty and you cannot refine it" is one of the most famous quotes of the war. According to Hart, Sherman did refine it. His evacuation received "the grateful acknowledgement of those who suffered it. So far as a deportation could be humane this was, establishing a precedent which later deportations have not maintained."[18]

It is obvious that Hart used Sherman's memoirs as his major source. He parroted Sherman's arguments that to follow Hood into Alabama was impossible—for if he had tried, it would have merely lifted Southern morale and depressed Northern morale. He accepted without question Sherman's claim that the "March to the Sea" was "not war, but rather statesmanship." Hart was very impressed with the army that Sherman marched through Georgia. He called it "the finest army of military workmen the modern world has seen." He was impressed because it was a veteran army, it was highly mobile, not tied to a supply line, and "stripped of all impediments, whether weight of kit or weaklings."[19]

In his biography Hart did do one thing that Sherman in his memoirs never did; he defended Sherman against accusations of cruelty in Georgia. The orders of what could be taken—and how—were strictly limited: soldiers were allowed to drive in livestock or pick fruit and vegetables within sight of the line of march, the cavalry and artillery were free to take horses and mules "discriminating, however, between the rich, who are usually hostile, and the poor or industrious, usually neutral or friendly." Sherman ordered that there should be no destruction of private property where the army passed through unmolested and that this decision lay solely with the corps commanders.[20]

Hart was not so naïve as to believe there was absolutely no theft or destruction in Sherman's line of march, but he argued that any excesses that did occur were not the fault of the general. Sherman and many top officers attempted to enforce these orders, but the large area the army covered made this almost impossible. The only punishment that could successfully deter pillagers was the death penalty. Permission from the president had to be granted to apply the death penalty. Not only was contact with the capital impossible until the campaign was over, but Lincoln's mercy was legendary within the enlisted ranks.[21]

Hart may have understood Sherman better than any other biographer, for the two men had a great deal in common. They were both elitists. Sherman saw the Civil War as "a war against anarchy." He would not have unleashed a mob of pillagers on the countryside. It would have been against what he stood for, control by the social elite, for "he hated any and every act which savoured of illegality."[22]

Sherman also deserved credit for George Thomas's victory in Tennessee, which occurred while Sherman was leading his army to Savannah. According to Hart, the invasion of Tennessee and the battles that ensued were acts of desperation brought on by Sherman's movements deeper into the interior of Georgia. The victory at Nashville "was pre-determined at Atlanta."[23]

In discussing Sherman's northward move through the Carolinas, Hart misread Sherman's memoirs, however. According to Hart, Sherman was relieved to discover his command would not be loaded on transports and sailed to Virginia. Sherman wrote in his memoirs that he hoped he and his command could be brought to Virginia as quickly as possible to take part in the final victory. Sherman throughout his career did not want command. His major concern was to avoid major defeat so that he would charge a high position in the postwar army. He asked Lincoln not to put him in command when he was sent to Kentucky under Robert Anderson. He tried to persuade Grant to remain in the West after he was promoted overall commander of the Union army. Once Sherman and his army were in Virginia, he would once again be subordinated to Grant.[24] That way, Grant would get to make the tough decisions. The defeat of Lee would bring enough glory to everyone and the pressure would be removed from Sherman. Had he succeeded in transferring to Virginia, Sherman would have avoided the entire ugly situation with the surrender of Johnston's army in North Carolina. Throughout his life Sherman's motivation never changed. His goal was to provide for his family; he had built an army career during the war on Grant's coattails and was sorry to see a chance to climb back on pass away.

Hart wrote that the march from Atlanta to Goldsboro, North Carolina, via Savannah was "the greatest march in modern history." Sherman's army covered over four hundred miles, averaging ten miles a day, even though they crossed five large rivers and the swamps of southern South Carolina. He lost no significant number of men to disease or the enemy. He brought pressure on General Lee and put his own army into a position to end the war if events did not go as planned for General Grant.[25]

Captain Hart's arguments contain one rather odd contradiction. On many pages he argued that Sherman was innocent of the charges leveled against him by so many Southern historians and defended Sherman by writing that his greatness was due to his purely military campaigns. Yet he concluded his book by stating that Sherman was a grand strategist for taking the war to the general population of the enemy and destroying its will to support its army.[26]

Not only did Hart's biography of Sherman contradict this but his written philosophy on later occasions showed he himself did not believe it. For example, Hart was close friends with the Oxford-educated archeologist and historian T. E. Lawrence, better known as Lawrence of Arabia, the mysterious hero of World War I, who was also the subject of a Hart biography. When Lawrence disappeared into self-imposed exile in order to avoid the hardships of being a celebrity and a national hero, Hart was one of the few men who knew he was Airman Second Class Shaw of the Royal Air Force stationed in rural India. Hart sent Lawrence one of the first copies of *Sherman*. Although Lawrence was no Civil War scholar (he asked Hart in a letter who Nathan Bedford Forrest was), he was a student of military history and a practitioner of that art. He had high praise for the book and Hart's arguments. He commended Hart for excluding footnotes, for which most scholars bitterly criticized him. His only complaint was that the biography was so well written that book reviewers would miss the military lessons Hart was trying to convey.[27] (This criticism must have had more to do with the intellect of book reviewers than Hart's work because his points were by no means discrete.) Hart and Lawrence exchanged letters on the subject of how to control rebelling natives in Africa and the possibility of using aircraft as a terror weapon. They both agreed that attacks on civilians stirred "up feeling of bitter hate and resentment" that was not conducive to ending rebellion.[28]

With the exception of the last five paragraphs of his biography, Hart did not portray Sherman as revolutionizing military strategy. He argued that Sherman used the same strategy as Scipio Africanus, arguably the greatest general of the ancient world, and any general who adopted this strategy had a much greater chance of success. In 202 BC, Scipio, with a Roman army fighting behind a shield wall, defeated the Carthaginian general Hannibal. In 1991, General Norman Schwarzkopf, with a multinational force and weapons so technically advanced they seemed like science fiction to those watching the war on television, defeated Saddam Hussein and the fourth largest army in the world. Both men used Hart's strategy.[29] Hart's work shows that Sherman did not revolutionize strategy but used accepted principles to win great success.

Hart's indirect method of warfare philosophy, however, had flaws as applied to the world wars. The initial German strategy of World War I, the Schliefan Plan, used the indirect method. They counted on the French not expecting an invasion through Belgium. The plan was within fifteen miles of being successful.

The French almost lost their capital to the Germans in August 1914 because they were so focused on offense, just not the indirect method. If the French had made a handful of better decisions they could have been in the German heartland, and Hart could have claimed that the French had used the indirect method. When the Western Front became stagnant after the first month, there was no longer any possibility of an indirect approach.[30]

Hart offered something for everyone and has successfully confused the issue of Sherman ever since. Captain Hart celebrated Sherman's genius as the inventor of modern warfare. By modern warfare he seemed to have meant that his indirect approach foreshadowed World War II, while Grant's grinding strategy was repeated in World War I. The historians who hold a negative view of the general also argue that he changed warfare and can look to Hart for giving him credit for inventing warfare that targeted the civilian population. The terminology of the indirect approach can easily be misinterpreted to mean attacks on civilians and the economic base as opposed to striking at the weak point of the enemy's line. Once the idea is accepted that Sherman was intentionally targeting civilians, it is easy to believe Sherman was guilty of all the atrocities laid at his door by Lost Causers. These assertions are problematic, to say the least.

Hart's later argument is problematic simply because war weariness had set in long before Sherman ever left Chattanooga. The Georgia legislature met in March 1864 to discuss offering peace terms. The people of the north Georgia Mountains had never been loyal to the Confederacy, and as the war dragged on southern Georgians lost their dedication to the Confederate cause. Taxes and conscription had more to do with this than Sherman. It seems unlikely that the "bummers" would have been allowed to operate alone or in very small groups safely in a region that was not already defeated. This was displayed in South Carolina, a state more loyal to the cause, where many Union soldiers were killed when they wandered too far from the main body of troops. Newspapers from other parts of the Confederacy, especially war-ravaged Virginia, chided Georgians for not resisting Sherman.[31] If one accepts that Sherman struck a blow at the economy of the South from which it could not recover, one must first consider the economy of the Confederacy in November 1864. Ignoring Columbus, Macon, and Augusta, three large industrial centers that were in fact bypassed by Sherman, the major contribution of Georgia to the Confederacy was agricultural. For this argument to stand true, the Confederate army would have had to have been well supplied with provisions up until Sherman reached Savannah. Nothing could be farther from the truth. The scarcity of Confederate resources is legendary, and the causes were diverse. The Confederacy could not feed its federal prisoners at Andersonville and Macon in the heart of Georgia long before Sherman's invasion. When

John C. Breckenridge became the secretary of war in January 1865 and reorganized that department, the flow of supplies to Lee's once starving army overwhelmed the railroad for the first time and the War Department depots had almost three million rations on hand.[32] Thus, Confederate armies in the field were better supplied after Sherman made his March to the Sea than before.

The idea that atrocities hurt the morale of an army or a people is counterintuitive. Historically, the type of behavior Sherman's army is accused of would rally an enemy's troops to fight harder. The Confederate government and its allies in the major newspapers of the South obviously believed this, as they published numerous propaganda stories about Sherman and other callous Union generals in order to motivate Confederate soldiers. Before Sherman had even accepted a position in the Union army, Jefferson Davis predicted that the North would behave that way in order to engender support for the Confederate cause.[33]

Sherman's army destroyed a great deal of railroad during his campaigns, but so did every other general during the war. It was by no means a strategy invented by Sherman, nor was the destruction of railroad necessarily an attack on the enemy's economy. Armies were moved by railroad, reinforcements and supplies brought up and positions evacuated. The Union was defeated at Chickamauga because Longstreet had brought a large force from the east by railroad. Sherman was a veteran of the army that had been defeated at Bull Run because General Johnston had reinforced General Beauregard by train.[34] Attacking a railroad was the equivalent of attacking an enemy's baggage train or of the British navy's attacking empty troop transport ships during the Napoleonic Wars.

Economic warfare also by no means originated with Sherman or the American Civil War. The most obvious example of this is a naval blockade. Both France and Britain blockaded one another during the Napoleonic Wars in order to hurt the economies of their foes and to make it more difficult for the enemy to supply his army.[35]

Hart has affected Sherman's reputation more than any other historian. His theories have been used and misused by historians ever since. Those who want to portray Sherman as a monster can use Hart's ideas of economic warfare as a stepping stone, and those who want to portray Sherman as a great general can misrepresent indirect warfare to show Sherman as the first modern general.[36]

The third British military man turned historian to weigh in on the issues of the American Civil War was Major General John Frederick Charles Fuller. In Civil War scholarship Fuller is best known for his dual biography of Grant and Lee. The Sandhurst-educated officer was decorated during the Boer War and World War I, in which he organized the first tank corps. He was an advocate for that weapon throughout the war and kept the tank from passing into obscurity.

Fuller was retired in 1930 and began his thirty-year career as a historian and a journalist. Like Hart, Fuller is seen as a revolutionary. He is often described as the father of the German Blitzkrieg strategy of World War II. In philosophy he had a great deal in common with Hart and Wolseley, for all of them were conservatives who disliked the modern warfare brought about by the Industrial Revolution. Although Fuller advocated the use of armored warfare coupled with close air support (all very modern concepts), he saw this as a way to bring back the old system when wars were fought by a professional elite.[37] This did not happen. World War II, with tanks and aircraft, was fought on a larger scale than any conflict in history. Ironically the tank that American factories poured into the war, disproving Fuller and Hart's theories that tanks would bring back small armies, was nicknamed "the Sherman" by the British army.

Fuller viewed the Civil War as "a struggle to the death between two societies, each championing a different civilization." He inserted the line by poet Stephen Benet in most of his books dealing with the Civil War, stating that the conflict was "the pastoral rebellion of the earth, against machines, against the age of steam."[38] It was obvious where Fuller's sympathy was. Fuller had no praise for Sherman. Unlike Hart, he did not see Sherman's army as the professional elite. To Fuller, Sherman represented the worst of modern warfare. We cannot know whether Fuller completely accepted the Lost Cause historians' view of Sherman's march through Georgia or simply did so because this view forwarded his argument that the armies of democracy unchecked by the steady hand of monarchy or totalitarianism was a very dangerous thing. He described Sherman's tactics as "a return to barbarism." Fuller took Sherman at his word. He liberally quoted the general, sometimes taking his words out of context and sometimes falling victim to Sherman's attempt to bolster his own reputation and the importance of the March to the Sea.[39]

Fuller invalidated most of his argument when he wrote that Sherman's officers resented the "savagery" of Sherman's "pillaging horde." Of the officers he cited as feeling moral outrage at Sherman were Jefferson C. Davis, Judson Kilpatrick, and William B. Hazen. But this choice of officers is problematic. Davis, for example, fought the war with a charge of manslaughter hanging over his head for killing a fellow officer. He also personally committed the worst act of the campaign, when he ordered the removal of the pontoon bridge over Ebenezer Creek, which left many of the freed slaves following Sherman to the mercy of Joseph Wheeler's Confederate cavalry. Many were so afraid of their treatment at the hands of Wheeler's Georgians that they plunged into the water and drowned before they could be rescued. Those who could not make it across were abandoned to the oncoming Confederate cavalry and an unknown fate. Unlike Fuller, most historians who accept the Lost Cause premise consider

Kilpatrick the worst of Sherman's officers. Had there been barbarism it is unlikely that Kilpatrick or Davis would have complained. Hazen, who does not have the thoroughly negative reputation of Kilpatrick and Davis, wrote his memoirs after the war. In them he supported Sherman and wrote that lawlessness and unnecessary destruction were almost nonexistent.[40]

General Fuller, Captain Hart, and Lord Wolseley were all traditionalists. As army officers they all to varying degrees were part of the British aristocracy. Each lamented the changes society was going through and the effect these changes were having on their profession. As an eyewitness, Wolseley saw the American Civil War as the harbinger of the wars of the twentieth century. He saw the British army of a bygone era in Lee and his Army of Northern Virginia, and while Sherman was no Lee, Sherman at least saw the importance of a smaller more professional army.[41] Hart's argument is almost identical to the arguments Wolseley had made more than sixty years earlier. Sherman voluntarily thinned his forces to make his army more mobile and more like the armies of the preindustrial age.[42]

Fuller's arguments differ from those of Wolseley and Hart. He offered Sherman's March to the Sea as evidence of the destructiveness of modern warfare. What Southern propaganda said about Sherman during the war fit Fuller's view that large, modern, democratic, industrial-age armies would only cause ruin and destruction. He did not argue that this was new or revolutionary but instead that it was a "moral retrogression." Fuller believed in small professional armies and the balance of power that marked Europe before World War I, even arguing that Adolph Hitler should have been left in power in order to balance the Soviet Union.[43]

Wolseley, Fuller, and Hart all saw as their ideal the small professional armies of the pre-industrial era. These English officers formed the background for the argument that Sherman fought the first modern war, even though the heart of their argument was that Sherman's famous march was reminiscent of an older form of warfare. Hart's argument that Sherman used economic warfare and Fuller's that Sherman fought a barbaric war led many Civil War and military historians of the post–World War II era to ask the question as to whether the Civil War was a total war. By this, they meant a war in which all of society, on both sides, was engaged—whether as soldiers, factory workers, or the numerous other ways that citizens could help the war effort—and thus all establishments were legitimate military targets.

The term "total war" was first used in 1921 by Italian general Giulio Douhet. He is considered the first true prophet of air power. Like Hart and Fuller, Douhet's theories were heavily influenced by his country's experience in World War I. Geography made it difficult if not impossible for Italy to wage offensive war. According to his book *Command of the Air*, long-range air power was the only way for Italy to strike at the other European countries. The target of strategic air power had to be the enemy's infrastructure. On his death in 1930, Douhet only had a few disciples, the most important being Billy Mitchell of the US Army Air Corps. Douhet's theories were not studied widely until World War II, when leaders were looking for philosophical explanations for what they were already doing.[44]

In 1948 John B. Walters culled a journal article from his dissertation titled "General Sherman and Total War" in the *Journal of Southern History*. Walters was a Lost Cause historian whose writings differed little from those that appeared in the pages of the *Confederate Veteran*. As the title implied, Walters argued that Sherman engaged in total war and made no distinction between combatants and noncombatants. He quoted a letter Sherman wrote to Salmon P. Chase in which Sherman defined war in terms of total war. In the letter Sherman concluded that "When one nation is at war with another, all the people of the one are the enemies of the other."[45] Walters concluded that Sherman in this letter was advocating brutality against Southern civilians. Even had Sherman been advocating such a policy, he would have written to the secretary of war or the commanding general not the secretary of Treasury. Sherman in that letter was making the commonsense argument that perhaps it was bad policy for the Union to be buying cotton from the Confederacy, an equivalent of the United States' selling gasoline to the Japanese during World War II.

Walters also used Sherman's policy of retaliation while in Memphis as proof that Sherman had adopted the revolutionary policy of total war. In Memphis, Sherman was dealing with guerrilla warfare. In dealing with guerrillas, retaliation was an accepted practice. The term "guerrilla" originated in the nineteenth century when the Spanish resisted Napoleon's invasion and occupation using irregular warfare. Napoleon and his generals used retaliatory methods in order to pacify the countryside.[46]

Walters argued that the retaliation against civilians supporting Confederate guerrillas around Memphis should "be considered as experimentation and rehearsal" for Sherman's actions in Georgia and the Carolinas. To cement this argument, Walters quoted one line from Sherman's memoirs that the South feared his army of Western men.[47] Of course, the reader just has to assume that the South feared this army because it destroyed a few abandoned houses along the Mississippi River, and not because of Shiloh, Vicksburg, or Forts Henry and Donelson.

According to Walters, the army of Confederate General Joseph Johnston and the mountainous terrain of North Georgia forced Sherman to institute discipline in his army, which explained why there was no wholesale destruction in north Georgia. Once the army came within reach of Atlanta this changed, Walters argued. He admitted that the orders Sherman gave his men were "in complete accord with the accepted rules of war," but Sherman's men knew what he really meant, that they should disregard his orders and run rampant across the countryside. These orders, he wrote, were only for the official records and future historians.[48] This argument contradicts much of Walters's early arguments that Sherman's orders and letters proved he was waging total war in Mississippi and Tennessee. Now, as Sherman was on the verge of using total war on a much larger scale, he decided that he should attempt to cover up his actions.

Walters's arguments were little different from what had been published in the *Confederate Veteran* between twenty and forty years earlier. Walters added an academic polish to the arguments that Sherman had destroyed one of the most productive regions of the Confederacy, making it much more difficult to supply Lee's army and showing the world the cause of the Confederacy was lost. For these arguments to be true, the Confederate armies would have had to have been well supplied and at least one foreign nation would have to have been considering intervention in December 1864.

Walters's article is full of errors. He chose his sources selectively. He only used Southern newspapers, for example. Many of these, such as the *Mobile Daily Tribune* and the *Richmond Daily Dispatch*, would have been isolated in 1864 and 1865 and forced to print rumor and propaganda. He used the memoir of one of Sherman's officers describing the destruction of a legitimate military target. A turn-of-the-century-era Southern writer grossly exaggerating the destruction also found its way into Walters's footnotes. This is done in such a way as to give the impression that Sherman's own officers agreed with the most grievous charges made against him.

In one example, Walters used Captain George W. Nichols's book. Nichols was aide-de-camp to Sherman and would have been to the front of one of the columns. Walters quoted him describing a large well-stocked plantation near Covington and saying he did not know what condition it would be found in once the entire column had passed it. Nichols did not know the fate of this plantation, and nor can anyone. He did not give enough information even to identify it. Walters assumed it was the plantation of Dolly Sumner Lunt Burge, and he quoted Mrs. Burge's very popular diary. A guard was posted at her door to keep soldiers from entering her home. The quote Walters used described the Union army carrying off the livestock and food from her barn, dairy, and smokehouse. According to Walters, what bothered Burge the most was that her slaves were driven off by the Union army. If Walters was correct and the plantation Nichols described was indeed Burge's, he did a great disservice to his reader by not discussing everything Nichols had to say about this plantation in Covington. The only reason Nichols even discussed that plantation was to describe the slaves: "a jollier set of negroes I never saw than these were when the blue coats came along." In a conversation Nichols had with one of the slaves he heard that they were told the Northern soldiers would commit atrocities against the slaves when the army passed through.[49]

The timing of Walters's submission to the *Journal of Southern History* could not have been better. His article was a simple rehash of all the Lost Cause arguments that had appeared in the *Journal* since its inception. Had Walters submitted his article earlier, it probably would not have caused much of a stir, but in the same year the article appeared, the United States performed the famous Marshall Island atomic bomb test and the Soviets completed their first nuclear reactor. The most destructive war in history was a very recent memory and the possibility of one even worse seemed a very real possibility. Walters's article about total war and its supposed origins in the Civil War was published when destructive war was a great concern to academics and the general population.

Walters was not the only one who wrote about Sherman in the late 1940s and early 1950s. In 1951 Earl Schenck Miers wrote *The General Who Marched to Hell*. Miers's book was as steeped in the Lost Cause argument as anything Walters wrote and often misquoted many of the same sources.[50] It did not, however, capture the attention of Civil War historians the way Walters did. With *The General Who Marched to Hell* there was no connection to the present. Even though the only real difference was the title, the idea of total war presented at just the right time allowed Walters to rise above his rivals.

In 1973 Walters turned the dissertation he used to write "General Sherman and Total War" into a full-length book titled *Merchant of Terror: General Sherman and Total War*.[51] There is very little difference between his article and his book except length. Walters went into more detail, but his arguments and strategies remained the same. He once again benefited greatly from timing. *Merchant of Terror* was at its heart antiwar. Sherman and his army are portrayed as terrorists, whose atrocities were worse than the Bataan Death March and set the precedent for Lieutenant William Calley's massacre at My Lai.[52]

Walters was once again the beneficiary of good timing. The publishing process began when the protest against the Vietnam War was at its peak. The US Army was portrayed as an evil force by Walters and by those protesting the Vietnam War. The idea of the agrarian underdog fighting for its independence against an industrial power willing to use atrocities to gain victory was the Lost Cause version of the American Civil War. This set the precedent for the portrayal of the American involvement in Vietnam the same way. If the US Army was capable of that type of behavior in 1864, why not also in 1968?[53]

Walters's arguments about the destructiveness of war were nuanced, and he allowed the reader to draw the parallels to the Vietnam War or any other war. This was not sufficient for the poet, novelist, playwright, and independent journalist James Reston, Jr., who feared that someone might not make the proper connections reading Walters's book. *His Sherman's March and Vietnam* was a combination of travel log through middle Georgia, history of the Civil War, and comparisons to the Vietnam War. Although Reston did not bother with endnotes or a bibliography, he borrowed so heavily from Walters, it is obvious that he wrote with an open copy of *Merchant of Terror* in front of him.[54]

Reston's main difficulty was how to portray Sherman as a brutal monster who destroyed Georgia while at the same time making fun of Southerners for believing Sherman was a brutal monster who destroyed Georgia. By touring Sherman's path, Reston did see some of the obvious flaws in the Lost Cause version of events. He noticed the large number of antebellum homes that still stand in areas that Sherman was supposed to have leveled. The myth that emerged around many of these homes was that Sherman had a romance as a young officer with one of the ladies of the house. As Reston pointed out, if this were true in half the cases, Sherman would have been "one of the great ladies' men of all military history."[55]

The argument that Sherman's march was not as hard on Southern mansions as some historians claim has appeared in much more scholarly form. In 1955 D. J. de Laubenfels, a professor of geography at the University of Georgia, used the journals and maps of Sherman's chief topographical engineer to trace Sherman's route through the state. Laubenfels wrote that his task was relatively easy since many of the buildings described by Captain Rziha were still standing in 1955. They were disappearing in the 1950s, and according to the author age and dry rot were the biggest enemies to antebellum homes in middle and south Georgia, not the Union army. According to Laubenfels the greatest damage done to Georgia was from loss of livestock and labor. Working livestock such as horses, mules, and oxen were more important than cows or pigs, but the Confederate army had impressed them long before the arrival of Sherman. Thousands of slaves followed Sherman's army into Savannah. This loss of labor was something from which Georgia would take decades to recover. Of all the land being cultivated before the war, only half was still being worked in 1870.[56] Even though Sherman carried away, as Southerners would say, a large part of Georgia's slave population, he only brought about the end of slave labor a few months earlier. Georgia's neighbor Alabama suffered as greatly from the loss of its labor force and its livestock as did Georgia without a large enemy army marching through.[57]

As one reads the introductory chapters of Reston's work, the impression is given that the obligatory flame on the cover might be misleading. However, when he began discussing Sherman's operations after the fall of Atlanta, his portrayal would have received an approving nod from Margaret Mitchell or Edith Drake Pope, editor of *Confederate Veteran*. Reston's hands were tied; if he continued arguing that much of what Southerners believed about Sherman was false, it would seriously hurt the parallel he was trying to make between the behavior of the US Army in the Civil War and its behavior during the Vietnam War.[58]

The comparison of the American Civil War and the Vietnam War is problematic, to say the least. There are similarities. There are claims of atrocities during both wars, and the scholar has to sift through decades of myths and politics to find the truth. Both wars still provoke a great deal of passion. From a purely military standpoint, the two conflicts could not be more different, however. While historians might debate whether the Civil War was a "total war," there is no comparable debate that the Vietnam War was a limited war. The actions and targets of the US armed forces were dictated by the White House.[59] One can only imagine what the outcome of that conflict would have been if a general with the mentality of a Ulysses S. Grant or William T. Sherman had been given free rein by a president whose only concern was to win.

Walters's obvious but unspoken parallels between Sherman's methods and the Vietnam War and men such as Reston who continued the argument in a more outspoken way built on the theory of economic warfare put forward by Hart. While much of the Lost Cause arguments, especially those dealing with race, have been dismissed by modern historians, those arguments dealing with Sherman have remained. It is the ties to Vietnam and the antiwar movement that have allowed the view of Sherman as a monster to remain in a time where other historical orthodoxy is torn down.

The Lost Cause version of Sherman is further cemented by well-meaning historians who attempt to answer "why" without stopping to question if this version is true in the first place. Canadian Civil War historian Michael Fellman would never consider himself a Lost Cause historian. His recent study of Robert E. Lee would not have received the approval of Douglas Southhall Freeman, the author of a multi-volume highly laudatory biography written in the 1930s. However, Fellman's *Citizen Sherman*, published in 1995, differed very little from the work of the Lost Cause historians or Southern wartime propaganda. Fellman repeated the Lost Cause myths about Sherman, from Sherman's hatred of the South to his cold-blooded destruction of Georgia and the Carolinas. Fellman took Sherman's atrocities for granted. He tried in *Citizen Sherman* to explain why Sherman was a monster without ever questioning if he in fact was, and he attempts to offer a psychological examination of General Sherman. He argues that Sherman had a great deal of rage. Apparently, this came from an unhappy childhood and his early career failures. When Sherman was stationed in South Carolina, he developed a hatred for the Southerners that would influence his action during the war.[60]

There are some serious errors in Fellman's arguments. For example, Sherman in fact enjoyed his time in South Carolina. Fellman uses complaints about military inactivity to say that Sherman was completely unhappy. He also uses selected complaints about some young men in South Carolina to say Sherman hated all Southerners. In truth, the only place Sherman really disliked was Ohio, and he spent his adult life trying to keep from having to return to his home state.[61] Obviously, because Fellman started with a faulty premise, there was bound to be a great number of inaccuracies in his work.

Historians have furthered an inaccurate image of Sherman in order to make their own points about American society or their own times. Usually this image is highly negative, as in Reston's work, but sometimes—more rarely—Sherman has been used to show the United States in a more positive light. Some later historians put a positive spin on the idea of total war in order to celebrate America's role in World War II or any of the more popular wars. They downplay Sherman's brutality only somewhat; the real difference is motivation. While historians such as Fellman give Sherman's motivation as hatred of the South, Victor Davis Hanson, the eminent historian of ancient warfare, made the argument that Sherman laid a path of destruction through the South in order to break the morale of the Southern people. His legacy, according to Hanson, is not that of Vietnam but of World War II, Eisenhower, and Patton.[62] Hanson's argument has many flaws, and it is obvious that his work is influenced very strongly by Hart's. Eisenhower and Patton struck at the German army. This was not the strategy of Sherman in Georgia as portrayed by so many historians. Striking at the German army resembled more the strategy of Grant in Virginia. The strategy of capturing Berlin was similar to the strategy of McClellan and every other Union general and newspaper editor whose sole focus was Richmond.

Hanson made his arguments in the 1999 work *The Soul of Battle*. The well-respected military historian fell into the trap of assuming the validity of the conventional wisdom about Sherman. Hanson examined three military leaders who used an army of volunteers to destroy their slaveholding enemies and then, to their credit, seized no power but simply disbanded their army and sent them home. William T. Sherman, Epaminondas of Thebes, and George S. Patton had a great deal in common.[63] Hanson was by no means attempting to disparage the US Army. He simply fell into the trap of assuming that the orthodox view was accurate. Hanson made the argument that total war can be a positive thing when it is used to defeat slaveholding tyrants. He failed to examine the question as to whether Sherman truly fought a total war.

The image of Sherman as the destructive warrior who changed the face of warfare, an image constructed by the descendants of Confederate veterans, has become cemented in American culture. It has become as difficult for modern historians to separate themselves from this portrayal of Sherman as it is to criticize Robert E. Lee even slightly. In *The Hard Hand of War*, Mark Grimsley examined the treatment of the Southern civilian population by the US Army. His thesis was simply that the goal of the North was the restoration of the Union, not the destruction of the South, and that civilians were treated with some pity. Grimsley showed that Sherman's policy in Georgia was not one of complete destruction. Orders were given to protect private property, especially the property of the working classes. Grimsley even suggested that Southern civilians held a kindlier view toward Northerners after Sherman's army had passed through.[64]

Disregarding the evidence he offers that Sherman made strong efforts to protect civilians and their property and was no more destructive than during other campaigns in the war, Grimsley compares Sherman's March to the Sea to the brutal tactics of the Hundred Years War. He takes Sherman at his word that the March to the Sea was in itself the point of the maneuver and not, as John Schofield argued, that it was the first step toward reaching Lee's Army of Northern Virginia. Grimsley justifies this seeming contradiction by showing that even though Sherman gave orders against unnecessary destruction, he assumed it would happen anyway and was lax in the enforcement of these orders. The proof Grimsley offers is that there were few cases of official justice carried out by the Union army in Georgia. Of course, that could very well be because the cases of destruction that did occur were done by deserters both Union and Confederate, Wheeler's cavalry, or Southern civilians taking advantage of the lack of authority in Sherman's wake. *The Hard Hand of War* does show, however, that Sherman's campaign was not unique in the annals of war nor was it as destructive as postwar Southerners claimed.[65]

In 1991 Charles Royster wrote *The Destructive War*. As the title implies, he argues that the Civil War was a violent episode in American history, a general thesis against which it is very difficult to argue. Royster begins with a balanced treatment of the occupation of Columbia. Using a wide variety of sources from both North and South, Royston shows that what happened at Columbia was the result of a breakdown of discipline on both sides. It was not part of a wider policy of Sherman to break the will of the Confederacy.[66]

It would be unfair to accuse Royster of being a Lost Cause historian. Even if he used sources that exaggerated the destruction, he does not argue it was according to the wishes of Sherman. He also argues against those in the twentieth century who blame Sherman for the mass killings of civilians. Royster argues that Sherman was not a war criminal as some writers have suggested. Wars are destructive and moving an army through an area brings destruction. Royster also parts with Lost Cause mythology by suggesting that the Confederates also fought a destructive war. He uses Stonewall Jackson as an example of Southerners who were using this type of warfare, which would not have been at all acceptable within the pages of the *Confederate Veteran*. Jackson was a protected figure. Mildred Lewis Rutherford, historian general of the UDC, wrote that any portrayal of Jackson as unchivalrous was "discourteous, cruel and revengeful."[67] Where Royster errs is in the suggestion that the Civil War was in any way special in the amount of destruction. Somehow before the Civil War, conflicts involved neat rules and those not in uniforms never suffered.

The most recent book written about Sherman, the almost seven-hundred-page *Southern Storm* by respected Civil War historian Noah Andre Trudeau is an almost hour-by-hour history of the March to the Sea. There was a great deal of destruction, as discussed in the book, but Trudeau concludes that Sherman was not nearly as evil as some have claimed. When John Shelton Reed, a University of North Carolina sociologist, reviewed *Southern Storm* for the *Wall Street Journal*, he must have assumed that Trudeau was simply rewriting Lost Cause mythology. In the review he wrote that Trudeau included how Southerners tricked Sherman into not destroying their homes, a mainstay of Lost Cause mythology concerning Sherman. Reed wrote that Masonic regalia often saved homes, a fact that Trudeau specifically discounts.[68]

The myth of Sherman is one accepted by many scholars at face value. Bruce Chadwick in his wonderfully written *The Reel Civil War* shows how Hollywood rewrote the history of the Civil War. He traces the origins of Lost Cause mythology and reveals how the vast majority of Civil War movies were overly pro-Confederate. Chadwick, however, takes at face value that Sherman was the worst monster of the war. He questions why more movies were not made about Sherman, since "his destruction of every small village in his way and the wholesale burning of Atlanta" most fit with Lost Cause mythology. Chadwick never questions that this behavior might have been the creation of the mythmakers he discusses.[69]

For non–Civil War historians it has become almost impossible to separate the myth from the reality. The myth has been repeated too often, and those writing general histories with only a little room to spare for Sherman simply include the myth with no discussion. James Morris in his survey-level textbook of American military history wrote that Sherman "carried total war to the South" and left a "60-mile-wide swath of destruction and desolation" and that he was revolutionary in the "directing of the destruction of war against civilian populations to destroy their morale and war making capabilities."[70]

In a 2002 philosophical work on war, Bruno Coppieters and Nick Fotion used Sherman to make a point about the conduct of war. Sherman is used as an example of realism in war. By realism, the authors meant an excuse to avoid the rules of civilized warfare. According to these authors, Sherman saw secession as a crime and thus the Northern soldiers could do anything they pleased. Coppieters and Fotion use as their evidence the evacuation and burning of Atlanta and quote the famous "war is cruelty" letter Sherman wrote to General Hood. They make their point successfully about justification before and during war, but these authors also are the victims of the Lost Cause mentality that dominates Civil War history. They imply, as so many do, that Sherman meant the destruction of Atlanta and the March to the Sea when he said "war is cruelty."[71]

The cruel act Sherman was referring to was the evacuation of the citizens with all their movable property—and even their slaves—if they would go voluntarily. Efforts were made to ensure the transfer of civilians to Confederate lines, and this was carried out with as little hardship as possible. In one of the few times Sherman would defend himself against this type of charge, he wrote to Hood that if the Union forces were such beasts, the civilians should be happy to be forced into the Confederate lines.[72]

One can almost forgive scholars for accepting the myth. It has become pervasive in popular culture—and among too many scholars. The myth has been evolving since before Sherman even began the March to the Sea. It is the creation of wartime propaganda, of generals (including Sherman) who were trying to bolster their reputations, of the tumultuous world of Gilded Age politics, of Southerners trying to explain and justify their loss, and of modern historians who shape the facts to fit their theories regarding the Civil War and other conflicts. In 1887 Field Marshall Viscount Wolseley wrote that, one day, "all the angry feelings roused by Secession" will be "buried with those which existed when the Declaration of Independence was written." One day, Americans will be able to "review the history of their last great rebellion with calm impartiality"[73] We are not there yet.

NOTES

INTRODUCTION

1. Cameron McWhirter, "Sherman Still Burns Atlanta: Despised Yankee General Wasn't as Evil as History Has Painted Him," *Atlanta Journal Constitution*, May 9, 2004.

CHAPTER 1

1. Ulysses S. Grant, *The Personal Memoirs of Ulysses S. Grant*, 1:149.

2. "Meeting of the Rebel Congress: Special Message of Jefferson Davis," *New York Herald*, July 22, 1861.

3. Lloyd Lewis, *Sherman: Fighting Prophet*, 22.

4. Ibid., 31–33.

5. William T. Sherman, *Memoirs of General William T. Sherman*, 2d ed., 14.

6. Freeman Cleaves, *The Rock of Chickamauga: The Life of General George H. Thomas*, 14.

7. There are some historians who credit Hebert with taking part in the murder of African American troops at the battle of Milliken's Bend. Other sources claim he had no combat experience in the war. The *Official Records of the Rebellion* do not clarify this minor controversy. Hebert is not mentioned in the Confederate reports dealing with the battle itself, but General Robert Taylor does mention him in reports immediately before and after the battle. That it is difficult to determine exactly where and what Hebert was doing on June 7, 1863, shows that he was not an important figure in the Civil War. *Tenth Annual Reunion of the Association of the Graduates of the United States Military Academy at West Point, New York, June 12, 1879*, 17.

8. Lee Kennett, *Sherman: A Soldier's Life*, 25–26, 38–39, 58, 61.

9. John F. Marszalek, *Sherman: A Soldier's Passion for Order*, 91–92.

10. Ibid., 105–6.

11. "Necessity of the Vigilance Committee," *Daily Evening Bulletin*, May 27, 1856; Kennett, *Sherman*, 70.

12. "We Are Informed on Good Authority," *Daily Evening Bulletin*, June 5, 1856; "Queries for General W. T. Sherman, the Avowed Advocate of the 'Law and Order' Party," *Daily Evening Bulletin*, June 3, 1856.

13. Marszalek, *Sherman*, 107–9; Kennett, *Sherman*, 70.

14. "Great Excitement in San Francisco," *Frank Leslie's Illustrated Newspaper*, June 28, 1856;

"Arrival of the Grenada: Casey and Cora Hung—Suicide of Yankee Robinson," *The Nebraskian*, July 16, 1856; "Details of California News: Funeral of King: Executions of Cora and Casey," *Daily Cleveland Herald*, July 1, 1856.

15. "John Sherman Is Probably the Youngest Representative from the State of Ohio," *Daily Cleveland Herald*, March 29, 1856.

16. Lewis, *Sherman*, 114.

17. "Messrs. Howard and Sherman of the Congressional Investigating Committee Arrived from Kansas Today," *Daily Cleveland Herald*, June 14, 1856.

18. "Affairs of Kansas: The Investigation," *New York Herald*, June 22, 1856; "Sherman and Wright," *Daily Cleveland Herald*, February 28, 1857; "Collision between Wright and Sherman," *Ripley Bee*, March 7, 1857.

19. Sherman, *Memoirs*, 148.

20. James D. Bilotta. "Helper, Hinton Rowen," in *Encyclopedia of Antislavery and Abolition*, ed. Peter Hinks and John McKivigin, 324; John McCardell, *The Idea of a Southern Nation: Southern Nationalists and Southern Nationalism, 1830–1860*, 84.

21. "John Sherman Bears the Seward Banner," *Daily Mississippian*, January 20, 1860.

22. "The Committees of the House," *New York Herald*, February 11, 1860.

23. Rachel Sherman Thorndike, ed., *The Sherman Letters: Correspondence between General Sherman and Senator Sherman from 1837 to 1891*, 76–77.

24. Marszalek, *Sherman*, 132; Kennett, *Sherman*, 86.

25. Sherman, *Memoirs*, 167–68.

26. Ibid., 171–83.

27. Ibid., 161; M. A. DeWolfe Howe, ed., *Home Letters of General Sherman*, 187–88.

28. Sherman, *Memoirs*, 154, 161.

29. Ibid., 184–85.

30. In fact, Sherman had no official rank as he had resigned from the army; the rank of colonel had been given to him by the state of Louisiana.

31. Sherman, *Memoirs*, 186; David Herbert Donald, *Lincoln*, 285.

32. Sherman, *Memoirs*, 188–89.

33. Ibid., 194–95.

34. "Battle of Bull Run Official Report of Col. Sherman, Brigade Commander W. T. Sherman, Colonel Commanding Brigade," *Daily National Intelligencer*, August 20, 1861.

35. Sherman, *Memoirs*, 210.

36. Kennett, *Sherman*, 11; Walter R. Borneman, *1812: The War That Forged a Nation*, 254.

37. Marszalek, *Sherman*, 154–55.

38. James McPherson, *Battle Cry of Freedom: The Civil War Era*, 297.

39. Bruce Catton, *This Hallowed Ground: The Story of the Union Side of the Civil War*, 41, 44.

40. Robert Anderson, General Orders no. 6, *The War of the Rebellion: A Compilation of the Official Records of the Union and Confederate Armies*, ed. Robert N. Scott (hereafter cited as *OR*), series 1, vol. 4, 296.

41. "General Sherman in Kentucky," *New York Herald*, October 13, 1861.

42. Marszalek, *Sherman*, 161–63; Kennett, *Sherman*, 138.

43. Sherman, *Memoirs*, 214.

44. Thorndike, *The Sherman Letters*, 136–37.

45. B. H. Liddell Hart, *Sherman: Soldier, Realist, American*, 118.

46. David S. Heidler and Jeanne T. Heidler, "Thomas West Sherman," in *Encyclopedia of the American Civil War: A Political, Social, and Military History*, 1763–64.

47. "The Naval Expedition," *North American and United States Gazette*, October 30, 1861; "Important from the Southern Coast: The Naval Expedition Moving Southward—Operations of General Sherman's Army at Port Royal," *New York Herald*, November 17, 1861.

48. Heidler and Heidler, "Thomas West Sherman," in *Encyclopedia of the American Civil War*, 1764.

49. "Gen. Sherman's Proclamation," *Daily Cleveland Herald*, November 14, 1861.

50. "Gen. Sherman's Proclamation," *New York Herald*, November 18, 1861; "Gen. Sherman's Affectionate Proclamation to the 'Rebels' of South Carolina: To the People of South Carolina," *Daily Morning News*, November 22, 1861. "In all the Appointments for Military Governors Made by Lincoln and Seward," *Charleston Courier*, June 26, 1862.

51. Herman Hattaway and Archer Jones, *How the North Won: A Military History of the Civil War*, 82; McPherson, *Battle Cry of Freedom*, 370–71.

52. Larry J. Daniel, *Shiloh: The Battle that Changed the Civil War*, 304.

53. "A Dispatch Received from Gen. Halleck," *Daily Cleveland Herald*, April 30, 1862; "General W. T. Sherman," *Boston Daily Advertiser*, May 1, 1862.

54. "Farragut and Sherman," *Daily Evening Bulletin*, May 8, 1862.

55. "Letter from Senator Sherman," *Newark Advocate*, May 9, 1862.

56. Thorndike, *The Sherman Letters*, 140.

57. Marszalek, *Sherman*, 194, 195.

58. "From Cairo and Below," *Milwaukee Daily Sentinel*, September 30, 1862.

59. John Bennett Walters, *Merchant of Terror: General Sherman and Total War*, 23.

60. "An Outrage Threatened," *Daily Morning News*, October 9, 1862.

61. Emmerich de Vattel, *The Law of Nations, or, Principles of the Law of Nature, Applied to the Conduct and Affairs of Nations and Sovereigns*, 92, 125–28, 351.

62. "Gen. Sherman's Mode of Enforcing the Fugitive Slave Law," *Daily Cleveland Herald*, August 6, 1862.

63. Allen C. Guelzo, *Lincoln's Emancipation Proclamation: The End of Slavery in America*, 70–73.

64. Ibid.

65. "Gen. Sherman Has Issued an Order that all Negroes Who Apply for Work Shall Be Employed as Laborers on Fort Pickering," *Milwaukee Daily Sentinel*, August 14, 1862.

66. "Gen. Sherman's Speech at Memphis," *The Liberator*, September 26, 1862.

67. "General Sherman Has Suppressed the Memphis Union Appeal," *Newark Advocate*, September 19, 1862.

68. Marszalek, *Sherman*, 198; Kennett, *Sherman*, 173.

69. "General Sherman's Expedition," *Daily National Intelligencer*, December 25, 1862.

70. "Sketch of General W. T. Sherman," *New York Herald*, January 5, 1863; "Maj.-Gen. William T. Sherman," *Frank Leslie's Illustrated Newspaper*, June 13, 1863.

71. "Death of General Sherman," *North American and United States Gazette*, June 11, 1863.

72. "Letter from General Sherman," *Lowell Daily Citizen and News*, June 19, 1863.

73. "Seven Months' Work of Gen. W. T. Sherman's Corps," *Daily Evening Bulletin*, September 8, 1863; "The Mississippi Campaign: Sherman's Operations before Jackson," *New York Herald*, July 28, 1863; "From Corinth, Miss.—Great Movements Bravery of Gen. Sherman," *Milwaukee Daily Sentinel*, October 23, 1863.

74. Marszalek, *Sherman*, 234.

75. Ibid., 238; Joseph T. Durkin S.J., *General Sherman's Son*, 7.

76. "Brig-General Sherman's Son, a Promising Lad of Nine Years, Died at Memphis on the 3d

Inst.," *Boston Daily Advertiser*, October 16, 1863.

77. "A Touching Episode of the War," *Cleveland Daily Herald*, October 16, 1863.

78. Hattaway and Jones, *How the North Won*, 458; "Gen. Sherman Succeeds Grant," *Wisconsin State Register*, October 31, 1863.

79. Cleaves, *Rock of Chickamauga*, 183.

80. Donald, *Lincoln*, 468.

81. "Glorious News from Chattanooga," *Lowell Daily Citizen and News*, November 27, 1863.

82. Ibid.; Hattaway and Jones, *How the North Won*, 461.

83. "General Sherman's Hasty March to Chattanooga," *Wisconsin State Register*, December 5, 1863.

CHAPTER 2

1. "City of Atlanta," *Daily Richmond Enquirer*, November 18, 1863; "Atlanta, Ga.," *Daily Evening Bulletin*, December 2, 1863.

2. "Sherman's Campaign—Another View of the Situation," *Milwaukee Daily Sentinel*, March 2, 1864.

3. W. J. Tenney, *The Military and Naval History of the Rebellion in the United States*, 503, 504; Hattaway and Jones, *How the North Won*, 507.

4. Buck T. Foster, *Sherman's Mississippi Campaign*, 22, 27, 32; Sherman to Halleck, January 12, 1864, *OR*, series 1, vol. 32, part 2, 74.

5. Hattaway and Jones, *How the North Won*, 520.

6. Tenney, *Military and Naval History*, 503, 504.

7. Sherman, report February 27, 1864, *OR*, series 1, vol. 32, part 1, 175–79.

8. Bruce Catton, *Terrible Swift Sword*, vol. 2 of *The Centennial History of the Civil War*, 131; Hattaway and Jones, *How the North Won*, 12.

9. "General Sherman's Progress," *North American and United States Gazette*, February 15, 1864; "General Sherman's Advance," *Lowell Daily Citizen and News*, February 25, 1864; "A Rebel Dispatch of the 14th Reports General Polk at Meridian, and Much Censured for Not Attacking Sherman," *Daily Times*, February 23, 1864.

10. "Sherman's Track," *Fayetteville Observer*, April 11, 1864.

11. "The Career of Sherman," *Daily Richmond Examiner*, March 22, 1864.

12. "Gen. Sherman's Destruction of Railroads, Etc.," *Daily Cleveland Herald*, March 17, 1864; "The Mississippi Papers Endeavor to Make Light of the Damage Done by Sherman to the Railroads in that State," *Milwaukee Daily Sentinel*, March 16, 1864.

13. Thorndike, *The Sherman Letters*, 227–28.

14. Kennett, *Sherman*, 239.

15. "Importance of Gen. Sherman's Operations in Georgia," *Daily Evening Bulletin*, June 25, 1864.

16. "Resume of Gen. Sherman's Campaign: The Battles near Resaca, Ga.," *Milwaukee Daily Sentinel*, May 23, 1864; "Sherman and Johnston," *North American and United States Gazette*, May 25, 1864.

17. See, for example, "From Sherman's Army: The Battle of Kennesaw Mountain," *Milwaukee Daily Sentinel*, July 2, 1864.

18. "To those who are familiar with Gen. Johnston's mode of fighting, and with the condition and morale of the Army of Tennessee, the quiet withdrawal of our army to the South side of the

Oostanaula wears an ugly aspect for Sherman," *Daily South Carolinian*, May 21, 1864.

19. "It is supposed that General Sherman now comprehends the wisdom of the well known warning he had from Winfield Scott," *Daily Richmond Examiner*, June 29, 1864.

20. "The Campaigns against Richmond and Atlanta Not Promising Well," *Daily Richmond Examiner*, September 1, 1864; "When McClellan Had General Command," *Chattanooga Daily Gazette*, September 1, 1864.

21. Kenneth Coleman, *A History of Georgia*, 191.

22. Mary Chesnut, *Mary Chesnut's Civil War*, ed. C. Vann Woodward, 642.

23. "A Broadside," *Newark Advocate*, September 2, 1864.

24. "A Letter from General Sherman," *The Liberator*, September 2, 1864.

25. Albert E. Castel, *Decision in the West: The Atlanta Campaign of 1864*, 73.

26. "Gibraltar of the Rebellion," *New York Tribune*, September 2, 1864; Hattaway and Jones, *How the North Won*, 624.

27. "The Loss of Atlanta," *Fayetteville Observer*, September 12, 1864.

28. Sherman, *Memoirs*, 571.

29. Brooks D. Simpson and Jean Berlin, eds., *Sherman's Civil War: Selected Correspondence of William T. Sherman, 1860–1865*, 750.

30. Walters, *Merchant of Terror*, xi.

31. Kennett, *Sherman*, 98–99.

32. Sherman, *Memoirs*, 637.

33. "The Gun Works at Augusta, Ga.," *Boston Daily Advertiser*, Thursday, June 30, 1864.

34. Sherman, *Memoirs*, 620.

35. Halleck to Sherman, September 26, 1864, *OR*, series 1, vol. 39, part 2, 480.

36. Horace Porter, *Campaigning With Grant*, 332, 333.

37. Sherman, *Memoirs*, 639–44.

38. Oliver Otis Howard, "Sherman's March from Atlanta," in Robert Johnson Underwood and Clarence Clough Buel, eds., *Battles and Leaders of the Civil War; Being for the Most Part Contributions by Union and Confederate Officers*, 4:iv, 663, 664; Wade Hampton, "The Battle of Bentonville," ibid., 700.

39. Sherman, *Memoirs*, 584.

40. Ibid., 585. One historian who took Sherman in this negative meaning was Albert Castel, who, in his seminal work *Decision in the West*, argued that the civilian evacuation of Atlanta was the harshest act of the war. Castel, *Decision in the West*.

41. William Clare, September 26, 1864, *OR*, series 1, vol. 39, part 2, 481.

42. J. Cutler Andrews, *The South Reports the Civil War*, 469.

43. "The Situation in Georgia," *Fayetteville Observer*, October 20, 1864; Simpson and Berlin, *Sherman's Civil War*, 731; *Columbia Daily South Carolinian*, November 20, 1864, quoted in Andrews, *The South Reports the Civil War*, 470.

44. Sherman, *Memoirs*, 664; Heidler and Heidler, "G. W. Smith," in *Encyclopedia of the American Civil War*, 1814–15.

45. Burke Davis, *Sherman's March*, 51.

46. "Wheeler's Cavalry," *Columbia South Carolinian*, December 29, 1864.

47. Catton, *This Hallowed Ground*, 358; John M. Schofield, *Forty-Six Years in the Army*, 344.

48. "We Regret to Hear," *Daily Cleveland Herald*, December 16, 1864; Kennett, *Sherman*, 334.

49. Duncan L. Clinch was a former congressman from Georgia, a general and a veteran of the Second Seminole War. Fort Clinch on the northeast Florida coast was named in his honor. Two of his sons served in the Confederate army, and his daughter, to whom Sherman was writing,

was married to Robert Anderson, of Fort Sumter fame. Sherman to Eliza Anderson, December 31, 1864, General Duncan Lamont Clinch Family Papers, Special and Area Studies Collection, George A. Smathers Libraries, University of Florida, University of Florida, Gainesville, Florida. Ironically, Sherman may have done much more to harm Anderson than those manning the guns in Charleston in 1861. Anderson was heavily invested in Georgia railroads and would be nearly broke at the war's conclusion. Robert Anderson to Elba Anderson, August 12, 1860, Special Collections and Archives, United States Military Academy Library at West Point.

50. Hattaway and Jones, *How the North Won*, 656–57.

51. Walters, *Merchant of Terror*, 181.

CHAPTER 3

1. Thomas L. Connelly, *The Marble Man: Robert E. Lee and His Image in American Society*, 209.

2. At the end of the war, there were 1,000,692 officers and men in the US army; by the end of 1866 that number had been reduced to 57,072. US Department of Commerce, Bureau of the Census, *Historical Statistics of the United States: Colonial Times to 1970*, bicentennial edition, part 2, 1142.

3. James M. Morris, *America's Armed Forces: A History*, 133–35.

4. Lewis, *Sherman*, 615.

5. Irene M. Patton, "The Civil War as Romance: Of Noble Warriors and Maidens Chaste," *American Heritage Magazine* 22 (April 1971): 48.

6. George Ward Nichols, *The Story of the Great March: From the Diary of a Staff Officer*, 35, 43–44.

7. Ibid., 37.

8. Ibid.

9. Ibid., 240; Sherman, *Memoirs*, 658–59, 815.

10. Joseph G. Rosa, "George Ward Nichols and the Legend of Wild Bill Hickock," *Arizona and the West* 19 (February 1977): 135.

11. Ibid.

12. Nichols, *The Great March*, 22.

13. Ibid., 106, 107.

14. "From General Sherman," *New York Times*, April 23, 1865.

15. William C. Davis, *An Honorable Defeat: The Last Days of the Confederate Government*, 182–84.

16. Marszalek, *Sherman*, 348.

17. Sherman to John Rawlins, May 9, 1865, *OR*, series 1, vol. 47, 33.

18. "From General Sherman," *New York Times*, April 23, 1865; John F. Marszalek, *Sherman's Other War: The General and the Civil War Press*, 190.

19. Marszalek, *Sherman's Other War*, 190, 191.

20. "General Sherman's Extraordinary Negotiation for Peace," *New York Times*, April 24, 1865; "News From Washington," ibid., April 26, 1865; "From General Sherman's Army," ibid., April 27, 1865.

21. "General Sherman's Armistice," ibid., May 22, 1865.

22. "News From Washington," ibid., April 26, 1865; Theodore Burton, *John Sherman*, 1; Lewis, *Sherman*, 84.

23. Marszalek, *Sherman*, 256–57; Kennett, *Sherman*, 145, 111; Connelly, *The Marble Man*, 14.

24. Sherman, *Memoirs*, 326–27.

25. Ibid., 328.

26. Grant, *Memoirs*, 644.

27. Sherman, *Memoirs*, 247–48.

28. William A. Byrne, "Uncle Billy Sherman Comes to Town: The Free Winter of Black Savannah," *Georgia Historical Quarterly* 79 (Spring 1995): 105.

29. Sherman, *Memoirs*, 248.

30. Heidler and Heidler, "Edward Pollard," in *Encyclopedia of the American Civil War*, 1539.

31. Edward A. Pollard, *The Lost Cause*, 82, 606, 616.

32. Ibid., 614–15.

33. Ibid., 615.

34. Joseph E. Johnston, *Narrative of Military Operations, Directed, During the Late War Between the States by Joseph E. Johnston, General, C.S.A.*; Craig L. Symonds, *Joseph E. Johnston: A Civil War Biography*, 361.

35. Johnston, *Narrative of Military Operations*, 421–29.

36. Symonds, *Johnston*, 365, 361.

37. Johnston, *Narrative of Military Operations*, 403.

38. Marszalek, *Sherman*, 496.

39. Symonds, *Johnston*, 364, 371.

40. "Sherman's Memoirs," *Milwaukee Daily Sentinel*, May 14, 1875.

41. Sherman, *Memoirs*, 229, 33, 51–53.

42. "Sherman's Book Again," *Georgia Weekly Telegraph*, May 25, 1875.

43. Sherman, *Memoirs*, 108–43.

44. David F. Boyd, "General W. T. Sherman and His Early Life in the South and His Relations with Southern Men," *Confederate Veteran* 18 (September 1910): 408.

45. "Sherman Insane," *Cincinnati Commercial*, December 11, 1861.

46. Sherman, *Memoirs*, 193, 214.

47. Anderson, General Orders no. 6, *OR*, series 1, vol. 4, 296.

48. Sherman, *Memoirs*, 202.

49. Kennett, *Sherman*, 138.

50. Ibid., 97–101.

51. Sherman, *Memoirs*, 215; Halleck to Edwin Stanton, April 13, 1862, *OR*, series 1, vol. 10, part 1, 98; Grant, *OR*, April 9, 1862, *OR*, series 1, vol. 10, part 1, 110.

52. Whitelaw Reid, *Cincinnati Gazette*, April 14, 1862.

53. Sherman, *Memoirs*, 246; J. Cutler Andrews, *The North Reports the Civil War*, 179.

54. Sherman, *Memoirs*, 243–46: Sherman, April 8, 1862, *OR*, series 1, vol. 10, part 1, 249.

55. "General Buell on Sherman's Memoir's," *Owyhee Daily Avalanche*, June 9, 1875.

56. Morris, *America's Armed Forces*, 83–86; Sherman, *Memoirs*, 235–40.

57. Kennett, *Sherman*, 193.

58. Sherman to Rawlins, January 4, 1863, *OR*, series 1, vol. 17, part 1, 608; Sherman, *Memoirs*, 436, 437.

59. Heidler and Heidler, "George W. Morgan," in *Encyclopedia of the American Civil War*, 1356–57.

60. Grant, *Memoirs*, 367–71.

61. Peter Cozzens, *The Shipwreck of Their Hopes: The Battles of Chattanooga*, 144, 161, 154.

62. Ibid., 247, 251–56; Grant, *Memoirs*, 385.

63. Sherman, *Memoirs*, 364.

64. Ibid., 362.

65. Cleaves, *Rock of Chickamauga*, 117,118; Walter H. Herbert, *Fighting Joe Hooker*, 247; Kennett, *Sherman*, 238.

66. McPherson, *Battle Cry of Freedom*, 743–56; John Keegen, *A History of Warfare*, 161.

67. Ibid., 271.

68. Hattaway and Jones, *How the North Won*, 607; McPherson, *Battle Cry of Freedom*, 753.

69. Sherman, *Memoirs*, 34.

70. H. V. Boynton, *Sherman's Historical Raid: The Memoirs in the Light of the Record*, 97; "Gibraltar of the Rebellion," *New York Tribune*, September 2, 1864.

71. "Sherman's Book," *Georgia Weekly Telegraph*, October 15, 1875.

72. Scholfield, *Forty-Six Years in the Army*, 292, 296.

73. Ibid., 300.

74. Sherman to Grant, October 9, 1865, in Sherman, *Memoirs*, 152.

75. Sherman, *Memoirs*, 137–70.

76. Ibid., 170; Marszalek, *Sherman*, 466.

77. Ibid., 243.

78. Ibid., 381–409.

79. Ibid., 395.

80. Ibid., 408–9.

81. Kennett, *Sherman*, 303–8.

82. Graham Cosmas, *An Army for Empire: The United States Army in the Spanish American War*, 12.

83. Sherman, *Memoirs*, 403–5.

84. Ibid., 403–4.

85. Marszalek, *Sherman's Other War*, 139, 157, 177

86. Lewis, *Sherman*, 616–17.

87. James R. Belpedio, "Orville Babcock," in *Encyclopedia of the American Civil War*, 157.

88. Lewis, *Sherman*, 589, 616–17.

89. Ibid.

90. Kennett, *Sherman*, 320.

91. Sherman, *Memoirs*, 205–6.

92. Herbert, *Fighting Joe Hooker*, 286; Cozzens, *The Shipwreck of Their Hopes*, 43.

93. Kennett, *Sherman*, 307; Sherman, *Memoirs*, 85.

94. John A. Carpenter, *Sword and Olive Branch: Oliver Otis Howard*, 241–42.

95. Ibid., 171, 191.

96. Ibid., 195, 196.

97. Ibid., 202–4.

98. Ibid., 207, 208.

99. Ibid., 231–33.

100. Boynton, *Sherman's Historical Raid*, 3.

101. Ibid., 7–9, 10.

102. Ibid., 230.

103. Ibid., 89.

104. Sherman, *Memoirs*, 152–70; Grant, *Memoirs*, 413.

105. Simpson and Berlin, *Sherman's Civil War*, 722–23, 727, 731, 747, 749–52; Grant, *Memoirs*, 543–52.

106. "Gen. Sherman's Memoirs," *New York Times*, December 28, 1875; "Sherman's Memoirs,"

Boston Daily Advertiser, October 20, 1875; "Sherman's Book Reviewed," *Bangor Daily Whig & Courier*, October 28, 1875.

107. "Kate Kleer, Houston Texas," *Confederate Veteran*, October 1906; "Close of the Confederacy," *St. Louis Globe-Democrat*, February 15, 1886.

CHAPTER 4

1. "Joe Hooker on Sherman," *Milwaukee Daily Sentinel*, June 4, 1875; Marszalek, *Sherman*, 422–25; Kennett, *Sherman*, 305–8.

2. "Joe Hooker on Sherman," *Milwaukee Daily Sentinel*, June 4, 1875; "Grant's List of Military Retainers on Whom He Can Safely Rely Is Growing Smaller Every Day" *Daily Arkansas Gazette*, January 3, 1875.

3. Symonds, *Johnston*, 366; John B. Hood, *Advance and Retreat: Personal Experiences in the United States and Confederate States Armies*, 2.

4. Richard M. McMurry, *John Bell Hood and the War for Southern Independence*, 196.

5. Ibid., 198, 200.

6. Kennett, *Sherman*, 330.

7. Hood, *Advance and Retreat*, 315, 237.

8. "Hurrah! for Jefferson Davis, Hurrah!" *Charleston Mercury*, January 16, 1865.

9. McMurry, *John Bell Hood*, 202.

10. Broeck N. Oder, "Richard Taylor," in *Encyclopedia of the Civil War*, 1923–25.

11. Richard Taylor, *Destruction and Reconstruction: Personal Experiences of the Civil War*, 194–95.

12. Oder, "Richard Taylor," in *Encyclopedia of the Civil War*, 1923–25.

13. Taylor, *Destruction and Reconstruction*, 194–95.

14. David F. Boyd. "A Professor under Sherman, a Major under Stonewall," *Daily Picayune*, July 12, 1896.

15. David F. Boyd. "A Professor under Sherman, a Soldier under Stonewall," *Confederate Veteran*, September 1910.

16. W. T. Sherman to John Sherman, February 1869, in Thorndike, *The Sherman Letters*, 327, 328; "Sherman in New Orleans" *Lowell Daily Citizen and News*, April 29, 1871; Jeffry D. Wert, introduction to James Longstreet, *From Manassas to Appomattox*, ix, x.

17. W. T. Sherman to John Sherman, February 1869, in Thorndike, *The Sherman Letters*, 327, 328.

18. "The New South: Letters from General Sherman," *St. Louis Globe-Democrat*, February 11, 1879; "General Sherman on the South," *Daily Arkansas Gazette*, February 16, 1879.

19. "Sherman and the South," *St. Louis Globe-Democrat*, September 16, 1879.

20. "Mr. Sherman in the South," *Daily Arkansas Gazette*, February 4, 1880; "Bourbon Sherman and the New South," *New Mississippian*, September 29, 1885.

21. Sherman, *Memoirs*, 166; "Radical Instructions," *Daily News and Herald*, January 15, 1868.

22. "What General Sherman Thinks and What He Said," *Georgia Weekly Telegraph*, May 9, 1871, and *Georgia Journal & Messenger*, May 9, 1871; "Both the President and General Sherman Recently Expressed Themselves in Favor of the Immediate Admission of Virginia," *Bangor Daily Whig & Courier*, October 18, 1869.

23. "The Radicals Are So Much Afraid That Sherman Will Be a Candidate for the Presidency," *Daily Arkansas Gazette*, November 14, 1867; "Sherman vs. Grant," *Daily News and Herald*,

November 22, 1867; "A Democratic Paper on Gen. Sherman," *Wisconsin State Register*, March 21, 1868; "Spirit of the Wisconsin Democratic Press: On Sherman as a Candidate for President," *Milwaukee Daily Sentinel*, November 26, 1867; "Sherman for the Presidency," *New Hampshire Statesman*, Friday, November 29, 1867.

24. Robert W. Cherney, *American Politics in the Gilded Age*, 27.

25. "Battles and Leaders of the Civil War," *News and Observer*, September 10, 1884.

26. Underwood and Buel, *Battles and Leaders of the Civil War*, 4:x, xiii.

27. Ibid., 4:260, 336, 671.

28. Daniel Oakly, "Marching through Georgia and the Carolinas," ibid., 4:672; Wade Hampton "The Battle of Bentonville," ibid., 4:700.

29. Craig E. Miller, "Give the Book to Clemens," *American History* 34, no. 1 (April 1999): 40.

30. Grant, *Memoirs*, 195–219; Sherman, *Memoirs*, 246–50; Grant, *Memoirs*, 212.

31. Grant, *Memoirs*, 644.

32. Boynton, *Sherman's Historical Raid*, 10; Grant, *Memoirs*, 561–62; Lincoln to Sherman, December 26, 1864, *OR*, series 1, vol. 44, 809.

33. Grant, *Memoirs*, 555–56.

34. Miller, "Give the Book to Clemens," 42.

35. Lewis, *Sherman*, 603.

36. Sherman, *Memoirs*, 559.

37. John A. Logan, *The Great Conspiracy: Its Origin and History*, 313.

38. John A. Logan, *The Volunteer Soldier of America*, v–xx.

39. Mary Logan, *Reminiscences of the Civil War and Reconstruction*, 97.

40. Lewis, *Sherman*, 389, 636.

41. Ibid., 437; Brooks D. Simpson, introduction to Jacob D. Cox, *Sherman's March to the Sea: Hood's Tennessee Campaign and the Carolina Campaigns of 1865*, xv, xvi.

42. Cleaves, *Rock of Chickamauga*, 302–5.

43. Cox, *Sherman's March to the Sea*, xv, xvi.

44. Ibid.; "The Cox-Grant Correspondence," *Daily Cleveland Herald*, November 1, 1870.

45. Simpson, introduction to Cox, *Sherman's March to the Sea*, xvi, xvii.

46. Ibid., 39.

47. Damon R. Eubank, "William B. Hazen," in *Encyclopedia of the American Civil War*, 959–60; William B. Hazen, *A Narrative of Military Service*, v.

48. Hazen, *A Narrative of Military Service*, 259, 312.

49. Ibid., 313–27, 414, 415, 416.

50. Ibid., 393–97.

51. Ibid., 348.

52. "The Burning of Columbia, S.C.," *Daily Cleveland Herald*, May 16, 1866.

53. Hazen, *Military Service*, 349, 353.

54. Ibid., 423, 420, 421.

55. Ibid., 259.

CHAPTER 5

1. Charles R. Wilson, *Baptized in Blood: The Religion of the Lost Cause, 1865–1920*, 51.

2. Jefferson Davis, *The Rise and Fall of the Confederate Government*, 1–15; Gaines M. Foster, *Ghosts of the Confederacy, Defeat, the Lost Cause, and the Emergence of the New South*, 73.

3. "A Rebel Rebuked," *Daily Inter Ocean*, June 9, 1881.

4. Davis, *Rise and Fall*, 443; "A Rebel Rebuked."

5. "A Rebel Rebuked."

6. Ibid.; Davis, *Rise and Fall*, 476–78; "A Rebel Rebuked."

7. Davis, *Rise and Fall*, 533; B. H Liddell Hart, *Great Captains Unveiled*, 91.

8. Sherman, *OR*, series 1, vol. 47, 22; "A Rebel Rebuked."

9. "A Rebel Rebuked."

10. William T. Sherman to Captain Lee, a letter reprinted in "General Sherman Seems to Have Been Considerably Stirred Up by the Publication of Mr. Davis' Book," *News and Observer*, June 29, 1881.

11. "A Rebel Rebuked."

12. "How Jeff. Davis Set Up Gen. Sherman," *Chicago Times*, quoted in *Daily Evening Bulletin*, June 21, 1881.

13. Ibid.

14. Herman Hattaway and Richard E. Beringer, *Jefferson Davis: Confederate President*, 340–41.

15. "How Jeff. Davis Set Up Gen. Sherman," *Chicago Times*, quoted in *Daily Evening Bulletin*, June 21, 1881.

16. *St. Louis Globe-Democrat*, November 15, 1881.

17. "The Vindictive Assaults on General Sherman," *Southwestern Christian Advocate*, November 24, 1881.

18. Field Marshal Viscount Wolseley, *The American Civil War, an English View: The Writings of Field Marshal Viscount Wolseley*, ed. James A. Rawley, 3, 4.

19. Ibid., xvi, xxix.

20. Ibid., xxv–xxvi, xix–xxvii; Sherman, *Memoirs*, 877–79.

21. Wolseley, *The American Civil War*, 198–200.

22. "Grant, Thomas, Lee," *North American Review* 144, no. 366 (May 1887): 437–50; Wolseley, *The American Civil War*, xxix.

23. Connelly, *Marble Man*, 1–3.

24. William T. Sherman quoted in "Sherman and Wolseley," *Daily Inter Ocean*, May 3, 1887.

25. Cleaves, *Rock of Chickamauga*, 1–3, 15, 55–61.

26. Lewis, *Sherman*, 644; William T. Sherman quoted in "Sherman and Wolseley," *Daily Inter Ocean*, May 3, 1887; "Sherman and Wolseley" *The North American*, May 2, 1887.

27. Kennett, *Sherman*, 334–35.

28. "Death of the Wife of General Sherman," *Daily Evening Bulletin*, November 28, 1888.

29. Marszalek, *Sherman*, 491.

30. Ibid.; "A Message to Congress," *Milwaukee Journal*, February 14, 1891; "The Wabash Makes Half Rates," *Daily Inter Ocean*, February 19, 1891.

31. Lewis, *Sherman*, 34.

32. "Rev. Father Sherman Arrives," *News and Observer*, February 20, 1891.

33. "Was Not a Catholic," *Milwaukee Sentinel*, February 16, 1891; "A Roman Catholic Sister Anthony Says Gen. Sherman Was Baptized," *St. Paul Daily News*, March 5, 1891.

34. "Sister Anthony America's Florence Nightingale Celebrates Her 76th Birthday," *Daily Picayune*, August 20, 1893; "A Roman Catholic Sister Anthony Says Gen. Sherman Was Baptized," *St. Paul Daily News*, March 5, 1891; "The Only American Women Who Have Ever Been Decorated by the Pope with the Rose of Virtue," *Daily Picayune*, June 5, 1892.

35. Cherny, *American Politics in the Gilded Age*, 25, 68.

36. Durkin, *General Sherman's Son*, 66–68.

37. "Senator Sherman on the Nicaragua Canal," *Daily Evening Bulletin*, February 9, 1891; "Sherman on Silver," *Morning Oregonian*, January 14, 1891; "It Was Terrible to Be Sure," *The Mississippian*, January 13, 1891.

38. "Extra: Dead," *St. Paul Daily News*, February 14, 1891; *Daily Picayune*, February 15, 1891; "Sherman Dead," *Atchison Champion*, February 15, 1891.

39. "General Sherman," *News and Observer*, February 15, 1891; "Cold in Death," *Galveston Daily News*, February 15, 1891; "General William T. Sherman," *Daily Mississippian*, February 17, 1891.

40. "Forgave Grant but not Sherman," *Daily Inter Ocean*, February 18, 1891; "The South at Sherman's Funeral," *Daily Inter Ocean*, February 22, 1891.

41. "A Day Off for Clerks," *Galveston Daily News*, February 20, 1891.

42. "General Sherman was Temperamentally Prone to Mix Truth and Exaggeration," *Morning Oregonian*, February 15, 1891.

43. "Reputation for Sand," *Galveston Daily News*, June 21, 1891; "Visiting Club Wins," *Morning Oregonian*, May 29, 1891; "Revolt Against John Sherman," *Milwaukee Journal*, June 15, 1891; "The Beast Is Dead," *Daily American*, January 13, 1893.

44. "The Reports from Mt. McGregor Yesterday," *St. Louis Globe-Democrat*, July 15, 1885; "The Coming Cortege," *Galveston Daily Press*, July 31, 1885.

45. "Grant and the South," *Milwaukee Daily Journal*, July 28, 1885; "Gen Grant's Burial Place," *Bangor Daily Whig & Courier*, July 27, 1885; "A Great Public Protest," *Milwaukee Daily Journal*, July 28, 1885; "A Pile of Money What Mrs. Grant Is Likely to Get from Gen. Grant's Memoirs," *Milwaukee Sentinel*, October 17, 1885.

46. "Gen. Howard Not the Author," *Boston Daily Advertiser*, March 7, 1891.

47. Henry Davenport Northrop, *Life and Deeds of General Sherman*, i.

48. Ibid., 527–32.

49. Ibid., iii; Kennett, *Sherman*, 99.

50. Faunt Le Roy Senour, *Major General William T. Sherman and His Campaigns*, v.

CHAPTER 6

1. Carol Reardon, *Pickett's Charge in History and Memory*, 91–93.

2. "General Sherman Left No Will," *Milwaukee Daily Sentinel*, March 1, 1891; "Unwarranted Gossip," *Morning Oregonian*, March 2, 1891; "Sherman on the Laws of War," *Daily Inter Ocean*, March 2, 1891; "Those Who Have Gone," *Daily Inter Ocean*, March 1, 1891.

3. "M'Kinley and Sherman," *Morning Oregonian*, July 2, 1891; "Just Wild Lunacy," *Boston Daily Advertiser*, July 10, 1891.

4. "Gen. Hayes on Sherman," *Daily News and Observer*, March, 4, 1891.

5. "Gen. Sherman's Family," *Daily Picayune*, April 21, 1891; "Statue of Sherman," *Daily Inter Ocean*, March 3, 1891.

6. "For Sherman's Monument," *Boston Daily Advertiser*, March 3, 1891; "To Build Sherman's Monument," ibid.

7. Porter, *Campaigning With Grant*, 317–20.

8. "Sherman Testimonials," *Daily Inter Ocean*, March 8, 1891; Durkin, *General Sherman's Son*, 117.

9. "Gen. Sherman's Statue," *Weekly Sentinel and Wisconsin Farm Journal*, April 9, 1891; "The Sherman Statue," *Daily Picayune*, March 14, 1891.

10. "The Statue of Sherman: Augustus St. Gaudens Chosen as the Sculptor; A Successful

Career," *North American*, April 28, 1891.

11. "Kilgore of Texas," *Rocky Mountain News*, May 21, 1892.

12. "Sculptors' Protest," *Atchison Daily Globe*, June 19, 1896.

13. "Sherman Statue Trouble," *Boston Daily Advertiser*, February 1, 1896.

14. "Sculptors' Protest," *Atchison Daily Globe*, June 19, 1896; "The Successful Sculptor Takes Umbrage at a Fancied Insult," *Daily Picayune*, February 1, 1897.

15. "Rohl-Smith Wins Again," *New York Times*, June 9, 1896.

16. "General Sherman's Statue," ibid., January 31, 1901.

17. "To Complete Sherman Statue," ibid., March 15, 1901.

18. "Decoration Day Events," ibid., May 30, 1903.

19. Kenyon Cox, *Old Masters and New: Essays in Art Criticism*, 141.

20. Ibid.; "Sherman Statue Unveiling," *New York Times*, October 14, 1903.

21. "Sherman Statue Unveiling," ibid., October 15, 1903.

22. William Judson Hampton, *Our Presidents and Their Mothers*, 214.

23. Theodore Roosevelt, *Addresses and Presidential Messages of Theodore Roosevelt, 1902–1904*, 250–55.

24. "Plan to Defeat Sherman," *Milwaukee Journal*, January 6, 1892; "Paul and Rachel," *Saint Paul Daily News*, January 1, 1892; "Reverend Thomas Sherman Has Much of the Spirit of Old Tecumseh in Him," *Daily Inter Ocean*, May 29, 1899.

25. "Sherman in Atlanta," *Georgia Weekly Telegraph, Journal and Messenger*, November 18, 1881.

26. David W. Blight, *Race and Reunion: The Civil War in American Memory*, 258–60; Reardon, *Pickett's Charge*, 85.

27. Longstreet, *From Manassas to Appomattox*, ix; Foster, *Ghosts of the Confederacy*, 19, 119–20.

28. "Among All the Objections," *Daily Cleveland Herald*, April 9, 1869; "Gen. Longstreet," *Vermont Chronicle*, April 10, 1869.

29. "There Has Just Been a Letter Written by General Sherman," *Daily News and Observer*, March 13, 1891.

30. Blight, *Race and Reunion*, 265.

31. "General Fitzhugh Lee's Visit to Brooklyn," *Frank Leslie's Illustrated Newspaper*, February 17, 1883.

32. "The Confederate Veterans Have Organized a Southern Grand Army," *Milwaukee Sentinel*, September 8, 1889; "The Auxiliary Association," *New Orleans Time Picayune*, April 23, 1889; "Keep the Lost Cause Green," *Commercial Appeal*, October 13, 1895.

33. Blight, *Race and Reunion*, 272, 273.

34. John A. Simpson, *Edith D. Pope and Her Nashville Friends: Guardians of the Lost Cause in the Confederate Veteran*, 25–26.

35. Ibid., 152.

36. Henry William Elson, *History of the United States*, 287; Karen L. Cox, *Dixie's Daughters: The United Daughters of the Confederacy and the Preservation of Confederate Culture*, 120–21, 124; "Letter to the Editor," *Confederate Veteran*, October 1906.

37. Blight, *Race and Reunion*, 272, 273.

38. Bessie Louise Pierce, *Public Opinion and the Teaching of History in the United States*, 138; McCardell, *Idea of a Southern Nation*, 178.

39. Lyon Gardiner Tyler, *A Confederate Catechism: The War of 1861–1865*, 2–12.

40. Ibid., 10, 11.

41. Pollard, *The Lost Cause*, 606, 607.

42. "Story of Mary Barnett," *Confederate Veteran*, August, 1899.

43. Gary M. Gallagher, *Jubal A. Early, the Lost Cause, and Civil War History: A Persistent Legacy*, 22.

44. "Grant's Liquor Drinking," *St. Louis Globe-Democrat*, January 24, 1887; "A Southern Woman's Strategy," *Confederate Veteran*, December 1899; "Blue Coats at Liberty Hall *Confederate Veteran*, July 1899; Cox, *Dixie's Daughters*, 43–45.

45. Thaddeus K. Oglesby, *Some Truths of History: A Vindication of the South against the Encyclopedia Britannica and Other Maligners*, 15, 30–31, 40; Mildred Lewis Rutherford, *Truths of History: A Fair, Unbiased, Impartial, Unprejudiced and Conscientious Study of History*, 3–10, 34–39.

46. Foster, *Ghosts of the Confederacy*, 123.

47. "In Sherman's Wake," *Confederate Veteran*, November 1932; May S. Mallard to May Jones, September 5, 1864, in Robert Myers, ed., *Children of Pride: Selected Letters of the Family of the Reverend Charles Colcock Jones from the Years 1860–1868*, 489.

48. Dolly Lunt Burge, *The Diary of Dolly Lunt Burge, 1848–1879*, ed. Christine Jacobson Carter, 158–65.

49. Foster, *Ghosts of the Confederacy*, 32; McPherson, *Battle Cry of Freedom*, 810; William C. Davis, *Look Away: A History of the Confederate States of America*, 261–79.

50. "In Sherman's Wake," *Confederate Veteran*, November 1932; Blight, *Race and Reunion*, 284, 286.

51. Blight, *Race and Reunion*, 284.

52. "Blue Coats at Liberty Hall," *Confederate Veteran*, July 1899; Davis, *Honorable Defeat*, 313–14.

53. "Fleming Dubignon's Pony," *Confederate Veteran*, July 1895.

54. W. C. Dodson, "Wheeler on Sherman's Flanks in Georgia," *Confederate Veteran*, December 1904.

55. John Bell Hood to Joseph Wheeler, December 1, 1864, *OR*, 1: XLIV, 916.

56. "General Wheeler's Command," *Fayetteville Observer*, January 19, 1865.

57. *Mobile Daily Advertiser and Registrar*, October 20, 1864, quoted in Andrews, *The South Reports the Civil War*, 467.

58. "How Errors Become Historic Facts," *Confederate Veteran*, April 1904.

59. "Why Sherman Did Not Destroy Augusta," ibid., May 1914.

60. Donald, *Lincoln*, 556; "General James W. Singleton Is Seriously Ill at Baltimore and Not Expected to Recover," *Daily Inter Ocean*, April 3, 1892.

61. "Why Sherman Snubbed Augusta," *Confederate Veteran*, August 1914; Felix H. Robertson, "Letter to the Editor," ibid., September 1914.

62. "Lt. Milford Overly," ibid., December 1903.

63. "Who Burned Columbia," ibid., August 1902; Sherman, *Memoirs*, 758–68; Oliver Otis Howard, *Autobiography of Oliver Otis Howard*, 2:111–27.

64. "The Mixed Claims Commissions," *New York Times*, September 29, 1873.

65. "Who Burned Columbia," ibid., May 7, 1873.

66. Sherman, *Memoirs*, 758–68.

67. "Who Burned Columbia," *New York Times*, May 5, 1873.

68. Sherman, *Memoirs*, 767.

69. "A Tribute to Wade Hampton," *Confederate Veteran*, May 1904.

70. Grant, *Memoirs*, 556.

71. "Letter from the Macon Telegraph," *Confederate Veteran*, January 1913.

CHAPTER 7

1. Schofield, *Forty-Six Years in the Army*, 332.

2. Donald B. Connelly, *John M. Schofield and the Politics of Generalship*, 1.

3. Schofield, *Forty-Six Years in the Army*, 15, 431–32, 435–36.

4. Ibid. xxv.

5. "Sherman in Georgia," *Daily South Carolinian*, November 20, 1864, reprinted in Andrews, *The South Reports the Civil War*, 470.

6. "Sherman's Retreat," *Augusta Daily Constitutionalist*, November 21, 1864, reprinted in ibid.

7. Schofield, *Forty-Six Years in the Army*, 309.

8. McPherson, *Battle Cry of Freedom*, 825; Davis, *Honorable Defeat*, 299–304.

9. Schofield, *Forty-Six Years in the Army*, 330 (quote), 331.

10. Ibid., 332.

11. Davis, *Look Away*, 232, 246.

12. "General Sherman Is Not Conquering Georgia," *Daily Richmond Examiner*, November 24, 1864.

13. "The Book of the Week," *New York Times*, December 18, 1897.

14. McPherson, *Battle Cry of Freedom*, 811–12; Schofield, *Forty-Six Years in the Army*, 243–45.

15. Schofield, *Forty-Six Years in the Army*, 300.

16. Connelly, *Schofield*, 152.

17. Ibid., 85, 99, 107.

18. Sherman to Schofield, March 28, 1876, quoted in Schofield, *Forty-Six Years in the Army*, 439.

19. "Villainy at West Point," *New York Times*, April 7, 1880.

20. Schofield, *Forty-Six Years in the Army*, 445–46.

21. "115 Years Late, He Won His Bars," *New York Times*, July 30, 1995.

22. Connelly, *Schofield*, 300.

23. Charlton W. Tebeau, *A History of Florida*, 310.

24. Cox, *Dixie's Daughters*, 142.

25. "How Wheeler Saved the Army," *Weekly News and Courier*, July 30, 1898.

26. "Reunion at Owensboro," *Confederate Veteran*, August 1902.

27. "Three Abolition Martyrs," *New York Times*, July 28, 1879; "Death of Alanson Work," *Hartford Courant*, July 7, 1877.

28. "Reunion at Owensboro," *Confederate Veteran*, August 1902; Cox, *Dixie's Daughters*, 118–19.

29. Marszalek, *Sherman*, 488.

30. Durkin, *General Sherman's Son*, 191.

31. Kennett, *Sherman*, 72.

32. Ibid., 57–68, 209–23.

33. Ibid., 161, 162, 191; "Jesuit Army Chaplains," *Milwaukee Sentinel*, May 17, 1898.

34. "Father Sherman" *New York Herald*, May 2, 1906; "Sherman on His March," *Atlanta Journal Constitution*, May 1, 1906.

35. Durkin, *General Sherman's Son*, 191; "Southern Congressmen Protest," *Atlanta Journal Constitution*, May 2, 1906.

36. Hampton, *Our Presidents and Their Mothers*, 214; "President Stops March of Sherman to the Sea," *New York Times*, May 1, 1906.

37. "Father Sherman Explains," ibid., May 7, 1906; "Why General Sherman's Name Is Detested," *Confederate Veteran*, July 1906.

38. Alice Fahs and Joan Waugh, *The Memory of the Civil War in American Culture*, 85.

CHAPTER 8

1. Cox, *Dixie's Daughters*, 6–7; Woodrow Wilson, *A History of the American People*, 4:196–97, 242, 257.

2. Henry E. Shepard, "Historic Ironies," *Confederate Veteran*, January 1918; "Conduct of the War," ibid., March 1921; Herbert Baxter Adams, *History of Higher Education in South Carolina*, 64.

3. Adam Hochschield, *King Leopold's Ghost: A Story of Greed, Terror, and Heroism in Colonial Africa*, 296.

4. Bruce Chadwick, *The Reel Civil War: Mythmaking in American Film*, 12, 38.

5. Ibid., 41, quoting *Moving Picture World*, April 17, 1909.

6. Ibid., 41–44.

7. "Negroes Oppose Film," *New York Times*, May 14, 1922.

8. Chadwick, *The Reel Civil War*, 74–75.

9. Ibid.

10. D. W. Griffith, *The Birth of a Nation*.

11. Ibid.

12. Chadwick, *The Reel Civil War*, 97.

13. Ibid., 188–89.

14. Victor Fleming, *Gone With the Wind*.

15. Chadwick, *The Reel Civil War*, 191.

16. Fleming, *Gone With the Wind*.

17. Hood, *Advance and Retreat*, 235–37.

18. Fleming, *Gone With the Wind*.

19. Chadwick, *The Reel Civil War*, 195–98.

20. Margaret Mitchell, *Gone With the Wind*, 338, 460; Chadwick, *The Reel Civil War*, 210.

21. John Ford, *How the West was Won*.

22. Ibid.

CHAPTER 9

1. Joseph H. Lemhann, *The Model Major-General: A Biography of Field Marshal Lord Wolseley*, 117–23.

2. Lawrence James, *The Savage Wars: British Campaigns in Africa, 1870–1920*, 251.

3. Hugh Dubrulle, "A Military Legacy of the Civil War: The British Inheritance," *Civil War History* 49, no. 2 (June 2003): 153–80.

4. Wolseley, *The American Civil War*, 67, 162.

5. Ibid., xxxiii.

6. Ibid., 66, 220.

7. "Sherman and Wolseley," *North American*, May 2, 1887 (quote); "Sherman's Reply to Wolseley," *Daily Picayune*, May 4, 1887; "Sherman on Lee," *News and Observer*, May 3, 1887.

8. Wolseley, *The American Civil War*, xxxiii–xxxiv.

9. Robert H. Larson, "B. H. Liddell Hart: Apostle of Limited War," *Military Affairs* 44, no. 2 (April 1980): 70–71.

10. Alex Danchev, "Liddell Hart and the Indirect Approach," *Journal of Military History* 63, no. 2 (April 1999): 313–14.

11. Albert Castel, "Liddell Hart's *Sherman*: Propaganda as History," *Journal of Military History* 67, no. 2 (April 2003).

12. Danchev, "Liddell Hart and the Indirect Approach," 315.

13. Hart, *Sherman*, 264–65.

14. Michael Evans, "Army Writer Came Close to Exposing D-Day Secrets," *London Times*, September 4, 2006.

15. Hart, *Sherman*, 106–10, 127–32, 206, 207.

16. Ibid., 220–21,236, 242, 264.

17. Ibid., 285.

18. Ibid., 309, 310.

19. Ibid., 325, 328, 331–32.

20. Ibid., 333.

21. Ibid., 334.

22. Ibid.

23. Ibid., 346–47, 350.

24. Ibid., 356; Sherman, *Memoirs*, 212–17.

25. Hart, *Sherman*, 378–79.

26. Ibid., 429–30.

27. T. E. Lawrence to B. H. Liddell Hart, May 3, 1930, in *T. E. Lawrence to His Biographers, Robert Graves and Liddell Hart*, ed. Robert Graves, 39–40.

28. Ibid., 40–41.

29. P. J. McNamara, "Liddell Hart's Indirect Approach and Its Applications to the Gulf War," National War College, Washington, DC, Defense Technical Information Center, November 7, 1991.

30. Barbara Tuchman, *The Guns of August*, 484–89.

31. Thomas Con Bryan, *Confederate Georgia*, 96–97.

32. Philip Van Doren Stern, introduction to John McElroy, *Andersonville: A Story of Rebel Military Prisons*, 7; Davis, *Honorable Defeat*, 27.

33. Mark Kneely, Jr., "Was the Civil War a Total War?" *Civil War History* 50, no. 4 (December 2004): 448.

34. Longstreet, *From Manassas to Appomattox*, 43, 436.

35. Richard A. Preston and Sydney F. Wise, *A History of Warfare and Its Interrelationships with Western Society*, 162.

36. One modern historian who is influenced by Hart is Lee Kennett. In *Marching through Georgia*, he argued that Sherman's brutality was a "psychological dividend" that helped end the war. Lee Kennett, *Marching through Georgia: The Story of Soldiers and Civilians during Sherman's Campaign*, 1–4.

37. David H. Zook, Jr., "A Memorial Appreciation of J. F. C. Fuller," *Military Affairs* 30, no. 2 (Summer 1966): 100–101.

38. J. F. C. Fuller, *The Conduct of War, 1789–1961: A Study of the Impact of the French, Industrial, and Russian Revolutions on War and Its Conduct*, 98.

39. Ibid., 107–10 (108).

40. Ibid., 110; Hart, *Sherman*, 333; Hazen, *Military Service*, 415–16.

41. Fuller, *Conduct of War*, 107–10; Hart, *Sherman*, 330–34; Wolseley, *The American Civil War*, xxxiii.

42. Hart, *Sherman*, 333.

43. Fuller, *Conduct of War*, 107, 309.

44. Mark E. Neely, Jr., "Was the Civil War a Total War?" *Civil War History* 50, no. 4 (December 2004), 434; James L. Stokesbury, *A Short History of Air Power*, 126–28.

45. John B. Walters, "General Sherman and Total War," *Journal of Southern History* 14, no. 4 (November 1948): 459, quoting William T. Sherman to Salmon P. Chase, August 11, 1862.

46. Ibid., 459–62.

47. Ibid., 466.

48. Ibid., 475–76.

49. Walters, *Merchant of Terror*, 163–64; Nichols, *The Great March*, 59–60.

50. Earl Schenck Miers, *The General Who Marched to Hell: Sherman and the Southern Campaign*, 236–39.

51. John F. Marszalek, Jr., "Review of *Merchant of Terror*," *Journal of American History* 61, no. 3 (December 1974): 784–85.

52. Walters, *Merchant of Terror*, xiii.

53. Jim Cullen, *The Civil War in Popular Culture: A Reusable Past*, 142.

54. James Reston, Jr., *Sherman's March and Vietnam*, 56–64.

55. Ibid., 29.

56. D. J. de Laubenfels, "Where Sherman Passed By," *Geographical Review* 47, no. 3 (July 1957): 381, 385, 388.

57. Peter Temin, "The Post-Bellum Recovery of the South and the Cost of the Civil War," *Journal of Economic History* 36, no. 4 (December 1976): 898–901.

58. Reston, *Sherman's March and Vietnam*, 56–59.

59. Morris, *America's Armed Forces*, 343–44.

60. Michael Fellman, *Citizen Sherman: A Life of William Tecumseh Sherman*, ix–xi.

61. Marszalek, *Sherman*, 51, 80, 95.

62. Victor David Hanson, "Sherman's War," *American Heritage* 50, no. 7 (November 1999): 58.

63. Victor David Hanson, *The Soul of Battle, from Ancient Times to the Present Day: How Three Great Liberators Vanquished Tyranny*, 258–59.

64. Mark Grimsley, *The Hard Hand of War: Union Military Policy toward Southern Civilians, 1861–1865*, 174.

65. Ibid., 190–91.

66. Charles Royster, *The Destructive War*, 5–8.

67. Royster, *The Destructive War*, 358; *Confederate Veteran*, February 1915, quoted in Simpson, *Edith D. Pope*, 51.

68. Noah Andre Trudeau, *Southern Storm: Sherman's March to the Sea*, 160–61, 349–50, 534–38; John Shelton Reed "From Atlanta to the Sea," *Wall Street Journal*, August 4, 2008.

69. Chadwick, *The Reel Civil War*, 75–76, 113.

70. Morris, *America's Armed Forces*, 119, 130.

71. Bruno Coppieters and Nick Fotion, *Moral Constraints on War: Principles and Cases*, 4–5.

72. Hood, *Advance and Retreat*, 235–37.

73. Wolseley, *The American Civil War*, 70.

BIBLIOGRAPHY

ARCHIVES

Anderson Papers. United States Military Academy Library at West Point, Special Collections and Archives.

General Duncan Lamont Clinch Family Papers. Special and Area Studies Collection, George A. Smathers Libraries, University of Florida, University of Florida, Gainesville, Florida.

NEWSPAPERS

Atchison Champion (1857–1892)
Atchison Daily Globe (1877–)
Atlanta Journal Constitution (1982–)
Augusta Daily Constitutionalist (1846–1875)
Bangor Daily Whig & Courier (1848–1900)
Boston Daily Advertiser, (1855–1929)
Charleston Courier, Tri-Weekly (1803–1873)
Charleston Mercury (1854–)
Chattanooga Daily Gazette (1864–1865)
Chicago Times (1854–1895)
Cincinnati Commercial (1817–1890)
Cincinnati Gazette (1828–1881)
Columbia Daily South Carolinian (1849–1867)
Commercial Appeal (Memphis) (1892–)
Confederate Veteran (1893–1936)
Daily American (Nashville)
Daily Arkansas Gazette (Little Rock) (1819–1897)

Daily Cleveland Herald (1835–1884)

Daily Evening Bulletin (San Francisco) (1855–1893)

Daily Inter Ocean (Chicago) (1874–1896)

Daily Mississippian (Jackson) (1833–1891)

Daily Morning News (Savannah) (1850–1868)

Daily National Intelligencer (Washington, DC) (1800–1870)

Daily News and Herald (Savannah) (1850–1868)

Daily Picayune (New Orleans) (1861–)

Daily Richmond Examiner (1861–1866)

Daily South Carolinian (Columbia) (1849–1867)

Daily Times (Leavenworth, KS) (1863–1864)

Fayetteville Observer (1833–1897)

Frank Leslie's Illustrated Newspaper (1855–1922)

Galveston Daily News (1874–1897)

Georgia Journal & Messenger (Macon) (1880–1882)

Georgia Weekly Telegraph (Macon) (1868–1869)

Hartford Courant (1823–1890)

The Liberator (1831–1866)

London Times (1788–)

Lowell Daily Citizen and News (1856–1879)

Macon Telegraph (1826–)

Milwaukee Daily Sentinel (1837–1995)

Milwaukee Journal (1882–1995)

The Mississippian (Jackson) (1851–1864)

Morning Oregonian (Portland) (1862–1899)

Moving Picture World (1907–1922)

The Nebraskian (Omaha) (1856–1861)

New Hampshire Statesman (Concord) (1823–1891)

New Mississippian (Jackson) (1882–1890)

Newark Advocate (Ohio) (1820–)

News and Observer (Raleigh) (1880–1899)

New York Herald (1802–)

New York Times (1851–)

New York Tribune (1841–1922)

North American and United States Gazette (Philadelphia) (1847–1876)

Owyhee Daily Avalanche (Ruby City, ID) (1874–1875)

Ripley Bee (Ohio) (1847–1868)

Rocky Mountain News (Denver) (1896–1899)

St. Louis Globe-Democrat (1875–1986)

St. Paul Daily News (1889–1894)

Wall Street Journal (1882–)
Weekly News and Courier (Charleston) (1896–1899)
Weekly Sentinel and Wisconsin Farm Journal (Milwaukee) (1891–1892)
Wisconsin State Register (Portage) (1861–)

MOTION PICTURES AND NOVELS

Griffith, D.W., director, producer. *The Birth of a Nation*. Mutual Pictures, 1915.
Fleming, Victor, director. *Gone With the Wind*. Produced by David O. Selznick. Selznick International Pictures, 1939.
Ford, John, director. *How the West Was Won*. Produced by Bernard Smith. Metro Goldwyn Myers, 1962.
Mitchell, Margaret. *Gone With the Wind*. 1936. Reprint, New York: Scribner, 1964.

SOURCES

Adams, Herbert Baxter. *History of Higher Education in South Carolina*. Washington, DC: Government Printing Office, 1889.
Andrews, J. Cutler. *The North Reports the Civil War*. Princeton: Princeton University Press, 1955.
———. *The South Reports the Civil War*. Princeton: Princeton University Press, 1970.
Blight, David W. *Race and Reunion: The Civil War in American Memory*. Cambridge: Harvard University Press, 2001.
Borneman, Walter R. *1812: The War That Forged a Nation*. New York: HarperCollins, 2004.
Boynton, H. V. *Sherman's Historical Raid: The Memoirs in the Light of the Record*. Cincinnati: Wilstach, Baldwin & Company, 1875.
Bryan, Thomas Con. *Confederate Georgia*. Athens: University of Georgia Press, 1953.
Burge, Dolly Lunt. *The Diary of Dolly Lunt Burge, 1848–1879*. Edited by Christine Jacobson Carter. Athens, University of Georgia Press, 1997.
Burton, Theodore. *John Sherman*. New York: Chelsea House, 1983.
Byrne, William A. "Uncle Billy Sherman Comes to Town: The Free Winter of Black Savannah." *Georgia Historical Quarterly* 79 (Spring 1995): 90–116.
Carpenter, John A. *Sword and Olive Branch: Oliver Otis Howard*. Pittsburgh:

University of Pittsburgh Press, 1964.

Castel, Albert E. *Decision in the West: The Atlanta Campaign of 1864.* Lawrence: University Press of Kansas, 1992.

———. "Liddell Hart's *Sherman:* Propaganda as History." *Journal of Military History* 67, no. 2 (April 2003): 405–26.

Catton, Bruce. *Terrible Swift Sword.* Vol. 2 of *The Centennial History of the Civil War.* New York: Doubleday, 1963.

———. *This Hallowed Ground: The Story of the Union Side of the Civil War.* New York: Doubleday, 1956.

Chadwick, Bruce. *The Reel Civil War: Mythmaking in American Film.* New York: Alfred A. Knopf, 2001.

Cherny, Robert W. *American Politics in the Gilded Age.* Wheeling, IL: Harlan Davidson, 1997.

Chesnut, Mary. *Mary Chesnut's Civil War.* Edited by C. Vann Woodward. New Haven: Yale University Press, 1981.

Cleaves, Freeman. *The Rock of Chickamauga: The Life of General George H. Thomas.* 1948. Reprint, Norman: University of Oklahoma Press, 1986.

Coleman, Kenneth. *A History of Georgia.* Athens: University of Georgia Press, 1991.

Connelly, Donald B. *John M. Schofield and the Politics of Generalship.* Chapel Hill: University of North Carolina Press, 2006.

Connelly, Thomas L. *The Marble Man: Robert E. Lee and His Image in American Society.* New York: Alfred A. Knopf, 1977.

Coppieters, Bruno, and Nick Fotion. *Moral Constraints on War: Principles and Cases.* New York: Lexington Books, 2002.

Cornish, Dudley Taylor. *The Sable Arm: Black Troops in the Union Army, 1861–1865.* New York: Longman's Green, 1956. Reprint, Lawrence: University Press of Kansas, 1987.

Cosmas, Graham. *An Army for Empire: The United States Army in the Spanish American War.* College Station: Texas A&M University Press, 1971.

Cox, Jacob D. *Sherman's March to the Sea: Hood's Tennessee Campaign and the Carolina Campaigns of 1865.* 1882. Reprint, New York: Da Capo Press, 1994.

Cox, Karen L. *Dixie's Daughters: The United Daughters of the Confederacy and the Preservation of Confederate Culture.* Gainesville: University Press of Florida, 2003.

Cox, Kenyon. *Old Masters and New: Essays in Art Criticism.* New York: Fox Duffield, 1905.

Cozzens, Peter. *The Shipwreck of Their Hopes: The Battles of Chattanooga.* Chicago: University of Illinois Press, 1994.

Cullen, Jim. *The Civil War in Popular Culture: A Reusable Past.* Washington, DC: Smithsonian Institution Press, 1995.

Danchev, Alex. "Liddell Hart and the Indirect Approach." *Journal of Military History* 63, no. 2 (April 1999): 313–37.

Daniel, Larry J. *Shiloh: The Battle that Changed the Civil War.* New York: Simon and Schuster, 1997.

Davis, Burke. *Sherman's March.* New York: Random House, 1980.

Davis, Jefferson. *The Rise and Fall of the Confederate Government.* 1881. Reprint, New York: Da Capo Press, 1990.

Davis, William C. *An Honorable Defeat: The Last Days of the Confederate Government.* New York: Harcourt, 2001.———. *Look Away: A History of the Confederate States of America.* New York: Simon and Schuster, 2002.

De Vattel, Emmerich. *The Law of Nations, or, Principles of the Law of Nature, Applied to the Conduct and Affairs of Nations and Sovereigns.* London: W. Clarke and Sons, 1811.

DeWolfe Howe, M.A., ed. *Home Letters of General Sherman.* New York: Charles Scribner's Sons, 1909.

Donald, David Herbert. *Lincoln.* New York: Simon and Schuster, 1995.

Dubrulle, Hugh. "A Military Legacy of the Civil War: The British Inheritance." *Civil War History* 49, no. 2 (2003): 153–80.

Durkin, Joseph T., S.J. *General Sherman's Son.* New York: Farrar, Straus, and Cudahy, 1959.

Elson, Henry William. *History of the United States.* New York: Macmillan, 1905.

Fahs, Alice, and Joan Waugh. *The Memory of the Civil War in American Culture.* Chapel Hill: University of North Carolina Press, 2004.

Fellman, Michael. *Citizen Sherman: A Life of William Tecumseh Sherman.* New York: Random House, 1995.

Foster, Buck T. *Sherman's Mississippi Campaign.* Tuscaloosa: University of Alabama Press, 2006.

Foster, Gaines M. *Ghosts of the Confederacy: Defeat, the Lost Cause, and the Emergence of the New South.* New York: Oxford University Press, 1987.

Fuller, J. F. C. *The Conduct of War, 1789–1961: A Study of the Impact of the French, Industrial, and Russian Revolutions on War and Its Conduct.* 1961. Reprint, London: Minerva Press, 1968.

Gallagher, Gary M. *Jubal A. Early, the Lost Cause, and Civil War History: A Persistent Legacy.* Milwaukee: Marquette University Press, 1995.

Grant, Ulysses S. *The Personal Memoirs of Ulysses S. Grant. 2 vols.* New York: Charles L. Webster & Co., 1885.

Grimsley, Mark. *The Hard Hand of War: Union Military Policy toward Southern*

    Civilians, 1861–1865. 1995. Reprint, New York: Cambridge University Press, 1997.

Guelzo, Allen C. *Lincoln's Emancipation Proclamation: The End of Slavery in America.* New York: Simon and Schuster, 2004.

Hampton, William Judson. *Our Presidents and Their Mothers.* Boston: Cornhill, 1922.

Hanson, Victor David. "Sherman's War." *American Heritage* 50, no. 7 (November 1999): 58–64.

———. *The Soul of Battle, from Ancient Times to the Present Day: How Three Great Liberators Vanquished Tyranny.* New York: Simon and Schuster, 1999.

Hart, B. H Liddell. *Great Captains Unveiled.* 1928. Reprint, New York: Books for Libraries Press, 1967.

———. *Sherman: Soldier, Realist, American.* 1929. Reprint, New York: Frederick A. Praeger, 1958.

Hattaway, Herman, and Richard E. Beringer, *Jefferson Davis: Confederate President.* Lawrence: University of Kansas Press, 2002.

Hattaway, Herman, and Archer Jones. *How the North Won: A Military History of the Civil War.* Chicago: University of Illinois Press, 1983.

Hazen, William B. *A Narrative of Military Service.* Boston: Ticknor and Company, 1885.

Heidler, David S., and Jeanne T. Heidler, eds. *Encyclopedia of the American Civil War: A Political, Social, and Military History.* Santa Barbara, CA: ABC-CLIO, 2000.

Herbert, Walter H. *Fighting Joe Hooker.* New York: Bobbs-Merrill, 1944.

Hinks, Peter, and John McKivigin, eds. *Encyclopedia of Antislavery and Abolition.* West Port, CT: Greenwood Press, 2007.

Hochschield, Adam. *King Leopold's Ghost: A Story of Greed, Terror, and Heroism in Colonial Africa.* New York: Houghton Mifflin, 1998.

Hood, John B. *Advance and Retreat: Personal Experiences in the United States and Confederate States Armies.* New Orleans: Hood Orphan Memorial Fund, 1880.

Howard, Oliver Otis. *Autobiography of Oliver Otis Howard.* 2 vols. New York: Baker and Taylor, 1908.

James, Lawrence. *The Savage Wars: British Campaigns in Africa, 1870–1920.* New York: St. Martin's Press, 1985.

Johnston, Joseph E. *Narrative of Military Operations, Directed, During the Late War Between the States by Joseph E. Johnston, General, C.S.A.* New York: D. Appleton and Company, 1874.

Keegen, John. *A History of Warfare.* New York: Alfred A. Knopf, 1993.

Kennett, Lee. *Marching through Georgia: The Story of Soldiers and Civilians during Sherman's Campaign*. New York: HarperCollins, 1995.

———. *Sherman: A Soldier's Life*. New York: HarperCollins, 2001.

Kneely, Mark, Jr. "Was the Civil War a Total War?" *Civil War History* 50, no. 4 (December 2004): 434–58.

Larson, Robert H. "B. H. Liddell Hart: Apostle of Limited War." *Military Affairs* 44, no. 2 (April 1980): 70–74.

Laubenfels, D. J. de. "Where Sherman Passed By." *Geographical Review* 47, no. 3 (July 1957): 381–95.

Lawrence, T. E. *T. E. Lawrence to His Biographers, Robert Graves and Liddell Hart*. Edited by Robert Graves. New York: Doubleday, 1963.

Lemhann, Joseph H. *The Model Major-General: A Biography of Field Marshal Lord Wolseley*. Boston: Houghton Mifflin, 1964.

Lewis, Lloyd. *Sherman: Fighting Prophet*. 1932. Reprint, New York: Harcourt, Brace, 1958.

Logan, John A. *The Great Conspiracy: Its Origin and History*. New York: A. R. Hart Publishers, 1886.

———. *The Volunteer Soldier of America*. New York: R. S. Peale & Co., 1887.

Logan, Mary. *Reminiscences of the Civil War and Reconstruction*. Carbondale: Southern Illinois University Press, 1970.

Longstreet, James. *From Manassas to Appomattox*. 1895. Reprint, New York: Da Capo Press, 1992.

Marszalek, John F. "Review of *Merchant of Terror*." *Journal of American History* 61, no. 3 (December 1974): 784–85.

———. *Sherman: A Soldier's Passion for Order*. New York: Macmillan, 1993.

———. *Sherman's Other War: The General and the Civil War Press*. Memphis: Memphis State University Press, 1981.

McCardell, John. *The Idea of a Southern Nation: Southern Nationalists and Southern Nationalism, 1830–1860*. New York: W. W. Norton, 1979.

McElroy, John. *Andersonville: A Story of Rebel Military Prisons*. New York: Fawcett, 1962.

McMurry, Richard M. *John Bell Hood and the War for Southern Independence*. Lincoln: University of Nebraska Press, 1982.

McNamara, P. J. "Liddell Hart's Indirect Approach and Its Applications to the Gulf War." National War College, Washington, DC, Defense Technical Information Center, November 7, 1991.

McPherson, James. *Battle Cry of Freedom: The Civil War Era*. New York: Oxford University Press, 1988.

Miers, Earl Schenck. *The General Who Marched to Hell: Sherman and the Southern Campaign*. 1951. Reprint, New York: Dorset Press, 1990.

Miller, Craig E. "Give the Book to Clemens." *American History* 34, no. 1 (April 1999): 40–47.

Morris, James M. *America's Armed Forces: A History.* Upper Saddle River, NJ: Prentice Hall, 1991.

Myers, Robert, ed. *Children of Pride: Selected Letters of the Family of the Reverend Charles Colcock Jones from the Years 1860–1868.* New Haven: Yale University Press, 1984.

Nichols, George Ward. *The Story of the Great March: From the Diary of a Staff Officer.* New York: Harper & Brothers, 1865. Reprint, Williamstown, MA: Corner House, 1972.

Northrop, Henry Davenport. *Life and Deeds of General Sherman.* Philadelphia: Globe Bible Publishing Co., 1891.

Oglesby, Thaddeus K. *Some Truths of History: A Vindication of the South against the Encyclopedia Britannica and Other Maligners.* Atlanta: Byrd Printing, 1903.

Patton, Irene M. "The Civil War as Romance: Of Noble Warriors and Maidens Chaste." *American Heritage Magazine* 22 (April 1971): 48–53.

Pierce, Bessie Louise. *Public Opinion and the Teaching of History in the United States.* New York: Da Capo Press, 1970.

Pollard, Edward A. *The Lost Cause.* 1866. Reprint, New York: Gramercy Books, 1994.

Porter, Horace. *Campaigning With Grant.* 1897. Reprint, Seaucus, NJ: Blue and Grey Press, 1984.

Preston, Richard A., and Sydney F. Wise. *A History of Warfare and Its Interrelationships with Western Society.* 2d revised ed. New York: Praeger, 1970.

Reardon, Carol. *Pickett's Charge in History and Memory.* Chapel Hill: University of North Carolina Press, 1997.

"A Rebel Rebuked." *Daily Inter Ocean,* June 9, 1881.

Reston, James, Jr. *Sherman's March and Vietnam.* New York: Macmillan, 1984.

Roosevelt, Theodore. *Addresses and Presidential Messages of Theodore Roosevelt, 1902–1904.* New York: GP Putnam's Sons, 1904.

Rosa, Joseph G. "George Ward Nichols and the Legend of Wild Bill Hickock." *Arizona and the West* 19 (February 1977): 135–62.

Royster, Charles. *The Destructive War.* New York: Alfred A. Knopf, 1991.

Rutherford, Mildred Lewis. *Truths of History: A Fair, Unbiased, Impartial, Unprejudiced and Conscientious Study of History.* Athens, Ga: United Daughter of the Confederacy, 1920.

Schofield, John M. *Forty-Six Years in the Army.* 1897. Reprint, Norman: University of Oklahoma Press, 1998.

Sears, Stephen. *George B. McClellan: The Young Napoleon.* New York: Ticknor and Fields, 1988.

Senour, Faunt Le Roy. *Major General William T. Sherman and His Campaigns.* Chicago: Henry M. Sherwood, 1865.

Sherman, William T. *Memoirs of General William T. Sherman.* 1875. Reprint, New York; Da Capo Press, 1984. 2d ed.; 1887. Reprint, New York: Library Classics of the United States, 1990.

Simpson, Brooks D., and Jean Berlin, eds. *Sherman's Civil War: Selected Correspondence of William T. Sherman, 1860–1865.* Chapel Hill: The University of North Carolina Press, 1999.

Simpson, John A. *Edith D. Pope and Her Nashville Friends: Guardians of the Lost Cause in the Confederate Veteran.* Knoxville: University of Tennessee Press, 2003.

Stokesbury, James L. *A Short History of Air Power.* New York: William Morrow, 1986.

Symonds, Craig L. *Joseph E. Johnston: A Civil War Biography.* New York: W. W. Norton, 1992.

Taylor, Richard. *Destruction and Reconstruction: Personal Experiences of the Civil War.* New York: D. Appleton and Company, 1879.

Tebeau, Charlton W. *A History of Florida.* Miami: University of Miami Press, 1971.

Temin, Peter. "The Post-Bellum Recovery of the South and the Cost of the Civil War." *Journal of Economic History* 36, no. 4 (December 1976): 898–907.

Tenney, W. J. *The Military and Naval History of the Rebellion in the United States.* New York: D. Appleton & Co., 1866.

Tenth Annual Reunion of the Association of the Graduates of the United States Military Academy at West Point, New York, June 12, 1879. New York: D. Van Nostrand Publisher, 1879.

Thorndike, Rachel Sherman, ed. *The Sherman Letters: Correspondence between General Sherman and Senator Sherman from 1837 to 1891.* New York: Charles Scribner's Sons, 1894. Reprint, New York: Da Capo Press, 1969.

Trudeau, Noah Andre. *Southern Storm: Sherman's March to the Sea.* New York: HarperCollins, 2008.

Tuchman, Barbara. *The Guns of August.* New York: Macmillan, 1962.

Tyler, Lyon Gardiner. *A Confederate Catechism: The War of 1861–1865.* Charles City County, Va.: Holdcroft, 1929.

U.S. Department of Commerce, Bureau of the Census. *Historical Statistics of the United States: Colonial Times to 1970.* Bicentennial edition. Washington, DC: U.S. Government Printing Office, 1975.

U.S. War Department, *The War of the Rebellion: a Compilation of the Official*

Records of the Union and Confederate Armies. Washington, DC: Government Printing Office, 1880–1901.

Underwood, Robert Johnson, and Clarence Clough Buel, eds. *Battles and Leaders of the Civil War; Being for the Most Part Contributions by Union and Confederate Officers.* 4 vols. New York: Yoseloff, 1956.

Walters, John Bennett. "General Sherman and Total War." *Journal of Southern History* 14, no. 4 (November 1948): 447–80.

———. *Merchant of Terror: General Sherman and Total War.* New York: Bobbs-Merrill, 1973.

The War of the Rebellion: A Compilation of the Official Records of the Union and Confederate Armies. Edited by Robert N. Scott. Washington, DC: Government Printing Office, 1890–1901.

Wilson, Charles R. *Baptized in Blood: The Religion of the Lost Cause, 1865–1920.* Athens: University of Georgia Press, 1980.

Wilson, Woodrow. *A History of the American People.* New York: Harper and Brothers, 1901.

Wolseley, Field Marshal Viscount. *The American Civil War, an English View: The Writings of Field Marshal Viscount Wolseley.* Edited by James A. Rawley. 1964. Reprint, Mechanicsburg, PA: Stackpole Book, 2002.

Zook, David H., Jr. "A Memorial Appreciation of J. F. C. Fuller." *Military Affairs* 30, no. 2 (Summer 1966): 100–102.

INDEX